15	16	17	18	19	20	21	22	23	24	25

Nr.

L ger: **Oflag 18 A**

Staatsangehörigkeit: **England**

Dienstgrad: **S/Ldr.**

Truppenteil: **R.A.F.**   Kom. usw.:

Zivilberuf: ~~verheirat~~   Berufs-Gr.:

Matrikel Nr. (Stammrolle des Heimatstaates): **33228**

Gefangennahme (Ort und Datum): **30.12.41 St. Palu** (Brest)

Ob gesund, krank, verwundet eingeliefert: **verw.**

e Personalbeschreibung

Kennzeichen:

arben im Gesicht , Narbe am rechl. Auge

d Anschrift der zu benachrichtigenden Person in der Heimat
des Kriegsgefangenen

ir Ministry London

Mrs. Th. Calnan, Butters Cottage

Wallingford Castle, Berks.

CALNAN, Th.   Wenden!

FREE AS A
RUNNING FOX

FREE AS A
RUNNING FOX

T. D. CALNAN

THE DIAL PRESS
NEW YORK

Originally published in England under the same title
by Macdonald & Co. (Publishers) Ltd.

Manufactured in the United States of America

I have waited nearly twenty-five years
to tell this story which would probably
never have been written if I had not, at
the late age of fifty-two, become a father
for the first time. I completed the last
chapter on my son's first birthday and,
when he is old enough to read it, I hope
that this book will help to bridge the
half-a-century gap between us.

Free as a Running Fox was written for
MARTIN ROWLEY CALNAN

T. D. CALNAN
Montanare di Cortona
April 1970

To the memory of my fifty friends and companions at Stalag Luft III who, without trial or sentence, were shot by Himmler's Gestapo after escaping from the great tunnel on 25 March 1944. Their names should not be forgotten.

P/O H. Birkland	F/Lt P. W. Langford
F/Lt E. G. Bretell	P/O T. B. Leigh
F/O L. Bull	F/O J. L. R. Long
S/Ldr R. J. Bushell	F/Lt C. A. N. McGarr
F/Lt M. J. Casey	P/O G. E. McGill
S/Ldr J. Catanach	F/O R. Marcinkus
P/O A. G. Christensen	P/O H. J. Milford
P/O D. H. Cochran	F/O J. T. Mondshein
S/Ldr I. K. P. Cross	F/O K. Pawluk
P/O H. Espelid	F/O H. A. Picard
P/O B. H. Evans	F/O P. P. J. Pohe
P/O N. Fuglesang	P/O B. W. M. Scheidhauer
Lt L. S. Gouws	P/O S. Skatzikas
P/O W. J. Grismann	F/Lt C. D. Swain
P/O A. Gunn	Lt R. J. Stevens
P/O A. H. Hake	P/O R. C. Stewart
P/O C. P. Hall	F/O J. G. Stower
F/Lt A. H. Hayter	F/O D. D. Street
P/O E. S. Humphreys	F/O P. Tobolski
P/O G. A. Kidder	P/O E. Valenta
F/O R. V. Kierath	F/O G. W. Walenn
F/Lt A. Kiewnarski	F/O J. C. Wernham
S/Ldr T. G. Kirby Green	F/O G. W. Wiley
F/O A. W. Kolanowski	S/Ldr J. E. Williams
F/O S. Krol	P/O J. F. Williams

Requiescant in Pace

Contents

FREE AS A
RUNNING FOX

Benson

LIFE at Benson was almost idyllic in those last days of 1941. The war was far away and in the peaceful, unchanging Oxfordshire countryside, the tempo of life was gentle. The pubs had plenty of beer and the talk was all farmers' talk, of partridge coveys, point-to-points and tractors.

Each of us pilots might fly four or five operational missions during the week and then we were certainly risking our necks. But the hot war with which we came into close contact when flying over Brest or Hamburg or Munich, never came back with us. As soon as we had landed and been de-briefed, it was forgotten.

All the local farmers, Tom Hedges, Dick Harris, Roger Bitmead, Richard Roadnight and so many others, kept open house for all the Benson pilots. I think they felt guilty that they were not in uniform. Each one of them, to a man, would have joined the services to fight the war, but they could not be spared. They were far more valuable as farmers, producing the food the country so badly needed, than as cannon fodder.

Invitations to dine or lunch or to shoot pheasant or partridges or pigeons or to go racing, were never lacking. We played squash with them, played poker with them and drank gallons of beer with them. Those were good days and they were good friends.

Boxing Day 1941 was one of those sublime days which, even after an interval of a quarter of a century, I still remember in every detail. Everything that happened that day was so traditionally English, so typical of the good life, the solid values and the serious pleasures of yeoman England, that it was a perfect example of that nearly mythical, rapidly vanishing way of life we supposed we were fighting to defend.

It was cold clear weather, with a moderate easterly wind and bright sunshine. I was off duty and had been invited by Dick Harris to shoot pheasant. There were only ten guns, most of them local farmers and nearly all of them excellent shots. There was Tom Hedges, Roger Bitmead and his father, Oliver Medley,

Richard Roadnight, Dick, Charles and Roland Harris, Duggie Sharpe and myself.

The first drive was to be through the woods on the top of Watlington Hill. I drew the outside position and came well forward of the line of guns, along the edge of the wood, to cut off any flankers. The beaters started their systematic drive through the wood, while the guns waited, their dogs behind them, lined out across the meadow on the downhill side of the trees. I was about fifty yards from the edge of the wood, moving parallel to it and towards the line of guns, keeping about a hundred yards ahead of the advancing beaters. No pheasant broke away my side of the wood and I took up my position at the corner, where I could see both the line of guns and the flank of the wood.

Suddenly the pheasants started breaking cover and there were repeated, excited cries of 'Over, over'. They came out of the woods high, because the trees were tall, and fast, because they were going downwind, right over the guns. Out of the corner of my eye I saw Dick take a high one in front of him with his first barrel and then another with his second barrel, just backwards of the vertical. The first pheasant fell right at his feet. The second towered up to a great height, stalled and then plunged to the ground about fifty yards behind him.

Nothing had come my way. No pheasant had broken out to the side of the wood. I had my gun half raised and was tensely expectant. The beaters were still moving forward and there had to be more birds to come.

Suddenly a magnificent cock pheasant came high out of the trees, wheeling south and away from the guns. I swung with him and fired, giving him a good bit of lead because he was moving across me and fast. I must have hit him in the head; his wings folded, he froze in the air and plummeted down, hitting the stubble so hard that he bounced.

That was all I needed. With my first shot I had cleanly killed a really difficult bird. I knew it was going to be a good day.

The next drive was through a field of kale, which lay about a mile away, downhill and downwind. All the pheasants which had got past the guns on the first drive were down there in the kale, as well as many others which had not yet been flushed. Dick Harris was not only one of the best shots I have ever seen, he also knew how to plan and organize a shoot, because he knew what the birds would do. The kale field, which he had planted deliberately for the purpose, was so situated that it was a natural refuge for the poor frightened pheasants which had just been driven from the wood. Being downwind and downhill and offering excellent cover, it was just what the pheasants needed. And they were all in there.

For this drive my place had changed and I was in the line of guns waiting at the end of the kale field. The beaters, protected by sacks tied round their waists, were having a hard time as the kale was high and thoroughly wet. The field was more than half a mile long and the going under foot was heavy with mud.

The first animal to break cover was a hare. I had it covered with my gun but did not fire immediately as I thought it was nearer to the gun on my left and was his target. My neighbour, however, did not fire so I took the hare about thirty yards behind me.

Then a covey of partridges came out of the kale, flying low and as fast as lightning. They were away to my right and I watched as the guns at that end of the line took two in front and four behind. It looked like good shooting to me and I was not surprised to see that Tom Hedges was at that end of the line. The dogs brought in the partridges.

The beaters were getting close and I knew that the pheasants would break any moment. I tried to relax, because my shooting was worse when I was tense.

The first pheasant over the guns was a hen, which got up early and crossed the line high. Somebody on my left disposed of it. I did not even swing, it was too far away. Then three pheasants broke out laterally from the sides of the kale field. Two went down to the flanking guns.

The real action started half a minute later. There were pheasants coming at me from all angles, low, frightened and fast. I missed my first target but got a fat hen with the second barrel. Re-loading quickly I took another hen in front of me but missed with the second barrel when I tried a long shot at a disappearing cock. The whole line of guns was firing fast and furiously. There was the shortest pause, just time to re-load. The beaters were within a few yards of the end of the kale. A beautiful cock pheasant took off fifty yards in front of me, climbing like a lift and coming straight at me. There was nothing else flying and I could sense all the other guns watching me. I swung along his line of flight and missed —well behind, I judged. I kept the gun on him and gave him the second barrel when he was almost exactly overhead. The cock folded and fell within five yards of me. Honour was saved.

There were two more drives before lunch. The beaters were well organized, the pheasants plentiful and the standard of shooting high. I was using a lovely short-barrelled Purdy, which Richard Roadnight had lent me. It was a beautiful gun and I was more than satisfied by my own performance. But I was beginning to get tired and very hungry. I was looking forward to lunch with greedy anticipation. In those hard-pressed days, rationing was severe and most of the population of England, including the RAF, ate dull, miserable meals. But the farmers of Berkshire and Oxfordshire, who produced their own butter and their own eggs, killing their own beef, their own pork, and their own poultry, could on special occasions indulge themselves and their friends.

I knew that a Boxing Day lunch prepared by Nancy Harris would be a gourmand's delight and a hungry man's heaven. Nor was I disappointed. On a long serving table, covered with a white damask tablecloth, there was one of the biggest cooked hams I have ever seen, a great sirloin of cold beef and a cold turkey which could not have weighed less than twenty-five pounds. There were also hot potatoes, roasted in their jackets, broccoli and brussel sprouts, cucumber salad and horseradish sauce. There was a whole form of Stilton and a mountain of butter. The bread was freshly baked.

But before getting down to the serious business of eating, there was our thirst to be taken care of. Dry martinis, gins and tonic and pint tankards of beer were being emptied faster than they could be refilled. The noise level of the conversation rose in inverse proportion to the level in the bottles. Everybody was thoroughly tired and very happy. It had been a wonderful morning's shooting.

It was well past two o'clock before Dick started carving. When everybody had finally been served and had taken the edge off their appetites, we got down to the traditional sweepstake on the day's bag, at a pound a head. Dick went round the table clockwise, noting the bids on the back of an envelope. I came late in the circle and I was able to listen to the opinion of many experts before making my own estimate. That morning we had already killed fifty-five head, mostly pheasants but with a few partridge, woodcock, hares and rabbits.

'Eighty-seven,' said Richard Roadnight. As we were going to end the day by shooting his ducks this meant that there were plenty of ducks and he expected us to shoot a lot of them.

'Seventy-nine,' said Tom Hedges. He obviously was not so sure about Richard's ducks.

When my turn came I put my money on seventy-eight.

It was a low estimate but I could see that lunch was going to take a long time and that there would be very little light left by the time we were finished. In any case, the standard of shooting was bound to have deteriorated. Alcohol and quick reactions do not go together.

My estimate of seventy-eight head was the lowest offered. Richard Roadnight looked disgusted. These low guesses almost amounted to an insult. He had plenty of ducks on his ponds and the bigger the bag we got, the prouder he would have been.

When we were all thoroughly replete and helped down the delicious Stilton with a few glasses of port, it was well past four o'clock. It took nearly half an hour to drive over to Richard's farm and by then the light was fading fast.

All the ducks had been driven off the pond and were circling high in the sky, waiting for a chance to come back.

I was positioned behind a barn. It was an excellent stand and I knew from experience that the ducks liked that approach.

They usually came in high over a row of tall elms, diving fast for the pond. They were in sight for two or three seconds and then disappeared over the roof of the barn. The pond was just beyond the barn and once they hit the water they were safe.

The later it got, the more anxious were the ducks to get back to their pond. Ducks do not like flying by night. Finally they started to come in, in big flights of twelve to fifteen birds, approaching the pond from every possible direction. There was no wind to influence their choice.

The light was now almost gone but, against the sky, they were clearly visible targets. We were supposed to be shooting only the drakes, but it was now too late to make the distinction.

All at once, all the guns were firing. The small space of sky above me was suddenly filled with silhouettes. All I could do was to pick one, swing along the line of flight, press the trigger and then try to get another duck with the second barrel. The difficulty was to re-load fast enough.

After twenty minutes it was all over. Most of the ducks which had not been killed were safely back on their pond. A few desperate ones were still circling and making suicidal attempts to reach their refuge. Richard called a halt. He blew his whistle and the day's sport was over.

At least, the shooting was over. The drinking and the gambling was to go in until the early hours.

Back at the Manor, we inspected the day's bag, which was laid out on the lawn. There were forty-one pheasants, twenty-one ducks, sixteen of them drakes which was good shooting in poor light, five partridges, one woodcock, one pigeon, five rabbits and three hares. I had won the sweepstake. Mine was the nearest guess.

The exhausted beaters were drinking beer from large tankards, waiting for their reward. We each contributed two pounds and they all went off happily to the local pub to spend their hard earned money. All of us retreated to the house to revive ourselves with stiff whiskies and soda.

Two bridge tables were set up and we played a few rubbers before dinner. The stakes were modest but the bids tended to be exaggerated and few made their contracts. After dinner there were not enough bridge players for two tables and so the game was changed to poker. There were seven of us sitting at the table and the level of betting was high from the outset. After a big hand, the pile of pound notes which was pushed across the table was of impressive proportions. I had to be cautious, the stakes were now uncomfortably high. If I was raised twenty pounds and held anything less than a full house, I quit. All that gave me the courage and the means to stay in the game was the money I had won on the sweepstake.

It was about eleven o'clock and many whiskies later that the game was changed to chemin-de-fer. The idea was to give the losers a chance to get their money back. Chemmy is a great leveller. Until then I had been losing slowly but steadily. But right from the first shoe, my luck changed. My first bank ran four times, my second six. The money began to flow my way. When the game finally broke up I had my pockets full of crumpled pound notes.

I was in bed by two o'clock, tired, happy and more than a little drunk.

Capture

EVEN in the early morning, 30 December 1941 promised to be one of those perfect winter days. There was no trace of cloud in the sky and all the trees and every blade of grass was covered with a silver crust of frozen fog. The temperature was a few degrees below zero and visibility was improving rapidly as the sun rose higher above the horizon. It was obvious that by noon the light would be excellent for high level photography.

I took off exactly at 11.30 in AA796, a dark blue Spitfire Mark V. It was a sweetly trimmed aircraft and handled like a feather. When fully tanked up it could fly to Danzig and back and still have ten minutes for photography over the target. There was nothing in the air which could match its speed. But it had no guns. They had been sacrificed to make way for extra fuel and the great thirty-six inch focal length cameras mounted in the fuselage. Its role was to get the pictures and run away from trouble.

I crossed the English coast 25,000 feet above Portland Bill, still climbing and on course for Brest, where I had a rendezvous with a big force of heavy bombers. Their task was to cripple the two German battlecruisers lying in the naval docks. Mine was to photograph the attack.

The Scharnhorst and Gneisenau constituted a very frightening threat to England's vital, but so vulnerable, supply line to America. Once loose in the Atlantic, either of the two German battlecruisers could sink every ship in every convoy on the ocean. And that might have meant the end of the war. The Navy had nothing to match them in speed or firepower and the torpedo bombers of the Fleet Air Arm and Coastal Command were something of a forlorn hope, even if they succeeded in launching their suicidal attacks before the Germans were safely out of range.

The situation at the end of 1941 was so critical that Bomber Command had been ordered to mount daylight attacks on these warships in Brest harbour. Already once before in that month of December, they had been bombed at high noon with a heavy cost in casualties to the bombers. But the results had been disappointing and there were indications that the two battlecruisers, as well as their escort cruiser the Prinz Eugen, might soon be fit to break out to the open sea. Now another attempt was being made to cripple them.

At 12.25 I was positioned a little to the north of the Rade de Brest, flying a short patrol line on alternate easterly and westerly headings. On one side of the aircraft I had a clear view of the line of approach of the bombers, on the other, of their targets.

My altimeter read 31,000 feet and I was flying just 500 feet underneath the critical condensation level. My Spitfire was leaving no give-away trail of white vapour, but any enemy fighter above me would necessarily leave a long plume of condensation behind it, visible for miles. Nothing below me would have the speed to catch me, so I felt safe.

The first wave of bombers was due to attack at 12.30 and I was watching the clock on the instrument panel in front of me. One minute to go and I could still see no sign of the bombers. Suddenly an immense carpet of flak bursts appeared in the air below me, not more than three miles north of Brest. As soon as my eyes had re-focused on the flak, I could see a compact group of Stirling bombers, surrounded by their weaving fighter escort, right in the middle of the shell bursts. Looking over the other side of my aircraft, I could see the gun flashes of the anti-aircraft batteries surrounding the harbour.

The bombers moved in relentlessly towards their target, so slowly that it was painful to watch. There was no weaving, no jinking, they appeared to be contemptuous of the sea of little brown mushrooms which were sprouting all around them. It took one second, perhaps two, for each mushroom to grow into a great ball of smoke and then, its lethal energy expended, to disappear and give place to a new crop.

For half a minute I watched the bombers take their terrible punishment. The familiarity of the scene, which I had witnessed only twelve days before in the same piece of sky, did nothing to diminish the freezing horror of watching violent death in the sunlight. One Stirling peeled away to starboard and went into a nearly vertical dive for the earth, trailing thick black smoke. I watched for parachutes, praying that the crew would have time to jump. So many of those pilots below were old friends, sitting on their personal pieces of armour plating, which they took with them on every raid, hoping to protect their genitals. I saw two other bombers, with engines on fire, drop rapidly behind the formation although they were still holding their heading for the target. Before it was time for me to turn in towards the dockyard, I had counted three aircraft which would never get to their target and three others which would never again see their home base. But the pilots and crews of these burning and broken aircraft were still holding their course, determined to keep them in the air for just that last desperate half minute necessary to bring them over the aiming point.

I turned in towards the target exactly above the bombers, my cameras switched on and my speed reduced to match theirs. I did all my photography undisturbed. The flak was all for the bombers. When the second and third waves of the attacking force arrived, I repeated the whole process and twice again briefly watched the holocaust.

When the last armour-piercing bomb had been dropped, I stood off from the target area for ten minutes to allow the smoke to clear. Then I went back to finish the film. When I set course for Benson it was a few minutes after one o'clock. My thirty-seventh operational mission was complete and I was happy because I knew I had some fine pictures.

I was not far north of Brest, steering 055°, when a burst of flak appeared in the empty, serene sky ahead of me. It was bright scarlet in colour and nearly accurate for height. But it was off line and some 300 yards in front of me. I jinked immediately, changing height and heading. I felt the adrenalin pumping into my bloodstream.

What worried me most was the colour of the burst. Red flak had been reported before at various points over the Reich and it was assumed that it was a directional indication to enemy fighters. I whipped into a steep turn to port, pulling all the 'g' I could without stalling. I could see nothing behind me except drifting flak smoke. Not a sign of a 109. Of course, there might be some bastard sitting right underneath me and turning with me. But at my speed and height I could not believe that it was possible for any enemy fighter to have got into that position.

In spite of the violent evasive action I was taking, I was still heading in a northerly direction and putting distance between myself and the angry bee-hive behind me, which was Brest. My eyes hardly left the rearview mirror. The flak bursts were still appearing, but in diminishing intensity.

The north coast of France was not far ahead of me when there was a sharp noise, like the popping of a champagne cork, and a little hole appeared in the top right hand corner of my windscreen. My adrenalin valves opened wide and I weaved like a weasel. Immediately, there was a dull thump right underneath the aircraft. Just as I was giving fervent thanks that the Spitfire was flying as fast as ever and that the controls were responding normally, a searing jet of living flame shot up from between my knees and played on my head and shoulders.

The pain was unbelievable and indescribable. I lost control of the aircraft and of myself. I writhed and twisted in every direction to escape from the burning petrol. I tore off my oxygen mask, ripping through the straps.

I do not know how long it was before the instinct to survive asserted itself and my brain started to work again. I had one and only one thought which was as clear as if it had been set up in neon lights in front of me.

Jump or you'll fry. A short concise message from my brain to my muscles.

The thinking took milli-seconds; the action many painful seconds.

I put my right hand back into the flames and took hold of the stick. Instinctively and without external reference, I righted the aircraft. I forced myself to accept the torture of the burning petrol spraying on to my face. As soon as the aircraft was level, I whipped back the hood with my left hand, pulled the triangular harness release catch and banged the stick forward with all my force.

Immediately I was out in space, still in a sitting position with my legs stretched out in front of me, as though on the rudder pedals. I caught a last glimpse of my Spitfire, curling away in the blue above me, streaming black smoke. But the agony was over and the fire had gone. Automatically, I felt for the ripcord of my parachute. I jerked it, there was a violent shock and I was dangling at the end of the rigging lines some 29,000 feet over the north coast of France.

My next impression was of complete, utter silence. I was alone in the desolation of space where nothing whispered and nothing moved.

For maybe two minutes I hung from my straps completely inert. I was enveloped by such an intense, pervading sense of peace that it had a physical effect on me. Possibly it was only relief that the agony was over. Possibly it was that inherent quality of the outer atmosphere, bordered by pure space, where there is only peace until man arrives.

When I started to think again, I was clear-headed and calm. I needed to assess my situation. Putting a hand to my face, I found that it was grotesquely swollen. The skin, which I delicately explored with my fingers, had the horrible texture of the crackling of roast pork. My eyes were so puffed up that I was only seeing through tiny slits. The right side of my face was covered in blood from a deep gash through the eyebrow. Because I had been wearing gloves, my hands were hardly burnt at all, except at the wrists and in small areas where the gloves themselves had burned away.

My eyes, thank God and all the saints, were undamaged. I was sure of this because, even if my field of vision was minute, I could see perfectly within those limits.

There was a dull pain in my right ankle and, wriggling my toes, I came to the conclusion that my boot was full of blood. Thinking back, I remembered that something had hit me in the leg when the explosion underneath me had occurred. The sequence of events immediately afterwards had not given me time to register the fact. There was a 10 inch gash on the front of my right thigh. Flying overalls, trousers and flesh were all cleanly cut, and the wound was bleeding copiously. The blood was running down my leg, helping to increase the level inside my flying boot, which was knee-length and so had a reasonable capacity.

It was disheartening to draw the conclusion that I was in no state to make a run for it when I landed, although I was well prepared, well briefed and over a country in which nearly all the population was friendly.

When I looked down to see where I was going to land, enlarging the aperture of my eyelids by the painful process of using a thumb and forefinger of each hand to force them open, all thoughts of escape were banished from my mind. I seemed to be suspended exactly over the coast, swinging through a wide, gentle arc. Petals on a daisy. She loves me, she loves me not. Dry land or wet sea.

I let my eyes close again and tried to remember what the met men had said about the winds. Because now, only the wind could save me. But I could only remember that the winds at my operating altitude were westerly. What the surface and medium altitude winds were, I had no idea.

If I landed in the sea, my chances of survival were so minimal that I needed a miracle. True, I was a strong swimmer, but that only made it worse. I also had a Mae West and an inflatable dinghy. But I doubted that, with my eyes closed, I could get that dinghy inflated. Mainly as a mental exercise I tried to evolve some boy scout method of deciding which way to swim, if I did fall into the drink. The best I could come up with was that I would certainly feel the heat of the sun on my burnt face. As it was not long after noon, the sun would be slightly west of south, so all I had to do was to keep swimming with the sun on my face. If this gave me little reassurance, at least it gave me a plan of action, which was, in itself, comforting.

My thoughts were suddenly interrupted by noise, the first I had heard since baling out. It was an aircraft, coming closer, closer, much too close. My parachute swung violently in the unseen aircraft's slipstream, spilling air and tumbling. Within seconds the noise had faded into silence and my parachute was stable again. I was cold with fear. The unwritten rules of air warfare said that you did not shoot at men dangling in parachutes. But I knew only too well that this rule, the only rule in the world which mattered to me at that moment, had been, on occasions, disregarded. And by our own fighter pilots, as well as the enemy. I had heard the stories first hand, straight from the mouths of the killers. They were rare, but they existed. Well decorated, cold-eyed, rather older than the average, they had survived very many fighter versus fighter duels. And they killed ruthlessly to stay alive. They were convinced that the only good German was a dead German: if you gave one a second chance, he might get you next time. Of course, they only told these stories when in drink and they may have been exaggerating. But in my position in space, dropping rapidly towards the English Channel or the French mainland, I tended to believe them.

I heard the 109 returning, the engine noise getting louder and louder. Then it was past me and I was still alive. He had not fired. What a very charming fellow.

I hit solid earth with a crash and fell over. My parachute collapsed immediately and so I did not have to go through that much too strenuous routine laid down for the case in which the parachute stays inflated and drags the unfortunate pilot across the countryside. I disengaged the harness and lay quietly resting on the ground while I waited for something to happen. I was in no mood to make things happen myself.

I found my cigarettes and lighter in the pocket of my overalls but, to my immense frustration, discovered that I could not hold a cigarette in my mouth. My lips had swollen to the diameter of golf balls and had no sensation of touch whatsoever.

I continued to lie there with a confused medley of thoughts passing through my brain. The early exhilaration and immense relief of having survived my adventure was wearing off. The harsh reality of the situation was beginning to surface above the level of my consciousness. I was finished. I had completed my last operational sortie. There were years of imprisonment ahead.

I waited passively, seeing nothing, because by now my eyelids had completely fused. I heard nothing, because there was an extensive silence around me. I thought of the .38 which I always carried in a shoulder holster under my left armpit. It was not the best of revolvers, but it was what we were issued with. I had spent long hours on the small-arms range mastering it and getting its feel. I could hit anything as big as a cow at twenty-five yards range ten times out of ten. The official reason for carrying this weapon was to be able to put a bullet into the petrol tank of my Spitfire, thus setting it on fire, should I make a forced landing in enemy territory. The fact that a .38 bullet probably would not have that result was well known to me.

I think that the real reason I carried the gun was that it was good for my ego and I had to live with my ego all the time. Our Spitfires were unarmed and I just could not think of myself as a fighting man unless I carried some sort of weapon. Even this relic from the Wild West had its moral value.

I took my beloved .38 from my shoulder holster and, with a long blind swing, threw it far away. Two packets of spare ammunition followed. My reasoning was that the Germans were bound to pick me up soon and I preferred to take the chance that some Frenchman would find it, rather than meekly hand it over to my captors. I had been ruminating for about ten minutes, when I heard a noise. It was indeterminate and definitely furtive.

There was somebody close by watching me, of that I was certain. It could not be a German, they did not need to be furtive. So it must be a Frenchman. A sudden surge of hope revived me. Maybe I had a chance after all.

I could speak reasonable French, quite fluent, intelligible and in a different class to that awful thing which we English were wont to describe as schoolboy French. I started to talk, but achieved no more than a croak. I persevered but it was nearly impossible to make the sounds I wanted. It was not surprising that my Frenchman, if he was there, made no answer. Immediately afterwards, the shouting started and I heard the unmistakable sound of Teutonic boots arriving at the double.

The fact that I could not see a thing put me at a disadvantage and added considerably to the confusion which ensued. My capturer-in-chief was obviously a German NCO, supported by two or three men. The fact that he knew less than half a dozen words of English and that I knew only two words of German, made the subsequent introductions difficult. It did not help matters, either, that I could not see any of the very expressive gestures he was making. The result was that his voice became more and more strident, went up half an octave in pitch and I began to feel alarmed for his blood pressure.

I sensed that it was high time that I made a positive contribution to the proceedings and pantomimed, in exaggerated gestures which he could see, but which I could not, that I was completely blind and had a broken leg. The situation then calmed down. The flying boot on my right leg was handled and a very impressive quantity of blood oozed over the top. I was searched and found free of weapons. My maps and personal papers had been disposed of during the long parachute drop down to earth. There was nothing incriminating on me. Rather to my surprise, nobody took my wristwatch.

Much more rapid progress was now made. It was established that I was an 'Englischer Flieger'. The German NCO, I gathered, also wanted to know where I had hidden my aircraft. Eventually I made a fine noise indicating an explosion and he was satisfied on this point.

Suddenly he was happy and friendly. Taking my arm to emphasize his point, he made the classic remark with which all Germans seem to have greeted their prisoners. It must be in their handbook.

'Fur sie ist der Krieg vorbei.'

And then he translated.

'For you the war is over.'

I could not think of a reply, in any language.

Two

MY impressions of the events of the rest of that day are disjointed and fragmentary. I remember having some difficulty in explaining to my captors that I could not walk and that they would have to carry me. I also remember a long uncomfortable journey over fields, hedges and ditches, carried by two unwilling German soldiers.

My immediate destination, as I gathered subsequently, was the German fighter base at Morlaix. There I was made comfortable on a couch in the mess and given first aid. I was told that my burns would be treated as soon as I reached the hospital. I was given a sedative.

I was by now in considerable pain and was glad to lie still and wait for the sedative to work. I soon sensed, however, that I was surrounded by an interested audience. One of them offered me a cigarette, which I wanted more than anything else in the world. When it became obvious to the donor that I could not smoke it, he solved my problem by producing a cigarette holder which I could hold between my teeth, without touching my burnt lips. I was more than grateful and lay back inhaling deeply, thoroughly enjoying the rather sweet flavour of German tobacco.

Then the questions started, in fair, if halting, English. As far as I could judge, my unseen questioners were all Luftwaffe pilots, full of professional curiosity and not unsympathetic.

I answered the easy ones, giving my name, rank and number. In reply to a direct question I also said that I was damned certain we were going to win the war and that the Germans had lost their unique opportunity at the time of Dunkirk. Soon I lapsed into a comatose silence. I had no strength to argue and was beyond the state of normal exhaustion. I found that I could doze off and become quite oblivious of my surroundings. My questioners were not professional interrogators and were not persistent. In fact, they were kind and considerate. They allowed me to sleep in peace and, some time later, brought me a boiled egg and some peppermint tea. One of them very patiently fed me minute portions of boiled egg on the handle of a teaspoon and, when I wanted to drink, a straw was put into my mouth so that I could suck up the tea without it touching my lips.

When, some hours later, an ambulance arrived to transport me to the naval hospital in Brest, a crowd of invisible Luftwaffe officers wished me goodbye and good luck. The donor of the cigarette holder insisted that I should keep it and I used it habitually during the rest of my time as a prisoner.

All I remember of the ambulance drive to Brest is that it was long and uncomfortable. I dozed most of the time. It was late at night when we arrived at the hospital where professional hands undressed me and a young German doctor examined me. He put a lint mask on my face which reached from the top of my forehead to below my chin. Slits were cut in the mask for my mouth and my nostrils, but my eyes remained covered. This worried me. I wondered whether I had been written off as blind.

The lint mask was thickly covered, on the side of contact, with a substance which had the consistency of axle grease and smelled disgusting. It was described, in German, as Leberöl and I translated this to myself as Liver Oil. I never knew what sort of liver oil it was, but certainly it had a very fishy origin.

The doctor also X-rayed my right foot and, when he had examined the plates, told me that I had a hunk of metal lodged in my ankle, plus a few broken bones and torn ligaments. I was wheeled into the operating theatre within the hour and went out like a light when they put the needle into me.

I awoke frightened and nervous, not remembering where I was

or how I got there. To my great relief, a voice from close beside me spoke in pure London Irish.

'How are you feeling?'

Everything came back to me with an overwhelming rush.

'Not bad. Certainly better than this time yesterday. By the way, what is the time?'

'Must be about two o'clock. I had lunch a couple of hours ago. I saved some for you but you did not surface.'

'And the date?'

'New Year's Eve, and the best of luck!'

'To you too, chum. Who are you, by the way?'

'Bill Joyce. Sergeant-pilot. Shot down in the big bomber raid on the 18 December. Flying a Hurricane.'

Laconic, but all the essential information.

'Watch it, mate,' I said to myself. 'This is probably a plant.'

'What happened?' I asked aloud.

'Cannon shell burst in the cockpit. Both legs full of shrapnel.'

'Did you bale out?'

'Sure did. The engine was hit and my elevator controls had gone. What happened to you? I saw them bring you in last night and you really were in a rough state. I thought you weren't going to make it. Glad to see you're with us again. And your eyes . . . ?' He was hesitant, afraid to ask.

The voice was eager, sympathetic, friendly. I immediately liked Bill Joyce. I had a strong desire to talk and tell my story. But at the same time I recognized the need to be very cautious. He could so easily be a phoney. The situation was ideal. I could not even see my companion to check the apparent truth of what he was telling me. PRU was a very hush-hush unit and I wanted, at all costs, to avoid giving any clue that it was where I came from. The Germans would want to know a very great deal about our highly successful photo-reconnaissance methods. At present, there was nothing to connect me with Benson or the PRU. My Spitfire and its cameras was probably at the bottom of the channel. I was hoping that I would be taken for a fighter pilot, which was routine capture in northern France and did not stimulate undue curiosity. I had to watch my step.

I had been silent for longer than I meant.

'My eyes are all right,' I said finally. 'I am pretty sure of that, although I'll be glad to open my eyelids again to prove it.'

Even though I spoke confidently, I realized that I had my own doubts and was afraid. But that was nonsense, I told myself. I could see perfectly well all the time my eyes had remained open during the long parachute drop. They could not have been burnt.

'What happened to you?' Joyce was being persistent.

'Look, Bill,' I said, 'if you don't mind, I'll tell you the story another day. Just now I don't know who I'm talking to and I don't know who may be listening. You get what I mean?'

There was no immediate reply.

'Tell me, Bill,' I asked, 'What's the situation here? Is there anybody else in the room? Are we guarded?'

Bill Joyce was only too eager to talk. He did not speak German and had been alone in the hospital for twelve days. He talked completely freely. He, at least, had no doubts at all that I was genuine. He told me that we were the only two occupants of a fairly large ward, except for one German soldier who never left the room until his relief arrived. This duty of guarding us was shared by two soldiers and Joyce knew both of them well. He said that they were docile, bored and armed with a rifle and a pistol. Neither spoke a single word of English and they were both grade three physically, not front line troops.

When I said that Bill did not speak German, I was exaggerating. He had learnt a number of words from the two soldiers and could ask for all the essential things such as eat, drink, bottle or bedpan. The sentries understood him without difficulty and would relay his requirements to the hospital staff, who seldom came near us, or even run errands themselves.

Bill had no difficulty in communicating with these sentries. He made it clear to the one on duty that I was a Major and therefore rated special treatment. On the strength of this, we got a cigarette each from the sentry, who was most impressed. I realized that life was going to be much easier for me with Bill there to organize and arrange the essentials.

Bill was ingenious. He had learnt his German phonetically by making the sentries repeat words over and over again until he could reproduce the sound. Then he wrote the words down inventing his spelling to correspond as closely as possible to the sounds he heard.

Whenever possible, he related the sounds to English words. For instance, Bill told me, if I wanted to know the time, all I had to say to the sentry was 'Fish paste'.

I tried it. I called the sentry and said 'Fish paste'.

'Ein Viertel vor elf, Herr Major.'

'A quarter to eleven,' translated Joyce.

It was not until many months later, after I had been studying German seriously, that I suddenly recognized what the mysterious fish paste really was. It was, of course, no more or less than 'Wie Spät ist es?' which, as every student of German learns very early, means what is the time.

Bill and I talked late into the night until I could no longer keep awake. I learnt a great deal of the organization of the hospital and of the personalities of the various people who came in contact with us. The hospital was full of German sailors, the majority of whom were crews of the German warships in the docks and harbour. A considerable number had been wounded during the bombing of the Scharnhorst and Gneisenau. Very recently, it appeared, an armour piercing bomb had penetrated the upper decks of one of the big warships and exploded in a crowded mess deck, killing a lot of sailors and causing a lot of shrapnel wounds. English airmen were not at all popular in the naval hospital at Brest at that time.

This largely accounted for the behaviour of the doctor. According to Joyce he was at heart a kind and humane man, as well as being a good doctor. He was, however, very worried about our presence in the hospital at that time, when bombing of the naval dockyard was a nightly occurrence and frequently took place by day too. Naval casualties from the docks and warships came into the hospital with sickening regularity. So unpopular was our presence that the doctor only dared give us the minimum of time and attention. When I got to know the doctor better I found that I entirely agreed with Joyce's judgement of him.

The time I spent in the hospital at Brest passed very slowly. Bill Joyce and the German nurse, whose responsibility I was, were both kindness itself during the first week, which was the most difficult. Still unable to open my eyes and hardly able to move any of my facial muscles, eating was one of my biggest problems. My food had to be cut into tiny pieces and then fed to me on the smallest of spoons. The space between my lips was sufficient to take a small hazel nut kernel and any movement of the jaw tended to stretch the burnt skin on my face, which was painful and to be avoided.

But Bill Joyce patiently cut up all the solid food provided and fed me with an egg spoon. The food was always cold by the time I got it into my mouth and I found that unless told exactly what I was eating I could not recognize the taste. The whole process of eating was so long drawn out and boring that I ate less than a quarter of what was provided. Soup was a staple dish; generous bowls containing a little meat and lots of vegetables, mostly potatoes. Anyone who has tried to consume a bowl of soup with an egg spoon will know how quickly the appetite vanishes after the twentieth little spoonful, although the contents of the bowl are not much diminished. What I most enjoyed was the thinly cut black German bread, spread with margarine. This could be easily and tidily cut into little pieces to suit my mouth and, most important, I could feed myself. Fortunately, black bread was the main course at breakfast and supper. Eaten with sliced sausage, or spread with honey or jam, I found that I could enjoy it.

After six days under my lint mask I was suffering from the most unbearable itching all over my face. The desire to scratch was very nearly irresistible. I had however been told, and readily believed, that to scratch would seriously damage and scar the skin. For days I had been pleading with the nurse and with the doctor on the rare occasions he came to see me to put a new mask on my face, covered with fresh, cool, soothing grease. But the answer had invariably been no. The longer I could leave the original dressing in place the better my face would heal. Vanity gave strength to my self-control, but by the sixth day the irritation and my frustration had reached such a pitch that I would grip the sides of the bed with both hands and scream and swear at the top of my voice to relieve my feelings. I found this helped considerably and it also had the effect of emphasizing very noisily the desperate state I was in. On the seventh day, the nurse, who was a very sympathetic girl, told me in the morning that the doctor would that day come and remove the mask. I would hate to have to live again through those three hours I waited for the doctor.

He came after our midday meal. Very carefully and very slowly he peeled the lint mask off my face. It stuck by my right eyebrow, which had been bleeding, and there he had to use scissors. Elsewhere it all came away cleanly. He asked me to open my eyes. I tried hard to do so, both separately and together, but the eyelids would not part. He told me that they must be opened and that to leave them any longer would mean a difficult operation to separate the eyelids. Then he put a thumb on my upper eyelid and a thumb on my lower and forced my left eye open. It was extremely painful but effective. He repeated the process on my right eye.

At first I could not see anything but a haze of light. My eyes were full of mucus and pus. But after they had been very gently bathed by the nurse I found that my vision was nearly normal.

I spent nearly three weeks in the naval hospital at Brest, with Bill Joyce as my friend and companion. It was not until I was able to see him that I realized the extent of his courage and the extraordinary strength of his spirit. From his voice I had made a mental picture of him and expected to find him a strong, cheerful and healthy individual, who was temporarily out of action because of some shrapnel splinters in his leg, but who would soon be up and about again. The Joyce I saw was thin, weak and pale, clearly in constant pain and with both legs in plaster. I soon discovered that he was far more seriously wounded than I and that his chances of ever walking properly again were remote. He was expected eventually to recover the partial use of one leg, but his other leg was so full of fragments of cannon shell that the task of removing them was beyond the scope of the hospital surgeons. He had already undergone two operations and although the bigger fragments had been removed and one leg was comparatively free of shrapnel, there remained in the other leg over fifty scattered pieces of metal. And there was little more that could be done for him.

Bill Joyce could not have been more than nineteen years old when he was shot down. I had only to close my eyes and listen to him talking to see him as he was before; a strong husky youngster, with blue eyes and thick black hair, always full of energy and enthusiasm, irrepressibly cheerful and continually active. The Bill Joyce in the bed next to mine at Brest had not changed in spirit, but he would be a cripple for the rest of his life.

With my eyes open, life in the hospital became much easier and much more interesting. I was rapidly recovering my strength and all that handicapped my activity was the lint mask on my face which I did not wish to dislodge. I had a plaster cast on my right leg which I soon discovered was quite comfortable to walk on, although I could do little more than hobble.

With Bill Joyce I could be much more frank and confiding. For long periods we were left to ourselves, except for the sentry at the door of the ward, who was too far away to hear what we were saying and would not have understood anyway.

During these periods we would discuss our future more than the present and the past. To my astonishment Bill was absolutely determined to escape before he was taken out of France to a prison camp in Germany. I had exactly the same plans, but whereas there was a remote chance for me, as soon as my face had healed and my ankle mended, for Bill there was no hope whatsoever. Even if he used crutches, he did not have a sound leg he could put to the ground. Such, however, was his courage and determination that he was quite incapable of admitting this to himself. And I did not have the heart to point it out to him.

For two weeks our main topic of conversation was escape. Bill had a variety of harebrained schemes, all of which had the virtue of simplicity. His general idea was to drop out of a hospital window in the middle of the night and find someone in the French Resistance to hide him before the Germans found him. Unfortunately the windows of our ward were on the first floor and the drop to the ground was twenty feet or so. Nevertheless Bill Joyce was gradually piecing together a plan of the hospital, so that he could pick the most likely window, and he was also trying to bribe the sentries to bring him a plan of the town of Brest. As soon as he could move himself on crutches, Bill was quite determined to get out somehow.

I was in less of a hurry. I knew that to stand any chance of making a successful escape I would have to be fit enough to walk fast and far. I calculated that I needed at least a month for my leg to mend completely and for my face to heal sufficiently. But while Bill had never given any thought to the problems of escape before he became a prisoner and knew little enough about it, I had read and re-read every escape story published and met and talked to some of the few who had already escaped from France since the German breakthrough in 1940. I had always considered it very likely that I would end my operational career as a prisoner, it was a common enough fate in the PR business, and I had therefore to some extent prepared myself.

As we were both confined to bed during the whole of our stay in Brest, I had all the time in the world to relate in as much detail as I could remember the stories of the more ingenious and adventurous escapes of the first world war. These we would discuss to discover whether there was in them any idea which we could use.

The move from Brest came without warning and much sooner than we expected. One morning the doctor informed us that a hospital train was leaving Brest that night and that, in view of the constant bombing, it had been decided to move us elsewhere. It was with great relief that we learned that our destination was not Germany but another hospital in France some hundred kilometres to the east. This was a welcome postponement of the journey into Germany which we so much dreaded.

Three

THERE was a long ambulance train drawn up at the station, painted a dirty white and with enormous red crosses on its roof and flanks. It was being loaded with German wounded. When our turn came to be carried on to the train, we were allocated two stretcher berths in a long carriage. The stretchers ran down both sides of the carriage in three tiers. I got a middle berth and Bill Joyce was put onto the stretcher below me. When the train moved out of the station, every stretcher was occupied. There must have been between fifty and sixty wounded in the carriage.

A guard with a rifle had accompanied us and now stood beside us, in the narrow corridor. He was explaining at some length and in a loud voice that we were English airmen. It was embarrassing and uncomfortable. We kept very quiet, feeling acutely unwelcome.

There were a number of seriously wounded in the train and many others who needed attention. Harassed nurses were constantly rushing up and down the corridor. Our guard was always in the way and was beginning to be a nuisance to these busy women.

The senior nurse arrived in crackling, starched linen. A tall, robust woman of about forty years of age, she had straw coloured hair, pale blue eyes and a hard mouth. A large nose spoiled an otherwise handsome face.

'You have to move,' she addressed the guard decisively. 'Go down to the end of the corridor and keep out of the way.'

'I can't do that,' the guard protested. 'My orders are to stand beside them and to shoot if they try to escape.'

'Escape?' She was contemptuous. 'These two won't try to escape. If they so much as move from their stretchers I'll hit them over the head with a bedpan.'

There was a roar of delighted laughter from the Germans in the bunks around us.

'Now off you go.' She drove the guard away. 'In this carriage I give the orders. There'll be no escape and no shooting.'

The guard retreated, muttering to himself. Bill and I lay in silence, gazing in awe at this extraordinary woman. I do not think either of us would have had the courage to face her when she was swinging a bedpan, even if we had been fully fit and mobile. As it was, Bill could not even stand on his feet and I could only hop on my good leg.

'My God,' whispered Bill from the lower bunk, 'it's damn lucky we're a couple of cripples. Imagine if we'd been fit and had tried to escape. She'd have slaughtered us.'

'Surely, you're not afraid of a mere woman, Bill. Why don't you call her back and ask for a bedpan?'

'I'm not going to even ask her for a bottle. I'd rather wet the bed.'

The train rumbled slowly through the night. It was not possible to sleep, the stretchers were too hard and there was no air to breathe. All around us men were moaning and there was one who screamed intermittently. The nurses kept running back and forth.

I lay on my bunk in semi-darkness, dabbing my eyes with a piece of gauze. They watered continuously and needed to be cleaned of mucus every few minutes. Before leaving the hospital at Brest I had persuaded our nurse there to prepare a whole boxful of little squares of sterilized gauze. If I had not had these with me I would have been most uncomfortable and probably would have had to

try and beg some from the German nurses on the train. I was glad
to be independent. I also had a water bottle and shared the contents with Bill. The thick atmosphere in the carriage made us
very thirsty.

It was after ten o'clock when the train drew in to a station. Our
guard came along the corridor to reclaim us and we were both
quickly carried on to the platform. There were no goodbyes. We
had not exchanged one word with the Germans.

Half an hour later, after driving through the deserted streets of
a blacked out provincial town, we were again in a hospital. It was
a relief to get into bed.

The place was Guincamp, a town of about 8,000 souls. The
hospital was a small one on the outskirts of the town, staffed entirely by Germans. The nursing sisters appeared to belong to some
religious order. The doctors and orderlies were army personnel.

The room we lived in was on the fourth floor, looking over the
garden in front of the hospital. It was a pleasant room, with plenty
of light coming from a large unbarred window. There were only
two beds in the room. We were thoroughly comfortable and efficiently looked after by the nursing staff, who nevertheless remained distant and uncommunicative.

Our doctor was a cheerful, fat Army Lieutenant who warned us
constantly not to make any stupid attempt to escape and took
good care to see that we did not. In the corridor outside our room
a guard was permanently stationed during daylight. He was
always positioned at the head of the stairs, where he also controlled access to the lift. There was no way out of the corridor
except past him.

At night, a guard was put inside our room where he sat in the
corner at a small table and read all night. The door to our room
was locked and the guard held the key.

Furthermore, our clothes had been taken away, including our
shoes. If we found a way out of the hospital we would have to
go barefooted and in our hospital pyjamas. This might not have
mattered greatly if we could have made early contact with the
French Resistance. But, so far, we had met very few French people.
There was a Catholic priest who dropped in to see us occasionally
and there was also a little girl of about twelve years of age who
came round with a collecting box for some orphanage. But we

could never talk to either of them alone and, obviously, escaping was not something we could discuss in front of the Germans. We could only hope that our presence in the hospital had been reported and that the French would find some way of getting in contact with us.

As the days passed and I got stronger, my frustration increased. I had the strongest of convictions that, compared with what I would be confronted with in a prison camp, getting away from the hospital in Guincamp should be child's-play. I knew I had to make an early effort to escape, that I had to find a way round the apparent difficulties.

Bill Joyce shared my views and although I was now certain that he was physically incapable of walking more than ten steps on crutches, he insisted that he was coming with me. I left it at that and we plotted together as if we were both going to escape.

There was only one way out of our room and that was via the window. It was easy to solve the problem of lowering ourselves fifty feet to the ground. The hospital was kept immaculately clean and employed a number of vacuum cleaners for this purpose. These machines were equipped with long lengths of electric flex which were stored in a cupboard in the lavatory down the corridor. With one or two coils of this flex, we could reach the garden below. I could easily steal the coils during a visit to the lavatory.

The next decision to take was whether to climb out of the window in daylight or at night. We argued over this for days. During daylight there was no guard in the room and, at certain periods, for instance immediately after lunch, we could count on being left undisturbed in our room for as long as two hours. On the other hand, on our way down to the ground, we would pass by at least three windows on the lower floors, all probably occupied by Germans and, if there was a sentry on the main gate, we would probably be in full view during our descent. Even supposing we were lucky enough to avoid being seen on our way down, we would find ourselves barefooted and in pyjamas in the garden below. No Frenchman could possibly be expected to take under his wings two fugitives in that condition. Particularly as one would be on crutches with both legs in plaster and the other hobbling painfully with one leg in plaster. It was really too much to hope for.

Going by night would eliminate the danger of being seen during our descent from the window and would offer the concealment of darkness during our subsequent journeyings. It was a much better proposition, except that it meant disposing of the guard in our room by violent means.

Bill had no qualms about this.

'We'll wait until, say, midnight,' he said, 'then you call the guard over and while he's talking to you, I'll hit him over the back of the head. We need an iron bar or something.'

I did not like it at all. In the first place I did not think the rules permitted violent action of that nature by a prisoner-of-war. Secondly, I thought it was not worth the very serious consequences we would be risking. If our prospects of escaping had been really good, or if it had been a matter of disposing of the last frontier guard who stood between us and freedom ten yards away, then I might have resorted to violence or manslaughter. But, just to arrive in the garden outside the hospital, barefooted, in pyjamas, with the high probability of being re-captured within the hour, did not balance an equation which might include murder. If caught, we would certainly be sentenced to death by a military court martial. I was quite certain that an escaper had to avoid these risks, unless he was already under sentence of death and had nothing more to lose.

Nevertheless we continued with our preparations, hoping we might find a way of modifying our plans and so avoiding violence. We started a concentrated campaign of persuasion to get the doctor to let us have our clothes back. I stole one length of flex, which would get us more than half way to the ground, and hid it in my mattress. I could steal another at the last minute.

I also found a weapon with which to hit the guard over the head. It consisted of a light metal tube, about a foot long, which I discovered while exploring the cupboards in the lavatory. At one end it was enclosed in a rubber handle for about three inches of its length. I could not imagine what purpose it served, but it looked ideal for our needs. It was too light to do any serious injury and the rubber handle would also help to soften the blow. I hid it under my pyjamas and stored it with the stolen flex inside my mattress.

We now had all the basic equipment to put our plan into practice. If only we could get our clothing back, particularly our shoes, we might have a chance of getting away. Or, at least, I might. I was sure that Bill would eventually have to admit that he did not have the strength to try.

On the other hand, I was feeling really fit. For three weeks I had been performing strenuous physical exercises whenever we were left alone. I could hop around on my good leg for half an hour at a time without pausing and my other leg would support my weight for a short time. I calculated that I could hobble away at a reasonably fast pace and cover a considerable distance. Once I was clear away, I could cut the plaster off my wounded leg which, I was sure, was now nearly mended.

I also exercised my arm and shoulder muscles for long periods every day and was certain that I could lower myself down the flex, when it came to climbing out of the window.

Bill had been provided with a pair of crutches and, with their help, could propel himself down the corridor to the lavatory with considerable skill. He admitted, however, that the leg he used to support himself was still very weak and knew he could only travel a limited distance.

We decided to be cautious and to test the strength of the electric flex we were going to use for our descent from the window. I attached a length to a ring bolt in the wall which served to secure the window shutters. Sitting on a chair with the flex held in my hands, I got both feet up against the wall. Thus I was able to apply all the force of both my arms and legs.

The flex showed no sign of breaking, but when the ring bolt came out of the wall, the chair went over backwards and I shot across the floor like a projectile, coming to rest against the door. The crash was deafening.

I was too stunned to move for a moment, but Bill's quick thinking saved the situation. He collected the flex and tucked it under his mattress. Then he distributed all the various objects from his bedside table artistically round the floor. The table itself he turned on its side. He added one of his crutches to the mess on the floor.

I picked up the overturned chair and opened wide the shutter, to hide the hole in the wall. When the nurse came in a moment later, I was lying on my bed reading and Bill was sitting on the edge of his, surveying the wreckage.

'I'm very sorry, nurse,' he was most apologetic, 'but my crutch slipped.'

Four

I WAS ready to go. We had been at Guincamp nearly ten days and I was convinced that I was quite fit enough for the Germans to decide to ship me to a prison camp deep in the Fatherland. I knew that unless I did something very quickly, the opportunity would go by.

Later that afternoon, I tackled Bill on the subject. I was embarrassed because of what I must say to him. But it had to be done.

'Bill, I can't wait any longer. If they give us our clothes back, I'm going out of the window, the same day. If they don't, I'll have to risk it anyway and go barefoot. But I'm going in daylight. I'll just have to hope I'm not seen on the way down and then run for it. I can move fast, even with this cast on my leg.'

Bill said nothing.

'Now, what about you? You'll never make it on crutches. Honestly, I don't think you'll even be able to lower yourself down the flex without breaking your neck as well.'

'Oh, I know that, skipper,' Joyce was quite resigned. 'I haven't got a chance. But it's done me good to fool myself that I might make it. If I come with you, it will hold you back to my pace and we'll both be caught. I've realized that for a long time. I just didn't want to face it.

'But why don't you go out at night,' he continued. 'You'll give yourself a much better chance. I'll knock out the guard for you.'

'No, Bill. No. It's out of the question. The penalties are too drastic. I'll take my chance in daylight. What you've got to do is get thoroughly fit and mobile, even if it takes you six months. You can escape from a prison camp—it's been done before. Or you might get an even better chance from a hospital. But you've got to wait until you can walk. Otherwise, it does not make sense.'

'OK, boss. Whatever you say.'

The German doctor came to visit us the next morning. He gave us a much more thorough examination than usual.

'I think your bones are mended, Major,' he said to me. 'We'll give you an X-ray very soon now and perhaps we can take off the cast.'

'What about me, doctor?' asked Joyce.

'I'm afraid you'll have to be more patient. Much more patient. We'll X-ray you too, but you are going to remain in plaster for a long time yet.'

Again I broached the subject of our clothes, reminding the doctor that he had twice promised to return our uniforms.

'I'm no longer confined to bed, doctor, and it really is undignified to have to spend the day walking around in these ridiculous pyjamas.'

The doctor smiled crookedly, as though at a secret joke.

'You'll have your uniform tomorrow, Major. You have my word as a German officer.'

Again that nasty smile.

'And when will you take off the plaster, doctor?'

'Very soon, Major. You seem to have made excellent progress. Your face, too, is healing nicely.'

When the doctor had gone, I turned to Bill.

'What did you make of that?' I asked. 'I think he's got something up his sleeve. He was too damned pleased with himself. You don't think that he could be planning to move us out tomorrow?'

It was a most uncomfortable and unsettling thought.

'No,' said Bill with conviction. 'We really aren't ready to be moved yet.'

As far as he was concerned, he was right.

'Well,' I said, 'if they bring my uniform tomorrow, particularly my shoes, I'm going out immediately after lunch. I don't trust that damned doctor. I'm sure he is plotting something.'

The next morning at seven o'clock, the senior nurse came in with our uniforms. I was delighted to see that my shoes were also there.

'X-ray in half an hour,' she announced. 'You can get dressed afterwards.'

When I had been X-rayed, the plaster cast was removed from my right leg. The feeling of lightness and mobility I experienced was exhilarating. I had the sensation that I could run for miles and break all existing records. In fact, when I put my wounded leg to the ground, it felt stiff and unpliant. But, at least, it bore my weight.

Bill, poor fellow, remained in plaster.

By the time the doctor came up to our room at ten o'clock, I was fully dressed and pacing the floor trying to exercise the muscles of my right leg. I had already visited the lavatory and stolen another length of flex and was all tensed up for the descent from the window.

Bill was fully dressed too, but lying on his bed, exhausted after the struggle of getting his trousers over his plastered legs. It had taken the help of a German orderly and myself to get him dressed.

'I hope you are happy, Major.' The doctor was smiling broadly. 'You are ready for a nice country walk?'

The bastard was way ahead of me.

'I'm feeling fine, doctor, and I'd like to thank you and the nursing staff for all the expert care I have had.'

I was saying the first things which came into my mind. I felt that I had to talk to distract attention from my purpose which, it seemed to me, was too obviously visible in my attitude and expression.

'Most kind of you to say so, Major. Now I have some excellent news for you. At exactly eleven o'clock we are leaving the hospital and taking a train for Germany. Please put your things together and be ready. We don't want to miss the train.'

I felt sick and cold with disappointment. I was going to end up in Germany without even having attempted an escape.

The doctor was still speaking, I had not been listening.

'I will be accompanying you,' he said. 'I have ten days leave and will visit my family in Düsseldorf. It is a great pleasure for me. There will also be two guards.'

He walked to the door and opened it.

'Herein,' he barked.

Two soldiers clomped in. They were young, alert men, armed with a rifle and a pistol.

'These two will not leave you alone for an instant from now until we arrive at our destination. Their orders are to shoot if you try to escape. I hope you will not be foolish.'

He turned and left the room. The two guards remained.

By the time we had been transported to the local railway station it was nearly one o'clock. We had not had our lunch and were both hungry. We were shepherded into the waiting room and the two guards, very unceremoniously, evicted all the other occupants. The doctor disappeared to talk to the station master.

The two guards were dour and uncommunicative. Not even Bill's incessant efforts to make conversation, using the extraordinary pidgin German in which he was now crudely fluent, drew any response. They remained aloof and watchful. We settled down to wait, and it was a long wait.

The train we were supposed to take never did arrive and it was after seven o'clock in the evening before we left Guincamp. We travelled all through the night, sleeping fitfully and uncomfortably in our second class seats. When, at long last, the train drew in to the Gare Saint Lazare it was past nine o'clock in the morning.

There had been no opportunity, not even a fleeting one, of escape. While we were in the compartment, one of the three Germans had always remained awake. If we went to the lavatory at the end of the corridor, one of the guards would escort us, closing himself inside the stinking little compartment with us.

The Gare Saint Lazare was thronged with Parisians. For the first time, my hopes revived. Maybe I could run into the crowd and disappear. The Germans would not dare to shoot and any Frenchman would help me. I had to make up my mind quickly. The doctor had told me that we were not leaving the train to cross the city. Our carriage would be shunted round to the Gare de l'Est, where it would be attached to another train bound for Frankfurt-am-Main.

There was a mobile newsstand on the platform, not far from our compartment. I asked the doctor whether I might go and buy a few papers to read during the journey.

'Of course, Major,' he answered politely. 'By the way, how is your leg feeling?'

He grinned at me, as if he knew the answer to his question. My leg, the one which had been in plaster, was now hurting abominably. Every muscle seemed to have seized and it was very painful even to put it to the ground.

'Hurting just a little, is it?' he continued. 'Don't let it worry you. It's a temporary effect. Do go and buy papers. We'll be watching you. And remember, Major, I can run much faster than you.'

I was beginning to dislike the man thoroughly. He was always one jump ahead of me. I hobbled painfully down the corridor and climbed down from the carriage. Two guards followed me. I walked over to the newsstand. The guards remained by the carriage door.

It was about a twenty yard walk and I was having difficulty in putting my weight on my right foot. I was in full uniform, such as it was, and long before I reached the news vendor, the attention of the crowd on the platform was focused on me. I had been recognized as a British airman.

There was a sudden silence and a certain tenseness in the atmosphere. People stopped moving and turned to look. The paper seller was standing there frozen, watching my approach.

'Je voudrais les journaux et quelque revues.'

'Mais oui, monsieur le commandant. Avec plaisir.'

Rapidly he assembled a great pile of newspapers, magazines and paperbacks. I looked back at the train. In the window of the compartment was the doctor, his pistol in his hand. The two guards were both standing where I had left them, at the carriage door. Their rifles were unslung and pointing in my direction. I turned back to the paperman.

'Combien je vous dois?'

'Mais rien du tout, mon commandant. C'est le moindre que je puisse faire.'

I felt he meant it and for a weak moment I was so touched that I felt near crying.

'Je vous remercie, monsieur. Vive la France.'

'Vive l'Angleterre.'

I tried to make my walk back to the train as dignified as possible, but I felt defeated. The doctor said nothing when I again sat down in the compartment. He tucked his pistol back into its holster. The guards came in and sat down in their appointed places.

The day's journey was the longest and cruellest I have ever experienced, but by six o'clock in the evening we had arrived in

Frankfurt. A deadly depression had settled on Bill and me from the moment we had left the Rhine behind us. Perhaps Bill sensed something of the ultimate finality of that frontier, for he was never to re-cross it.

Durchganglager Luftwaffe was a tram ride from Frankfurt station. It was the most ordinary of journeys but to us it had a nightmarish unreality which was frightening. We were travelling in a common tram, crowded with ordinary people who did not know who we were or, if they did, did not care. They were all free to ring the bell and get out at the next stop. If we had tried, we would have been shot. It was such a degrading and undignified way of entering captivity that it corroded the little courage we had left.

The gates of Dulag Luft closed behind us. Our escorts from Guincamp departed. Bill and I were separated and were not to meet each other again for a very long time. I still had his razor and he had my pullover.

I hated Dulag Luft. It was one of the most unreal and unpleasant places in which I ever was confined. The initial solitary confinement was nothing, nor were the repeated interrogations and the trick questions. What was really uncomfortable was the atmosphere of the prison camp itself, after one had been released from the cells and joined the other air force prisoners held there.

It was very difficult to put one's finger on what was wrong with the place. But it was a feeling which grew stronger as the days passed. When I left Dulag Luft, after a stay of two weeks, I had not resolved the problem to my complete satisfaction.

Life was comfortable there. The beds were good, the food dull but adequate. It was full of new prisoners, most of whom were old friends. All of us were held there for a short time before being transferred to larger prisoner-of-war camps deeper inside Germany.

Looking back on that experience, analysis is now easier, perhaps too easy. Dulag Luft had a so-called 'permanent staff' of British officers who remained there to shepherd the newcomers into the German system. Normally new prisoners went to Dulag Luft for interrogation and departed to other camps within two or three weeks. The Germans found it convenient and practical to keep a small staff of prisoners at Dulag Luft who provided continuity of organization on the British side.

We newcomers found ourselves treated as second class citizens by our own kind and were very ready to resent this. They were the directing staff, we were the new course of pupils. Their task was to indoctrinate us, equip us with the German supplied clothes and despatch us elsewhere. They messed separately from us and ate better food. They had their own reserves which had accumulated over the months. We were fed communally and took what was provided, which was not always a great deal. They had the superiority of experience and an unfounded authority. We were ignorant new boys.

They lived their comfortable, withdrawn lives and were normally well able to put down any budding revolt among the latest arrivals. The truth is that they were doing a very necessary job efficiently; the doubt which arose in the minds of more than one of the transient newcomers was whether their efficiency was not of more assistance to the Germans than to the RAF. It was an unpleasant thought which only rarely surfaced. What we did not know and could not be told was that these men were performing a very essential function within our overall intelligence network. They too would have liked to move on to a permanent prison camp, but the problem of replacing them was not easy to solve.

We newcomers did not know this and, more than once, bitter arguments erupted. The most delicate subject was escape. So many of us, frustrated at not having got away while we still had an excellent chance in France or the Low Countries, were trying too hard.

A new boy, aggressive, even truculent, would corner one of the staff.

'Listen. I want to try a tunnel from the top block, at the north end. Can I do that? I'm asking you officially.'

'Well, you see, there's nothing to stop you trying, really. But you won't be here long enough. Why don't you wait until you get to a permanent camp?'

'What do you mean, not long enough? That block is ten yards from the wire. We could get a tunnel out in three days, maybe two.'

'I wouldn't count on that, old boy. What about the dispersal and the shoring? It would take you ten days at least. I know. We've tried it.'

Sometimes this would be the end of the conversation. Occasionally, it would go further.

'I don't give a tinker's cuss for what you've tried. I can do it in three days and if I'm moved before it's finished I can assure you that someone else will take over. What do I care? Maybe you'd even like to go out yourself.'

The last sentence was added with malice.

What was the poor permanent staff to do with these hotheads? The top block, at the north end, where it was only ten yards from the wire, stood on ground which was honeycombed with old tunnels. The Germans had discovered every one and controlled the terrain more carefully. To the old stager, the idea was boringly stupid. The new boy was just another ignorant, impetuous headache.

I was glad to leave Dulag Luft, after a stay of two weeks. I had quarrelled badly with authority and got nowhere.

'Why don't you wait until you get to a permanent camp?'

This was always their answer. And in my case, as had happened before me and would happen after me, they had the last word.

Spangenberg

SPANGENBERG is a grim medieval castle perched on the top of a conical hill, in the very heart of Germany, not far from Kassel. Who built it, or what its function is in peace time, I never knew. In times of war, it is turned into a high security prison. French prisoners scratched their names on its dungeon walls during the Franco-Prussian war in the 1860s; British prisoners were interned there in the Great War of 1914–18; I added my name to the lists on its walls in 1942.

We arrived at Spangenberg station on 17 February, a small party of RAF officers, not more than forty strong. We were all new prisoners with little experience and few belongings.

During the train journey from Dulag Luft our Luftwaffe guards had been alert and watchful. As we were travelling in broad daylight, there was no hope of jumping off the train unobserved and a high probability of being shot if one had risked it. Nobody tried. I, myself, had no intention of trying to escape because I was far from being fit. My ankle was still very weak and I could only walk with the aid of two sticks. I was perversely relieved that no real chance of escaping from the train had offered itself. Studying the possibilities, I concluded that escaping from a train would have to be a night operation, but that it was certainly possible. I determined to be fully prepared for the next train journey, whenever it occurred.

When we de-trained at Spangenberg station, we were handed over to German guards. It soon became evident that these soldiers were rougher and more short tempered than our previous Luftwaffe guards had been. The kindred spirit which the Luftwaffe liked to claim existed between airmen was certainly lacking.

While the German Army was a new experience for us, it soon became obvious that they had not encountered the RAF before. Perhaps what bewildered them most was that we did not comport ourselves with the dignity and decorum which is to be expected from officers. The Germans react well to professionally correct behaviour and parade ground manners, but they are completely lost when they find themselves confronted with an undisciplined and unruly mob of overgrown schoolboys, which is how we were behaving. The German captain who commanded the guard party was near apoplexy before he had us lined up in columns of five and counted.

RAF aircrew have never had a great reputation for being smart on parade, although, when the occasion demands, they can perform the necessary drills with due soldierly precision. Our arrival at Spangenberg, however, did not seem to be one of these occasions and the fussy German captain did not impress us. It was also difficult to feel in the mood for disciplined behaviour when, because of our attire, we felt and looked like a shambling rabble of refugees.

In the whole party, no one had a uniform cap, most were bareheaded and a few wore woollen Balaclavas. I had on a Polish army greatcoat which was long enough to touch the ground when I was standing. It was a quite shapeless garment and the sleeves were at least six inches longer than my arms. I had carefully selected it from the pile offered at Dulag Luft as giving the maximum amount of wrapability when used as a blanket. For the German winter was freezing cold and at night one needed all the covers one could lay hands on. Most of the others had equally grotesque garments, provided by the Germans from captured stores. Complete uniforms were rare in our party, the one outstanding exception belonging to Tony Barber, who was resplendent in an army lieutenant's uniform, complete with Sam Brown.

Tony Barber was an Army officer who had been lucky enough to get himself seconded to the RAF and had come to Benson to fly with PRU. He had had engine failure on a high level reconnaissance mission in a Spitfire and had had no alternative but to bale out calmly and land in the hands of the enemy. His uniform had not suffered. But many others among us had survived violent crash landings, burning aircraft or days and nights in a dinghy in the North Sea. Uniforms do not stand up to that kind of treatment.

After some twenty minutes of complete chaos, during which time German tempers had risen to the danger point, we were finally assembled in the station yard in some sort of order and marched off.

To our surprise our destination was not the fortress on the hilltop but a rather picturesque prison situated right in the middle of the village of Spangenberg, alongside the river. This was known as the lower camp and was administered together with the castle. The official name of the two prisons, the one in the village and the other on the hill, was Oflag IXA/H.

We were only there for a few days and I remember it as an unreal, surprisingly pleasant interlude. Geese and ducks paddled about in the river, right under our barred windows. On the far bank we could observe the normal bustling life of a German village. For the first time in many months we saw women, indeed the inhabitants of the village seemed to be mostly women and children. The sturdy, buxom, rosy cheeked country girls were a glad sight and we never tired of watching them. But they reminded us painfully of the enforced celibacy we were enduring and would have to endure for the remainder of our captivity.

The Lower Camp was occupied by Army officers, who had already been in captivity for a long time. They had developed the basic Kriegie philosophy, which we had yet to learn and which came with experience. I find it difficult to define this philosophy. Oversimplifying, one might say that our behaviour came to be governed by just one material factor—Red Cross food parcels. When these were available, we filled our empty bellies, laughed and were energetic. When there were none we retired into our shells and hibernated, both mentally and physically. Many prisoners took to their beds and stayed there.

The other governing rule was to live for today and close one's mind to the future. We made ourselves as comfortable as possible and our most precious possessions were warm blankets and woollen sweaters. We developed an exaggerated selfishness but remained very aware of it and were glad to salve our consciences by being generous when generosity was called for. This was why old time prisoners, well endowed with the riches of prison camp life, were usually kindness itself to new arrivals whose total wealth was often no more than the clothes they stood in.

Many of the prisoners in the Lower Camp at Spangenberg had been captured in Crete. They had only just then arrived in Germany and were gaunt, hungry men with short tempers. They had survived incredible hardships and near starvation in Salonika and an unending journey across Europe, crowded forty to a cattle truck, most of them suffering from dysentery. We listened to their stories and admired them. Certainly, we had had an easy time. We hoped never to be reduced to their state but we learned a lot from them of how men live when their only preoccupation is to survive for another day.

It was a clear, sunny morning when we, the RAF contingent, were moved from the Lower Camp. After the usual shambles of being lined up and counted, during which German tempers got very frayed, we marched out through the gate.

The road circled round the hill, climbing steadily. For about the first kilometre, I walked with the column and then decided I had had enough. I could hardly put my right foot to the ground and the ankle had started to swell alarmingly. It had been foolish of me to expect that my ankle would stand up to so long a walk. But the forbidding sight of the castle on the hill top, which was to be our prison, had given me the idea of enjoying a last country walk before the gates slammed shut behind me.

I dropped back behind the column, with an armed guard in close attendance. Sitting down on the grass verge, I waited to see what my captors would do now. The familiar pandemonium developed with gratifying speed.

The soldier who was guarding me yelled for the Feldwebel. The Feldwebel came running back and started shouting at me. I pointed to my bandaged leg. He then galloped back after the still advancing column to report to the Leutnant, who in turn reported to the Hauptmann.*

It seems to be a regulation in the German Army that when reporting to someone senior in rank, one must shout with all the power of one's lungs. The noise was deafening, even in the peaceful countryside. Orders were screamed up and down the line and eventually the column was brought to a halt. The top brass marched menacingly towards me followed, at regulation distance, by a descending order of NCOs.

As one man, the group of prisoners collapsed on to the grass verges at the side of the road and lit up cigarettes. Immediately,

* Captain.

the captain and his retinue turned about and rushed back up the road, screaming at the prisoners.

'On your feet!'

'Put out those cigarettes!'

'Discipline! There must be discipline!'

Nobody took the slightest notice.

Eventually, the captain and his posse headed back towards me. As they approached, I put out my cigarette, thinking that further provocation would be superfluous and probably dangerous. So far, the incident had been amusing and it was a definite victory for us in the long contest of one-upmanship which was one of the few ways in which we could engage the enemy.

Gamesmanship was a closed book to the Germans; they did not know the rules of the game or appreciate its finesse; they had never heard of Stephen Potter. To us it was an outlet for our frustration and an antidote to our despair. To infuriate our captors, to make them look ridiculous, was the best morale builder we had. The satisfaction of winning a small and temporary victory was very sweet and gave renewed courage, during the blacker days of the war.

Basically, however, this was not a game but a serious policy. Our first duty as prisoners was to escape, but opportunities to attempt this only occurred rarely. Our second duty was to force the enemy to divert as many troops as possible to the tasks of guarding and administering the prison camps in which we were lodged. The most effective way we could achieve this was by being difficult to handle and by making as great a nuisance of ourselves as possible. Attempts to escape, even if they seldom succeeded, had a very high nuisance value and in all established camps wherever we found ourselves, first priority was given to escape activities. But at all times the ploy of gamesmanship continued without pause. Stephen Potter would probably agree that the exact definition of the game was lifemanship.

The infuriated Germans were now drawn up all round me in battle order. The fat captain was already red in the face from his exertions. As he started screaming at me I watched the swelling veins in his neck and began to be seriously concerned that he would burst a blood vessel. Suddenly he stopped shouting and glared at me with malevolent, bloodshot eyes. Obviously, I was expected to reply, but I had not understood a word. I did my best to look blank, uncomprehending and, at the same time, encouraging. I must have had quite a fatuous expression on my face.

After a painful thirty seconds of complete silence, the captain turned about, looking rapidly round his retinue.

'Where the hell is that bloody interpreter?'

Everybody jumped to attention and booted heels clashed together like castanets.

'Sofort, Herr Hauptmann.'

They all started running in different directions, all yelling for the Dolmetscher. But the missing Dolmetscher had goofed off. He was, in fact, comfortably riding in the back of the horse drawn cart which was bringing our kit bags up the hill. Just when the panic and confusion was at its height, the cart arrived and the unfortunate interpreter jumped down, buttoning up his tunic and straightening his cap.

'Zu Befehl, Herr Hauptmann.' He saluted the captain with great verve, but he was white as chalk in the face.

I could not follow the subsequent conversation but I would not have been surprised to hear, the next day, that the interpreter had been shot at dawn or, at least, posted to the Russian front.

The interpreter turned to me.

'Why march you not?'

'I am wounded.' I tapped my bandaged leg with my stick.

'Why have you not said so before we start?'

'Nobody asked me.'

'You will be strongly punished if you are not saying the truth.'

'Call a doctor.'

The interrogation went on for a long time, long enough for everybody to calm down and for the main column of prisoners to smoke a second cigarette. Finally I was put on to the baggage transport, where I made myself comfortable. The Dolmetscher was made to walk.

Now that the baggage cart had caught up with the column, the horses had no difficulty in keeping station a few yards behind. The steepness of the winding road was beginning to tell, more on the marching men than on the horses. By the half way mark I could see that the boys were beginning to tire.

In the circumstances it was a mistake to start singing. For one thing we were going to need our breath to climb the hill; more to the point it annoyed the German soldiery who had taken a thorough dislike to us. We sounded far too cheerful.

I suspect that it was Bill Jennens who started the singing. He was the adjutant of our party, a great wing forward and with a voice like a bull. I am sure that he thought that a few rousing songs would revive our flagging spirits and get us up the hill with the minimum of pain.

'Pack up your troubles' went off well and the column took on a noticeable marching rhythm. 'Roll out the barrel' followed and I could observe from my ringside seat, that the rate of progress had definitely improved. But the next song, 'We're going to hang out the washing on the Siegfried line', was a disaster.

I do not believe that the Germans understood the words. Maybe the reiteration of the word Siegfried made them suspicious, maybe we were being too arrogantly cheerful. The net result was that some guards lost their tempers and swung the butts of their rifles, inflicting very painful damage on the more vulnerable prisoners at the sides and back of the column.

The singing died as suddenly as it had begun and the last mile of the climb was covered in sullen silence. One victim of a rifle-butt blow to the kidneys joined me in the wagon. He had been at the back of the column, where the guards had been able to hit from behind. He was by no means fit having only recently got over a cure of near frost-bite in both feet. Two days and nights in a dinghy in the North Sea usually resulted in frost-bite at that time of the year, if you were lucky enough to survive the ditching.

'Bloody stupid, adolescent behaviour.'

He was not only hurt but very angry.

'Not stupid,' I answered. 'We had the right idea, we just went too far. It's a matter of judgement.'

'You can't tell me that it was not stupid and irresponsible to start singing about the Siegfried line.'

'There I agree with you, it was a very bad choice. But the principle of the thing is right—don't you agree? Infuriate the goons, make them flap and panic, harass them, disturb them—that's what we have to do.'

'Not at the expense of my kidneys,' he answered, rubbing his back.

'I'm sorry about that,' I said, 'and I do agree that this last effort was below standard. On the other hand, you have to admit that these Germans now respect our little RAF contingent. They know they are going to have to watch us very carefully and that, in itself, is a victory. Quite apart from the fact that we destroyed the fat captain in that shambles at the station when we first arrived and again just down the hill when everybody sat down on the roadside.'

'That's all very true. But suppose those bastards had started shooting instead of just slogging us. What then? Would that have been clever?'

It was a critical question and I thought carefully before replying.

'No. The game as it should be played must at all costs avoid violence and injury. Violence is their weapon and we have no defence against it. If we provoke it we are the losers, as in this case. I think that there are two vital lessons to learn from our experience of this morning.'

'And what are they?'

'I suppose it really boils down to one principle. Attack the system but not the individual. Which means, never bait or try to infuriate a German soldier with a gun because he, as an individual, has a very human limit of self-control and, if pushed too far, may well press the trigger. On the other hand, with a German officer you can go almost to any limits, because he represents the system with all its rigid discipline and blind obedience. No German officer, however much you provoke him, would ever shoot you out of hand or even hit you. He will have you thrown in the cooler but he will not lose his self-control and get violent. So we should bait the officers but lay off the soldiers.'

'Maybe,' he was doubtful, 'you have something there. But it does mean that we have to be in control of ourselves. We can't let just anybody start a riot. Somebody has to give the orders and take the responsibility.'

'I entirely agree with you,' I answered. 'We must have discipline among ourselves and respect our own authorities. The Army can teach us a lot, although in my opinion they go too far and are too rigid. But I am pretty sure that we will develop a typically Air Force compromise, which will work.'

'Let's hope you're right.'

Two

WE halted on the castle drawbridge, in front of the massive main gates. Towering 120 feet above us were twin keeps which guarded the drawbridge. The moat below us was dry, some seventy feet deep and equally wide. It completely surrounded the fortress. When the gates were finally opened, we marched into the court-yard to find an unexpected reception awaiting us.

The 51st Highland Division, commanded by General Fortune, was on parade to welcome us. It was a very heartening sight and a courtesy which took us completely by surprise. The 51st was smart and orderly, all were wearing proper uniforms and looked like officers. We felt shamed and self-conscious as we tried to trans-form ourselves from the ragged mob we were into a disciplined body of RAF officers, but our long Polish greatcoats and Bala-clava helmets were too much of a handicap and the result was ludicrous.

We received the warmest of welcomes.

Inside the castle, where we lived for nearly three months, we rapidly settled into our individual and collective routines. Cold and hunger were our major preoccupations. No Red Cross food parcels had arrived at the camp and the German ration, as always, never filled our stomachs. We survived on a daily diet of a hand-ful of potatoes boiled in their skins, some thin soup and a tiny ration of bread. The Germans also provided acorn coffee and mint tea. Twice a week there was an issue of a litre of watery beer per man. But what we lacked was solid food.

From Dulag Luft where, compared to our present plight, life had been featherbedded luxury, we had all brought with us a small stock of cigarettes. These were in sealed tins of fifty, which is how they were shipped to us, through Red Cross channels. Soon the last tins of fifty were being opened and there was not even a rumour of any new supplies coming in. I can still remember the in-tense sensual pleasure we enjoyed when opening a sealed tin of fresh cigarettes and deeply inhaling the aroma of tobacco. It was almost as satisfying as smoking and, whenever a new tin was opened, it would be handed round the tobacco starved company so that each man could breathe his fill of that delicious scent. But generosity went no further than that.

Most people saved the butts of their own cigarettes. When their stock of fresh cigarettes was exhausted they would roll themselves cigarettes from the tobacco provided by the butts. A careful smoker could get twelve second-run cigarettes from a tin of fifty. They were strong but satisfying.

The RAF contingent lived all together in one enormous barrack of a room which was known as the Arab Quarter. We slept in two-tier wooden bunks which lined one wall of the room. A few stools and benches and two great solid tables completed the furnishings. It was at these tables that we passed most of our day, writing, reading, drawing maps, playing cards, chess or backgammon.

The army prisoners were in a different class altogether. They had been in the bag since Dunkirk and had learned long ago how to make the best of their lot. They had also had time to receive clothing and food parcels from home and were, as a result, warmly dressed and had small private hoards of food and cigarettes. They were also most kind to their poor relations, the RAF. They provided us with much appreciated woollen sweaters and with cigarettes when they were rich in this luxury. Occasionally, they invited us individually to tea, and these invitations were much sought after.

I remember very clearly the first tea party to which I was invited. There were three army officers living together in a room high up in the castle tower, with a glorious view over the valley below. They slept in real beds with sheets, blankets and pillows. There was a stove giving out a lot of heat and the room was homely with photographs, decorations and personal belongings. There were even chairs to sit in. They were most enviably well organized.

The tea was a miracle. All sorts of Fortnum & Mason goodies to eat, real Indian tea poured from a real teapot, canned milk and no shortage of sugar. It was difficult to exercise enough self-control not to be greedy. And after tea a cigarette. What luxury!

I felt only a qualified envy for this high standard of living, in comparison with our lot in the Arab Quarter. The food and the cigarettes I certainly coveted. But the comfort seemed then to be too resigned an acceptance of imprisonment. It gave to it a permanence which I was not ready to think of. In those days my thoughts were only of escape and I was sure that the opportunity would come soon.

When I met them at Spangenberg, these Army officers had already been prisoners for nearly two years and, with the disastrous war news that kept coming in at that period—the fall of Singapore, the fantastic German advances into Russia—they could not be blamed for thinking that they had many many years of imprisonment to endure. Unlike us, they had little hope of being moved elsewhere and Spangenberg castle certainly gave the impression of being escape-proof, although, less than a year before, the contrary had been proved.

The story was a remarkable one which always gave us hope and encouragement whenever it was re-told. I heard it first hand from John Milner, who impersonated one of the German officers, although I no longer remember the exact details of the dramatis personae involved. It was the classic example of the perfect walk-out, meticulously planned and brilliantly executed.

The Swiss Red Cross had the responsibility and the right to visit prison camps both in German and British territory, to see the prisoners were not being ill-treated and that the rules of the Geneva convention regarding the treatment of prisoners-of-war were being obeyed. It was a most useful and efficient organization. Far more than that, it saved our lives. For it was this organization that ensured the delivery of Red Cross food parcels to prison camps in Germany. Without these food parcels many of us would slowly and painfully have died from malnutrition—as did the Russian prisoners who did not come under the protection of the Red Cross. A visit by the Swiss Red Cross was always an event in any prison camp. It gave the opportunity of putting one's complaints clearly to the Swiss, in the presence, of course, of the Germans—for the Swiss were carefully and painstakingly neutral. The result, even if it only lasted for a few days, was always an improvement in rations and general conditions.

One day in 1941 a Swiss Red Cross commission had arrived at Spangenberg. As usual, the visit had been pre-announced well in advance and the German Kommandant had had the camp cleaned up and had issued a few extra boiled potatoes at midday.

When the Swiss commission arrived at the main gate, it was welcomed with due Teutonic ceremony by two officers of the prison staff, conducted across the castle courtyard and up the winding staircase to the Kommandant's office. The Swiss commission consisted, let us say, of a Swiss colonel in uniform and two civilians in plain clothes. All carried briefcases.

About an hour later a Swiss colonel in uniform and two civilians, all carrying briefcases, and escorted by two German officers, re-crossed the courtyard to the main gate. There the party halted while the Swiss colonel, in good German, thanked his hosts for their courtesy and apologized for the short duration of his visit, saying that train connections forced him to leave immediately.

The Germans shook hands with each of the Swiss in turn and saluted. In the best of parade ground voices, a German officer ordered the guards to open the gate. Both sides bowed politely to each other, the guards presented arms and the Swiss commission walked briskly over the drawbridge, down the hill and out of sight.

Each one of the Swiss commission which had just walked out of the main gate was, as must now be obvious, a British officer suitably disguised. The two escorting German officers who had shaken hands with the Swiss—and remained inside the gate—were also British officers in German uniform.

The whole act had been watched, from various discreet vantage points, by nearly every prisoner in the castle. Their hardly repressible joy at its complete success was only to be matched by the delicate anticipation of being able to watch, and quite openly, the terrible panic which was bound to occur when the real Swiss commission tried to leave.

Eventually, the true Swiss commission, having completed its work, descended to the courtyard. The Kommandant accompanied them, with a number of other officers. Lookouts flashed the news round the prisoners and within a minute every window overlooking the courtyard was crowded with a happy, expectant audience. There was no longer any need for secrecy, within seconds the Germans would know what had happened.

Every detail of the scene which ensued was savoured with malicious relish. The terrible consternation of the guard commander when he saw a second Swiss commission approaching. The bewilderment and mounting fury of the Kommandant at the way the gate guards were acting. The questions, the answers, the shouting, the screaming, the confusion and the panic. And finally the derisive cheers from the exultant prisoners. Perhaps it was only a tiny local victory but for those prisoners it partly revenged Dunkirk.

Life in the Arab Quarter was at least amusing. We were, each one of us, slowly beginning to come out of our shells and get to know our companions. Digger Larkin, who had the thankless and frustrating responsibility of being the senior RAF officer, and as such answerable for all our misdeeds, turned out to be an accomplished guitarist with the longest repertoire of barrack room ballads and bawdy songs I have ever heard.

Digger, the calmest and most imperturbable of Australians, would keep us amused until the small hours with his songs, accompanying himself on a guitar he had miraculously obtained.

There were Canadians among us and a surprisingly high proportion of Americans. These latter were young US citizens who, either for the hell of it or because they felt strongly about Hitler, had made the long and difficult journey to England to join the Eagle squadron, which was manned entirely by Americans.

Danny, for instance, claimed to be a Red Indian although he looked like a fat, pudgy Brooklyn businessman. Late at night when we lay sleepless with cold on our straw filled mattresses he would tell us wild stories of life in the Indian reservations. We did not believe a single word, but it was most entertaining. Fes Fessler, a giant of a man, spoke little, but when he did his American vernacular was most effective and he usually had the last word. I will never forget the occasion when a senior officer walked in unexpectedly and rather arrogantly ordered us to do something very trivial, like get out of bed or stand up or sit down. The senior officer concerned was from our side, not a German.

There was a moment's resentful silence. Then Fes's deep voice echoed through the barrack room.

'Go blow it out your ass.'

The senior officer wisely retreated under cover of the general laughter.

Marcus Marsh was the oldest of our group. He could easily give twenty years to any of us. In England he was a well known racehorse trainer, and had already achieved the great life's ambition of all trainers. The proudest day of his life had been when he led in Windsor Lad after winning the Derby. In spite of his age, Marcus had found a loophole which permitted him to join the RAF as an air gunner. There were few professions which were more dangerous.

I had seen Marcus in the paddock at race courses all over Southern England, invariably dressed in a smart, belted camel hair coat and a brown trilby pulled well down over his eyes. This elegance was now gone and Marcus, in his well worn battle dress, looked as unkempt as any of us.

His pale, almost bleached hair was thin on his scalp although he had a thick thatch at the back and sides of his head. Perhaps he was a little overweight but he had a relentless energy. He simply could not be unoccupied and was always the first to volunteer for any job which would serve the community. As long as he was working, he was happy.

Too old for the rigours and exertions of the escape game, Marcus confined himself to helping others to prepare for escape. When it came to intrigue and plotting he was in his natural element.

I think imprisonment was a heavy burden on Marcus. He was sometimes morose and solitary. But when he came to life, he had a bluntly devastating manner of expressing himself and an acute sense of humour which could be very caustic.

We all liked and admired Marcus. He had something we all lacked, a deep experience of life. He had made his living among the racing fraternity of England, one of the hardest schools in the world. As well as being an excellent judge of horse flesh, he was a very shrewd judge of men. Beneath the surface of his incessant activity, there was a serenity which we envied.

Another imperturbable and entirely self-sufficient character was Squadron Leader Woods, an Australian. Woody might have been playing the part of the eccentric inventor, for all the interest he took in normal everyday events. He was always utterly absorbed in his latest scheme to escape. He dedicated his whole day to map-making, or carpentry, or drawing carefully accurate plans of the castle. He got so involved in whatever he was doing that he would forget to eat. His ideas were always original and often weird.

There was also Barney Runnacles who, on the outbreak of war, had left his home in the Argentine and come all the way to England to join the RAF. The first thing one noticed about Barney was his luxuriant beard, which made him look like a Greek Orthodox priest. A beard was most uncommon in the RAF and was also strictly illegal. No less than the sovereign's permission was required to grow one. As Barney was only a young and junior pilot officer, there were irritable senior officers in plenty to tell him to go and shave, who indignantly quoted chapter and verse from our bible—King's Regulations and Air Council Instructions—where it was laid down that only the upper lip might be left unshaven. But Barney took no notice and never shaved while he was a prisoner. He was one of the outstanding characters of the Arab Quarter, irrepressibly cheerful, friendly and popular with us all. The fact that he also spoke excellent German was of immense help to us.

There were, of course, many Englishmen among us, although we formed the barest of majorities. A lot of other nations were fighting our war with us and it was heartening just to look around our own small community, to listen to the many accents and to appreciate the immense potential of the universal opposition which was building up against these confident, arrogant Germans. We knew then that we were going to win, in spite of Pearl Harbor and the Japanese, in spite of Tobruk, in spite of Singapore, in spite of the bombing of London.

One little trio of Englishmen came from PRU at Benson. We had all been shot down within a few days of each other. Tony Barber, Charles Hall and myself. There were a number of others, too. Oliver Philpot who, a year and a half later, was to make his remarkable escape via the famous wooden horse. Stafford Crawley, tall, studious and reserved, who wrapped a permanent cloak of mystery around himself. Bill Jennens, about whom there was no mystery at all. He was big, noisy, extrovert and a great rugby player. Bob Tuck, highly decorated and handsome, one of our fighter aces. Roy Smallwood, quiet and pleasant, who was to become one of the best tailors of German uniforms, as well as civilian clothes in Stalag Luft III. We all lived together, laughed, quarrelled and were hungry.

During the period before lights-out, the Arab Quarter was usually turned into a gambling casino. Seven and five card stud, Red Dog, Slippery Sam, dealer's choice, nothing was too wild. Bridge parties were relegated to the bottom level of the two tier bunks because there was no room for serious stuff at the available tables. The casino flourished and soon the army started coming in to lose their money to the RAF. The money in use was the most counterfeit of all time—Lagermarks. These specially printed notes were issued to us monthly by the Germans in accordance with a scale which depended on rank. I, as a squadron leader, was paid, let us say, a hundred Lagermarks a month. The supposed value of the Lagermarks was deducted from my pay at home at a pre-war exchange rate which was completely unreal and grossly in favour of the Germans. The Lagermarks, which we had no way of refusing, had no purchasing value whatsoever. They could only be spent in the German-run canteen in the castle where, apart from paying for the two litres of beer per week which were issued to us, one could buy only pencils, erasers, razor blades and an inferior hair oil.

Needless to say, most prisoners gambled away their stock of Lagermarks with reckless abandon. To us they had no value, although we were paying for them at home, at a ridiculously exorbitant rate of exchange. I calculated that the Lagermark racket must have cost me many hundreds of pounds in real money during the term of my imprisonment. In many prison camps, Lagermarks were used to paper the walls. Not that they were decorative, but it was a gesture of protest which gave us some satisfaction if no redress. Apparently, the British authorities expected us to save all the Lagermarks which we did not spend, take them back to England and trade them in for a credit. They did not seem to understand that no prisoner of war can accumulate and preserve property. If we escaped, which was our duty, there was no certainty at all of coming back to the same camp. And even one's closest friend was not going to look after a heap of dirty Lagermarks when his own had already been donated to the camp latrine for a more immediate purpose.

Three

It was natural that Charles Hall, Tony Barber and I should plot escape together. We had known one another at Benson, before being shot down and we still felt that we all belonged to the same unit. Charles and Tony had very different characters. Tony, tall and red-headed, was always absolutely sure of himself and never stopped talking. Charles was much more reserved, more uncertain and comparatively quiet. Charles badly wanted to escape but did not really believe it was possible. Tony had no doubts that he would escape and was full of ingenious ideas. Charles was very practical and methodical. He could make things with his hands, even when the primary tools were lacking. Tony was a theorist and a brilliant planner.

Together the three of us explored every idea, however farfetched, which any of us could conceive as a possible means of getting out of the castle. Tunnelling to freedom was obviously out of the question. It would be necessary to start well below the level of the moat and would have meant boring through hundreds of yards of rock. A great well shaft went vertically down to an unknown depth underneath the castle and there was said to be a secret passage cut through the mountain which led from the side of the well shaft to the open hillside below the castle. But nobody had ever found it and exploring the well shaft was a terrifying and difficult operation.

The only other ways out were across the moat or through the main gate. The moat was a formidable obstacle. Getting down into it was not an insuperable problem, one could get out of a window and lower oneself down on a makeshift rope. But climbing out of the moat again would have been as difficult as scaling the north face of the Matterhorn. There was also the small detail of the sentries who patrolled the far side of the moat.

The Australian Woody was convinced that he could get over the moat via the electric cables which served the castle. These power lines crossed high over the moat to reach the outside wall of the castle close to a window.

Woody had designed and was starting to construct a wooden trolley which he intended to hook on to the electric cables from the nearby window. The trolley was equipped with little wheels to give it mobility. As there was a distinct downhill gradient from the point of attachment of the power lines at the castle wall to the pole on the other side of the moat, Woody's plan was to ride across the moat under gravity, clinging to the bottom of the trolley. He then hoped to climb down the pole on the other side without electrocuting himself.

Woody could not be persuaded that the sag in the power lines, which would result from the addition of his weight and the trolley's, would mean that the last part of his traverse would be uphill and that, consequently, he would be left dangling from his trolley 100 feet above the bottom of the moat.

He was still working on various fantastic solutions to this difficulty when he was suddenly moved from the castle to another camp. I am sure this saved his life.

With Tony and Charles, I continued to examine and discard every idea our imaginations presented, concentrating on a way past the guards on the main gate. Another Swiss commission type of escape was out of the question, the Germans would not be fooled a second time. Hiding ourselves on the various carts, wagons and trucks which came into the courtyard was a possibility, but the thoroughness with which these vehicles were searched on their way out convinced us that it would only mean immediate discovery and ten days in the cells.

Relieving the guards on duty with a platoon of prisoners dressed in German uniforms was a classic method, attempted more than once. But the making of goonskins* and dummy rifles took a long time and we knew that we were only temporarily at Spangenberg. Furthermore, the German community there was a small one and they all knew each other well. A scheme like that could only have a chance of success in a very big prison camp.

'There is one perfect way out,' I said one morning, after a sleepless night during which my brain refused to stop working.

'Do tell.' Charles was sceptical as usual.

'Well. You know that twice a week the RAF party gets taken out of the gate over to the gymnasium on the far side of the moat. If we could hide up on that side of the moat and the evening appell could be rigged, we could be off down the mountain as soon as it was dark and have at least twelve hours start.'

'You're not serious,' said Charles indignantly. 'They count us out through the gate and they count us in again. If there are two missing they'll find us within minutes.'

* A faked German uniform.

'I know that, our problem is to falsify the counting.'

'Well, if you can think of a way of doing that, I'm with you. Have you really got an idea about how to do it?'

'I've got one or two, but nothing has really gelled. I'd like you to think about it too. After all, the count has been faked on appell a number of times with complete success. We might be able to apply the same methods.'

The appell was the twice daily parade of prisoners at which we were carefully counted, so that our captors could ascertain that we were all still there. Whenever a successful escape took place every possible ruse was employed to disguise the fact that any prisoners were missing. This gave the escapers valuable time to put distance between themselves and the camp before a general alarm was raised. It could only be done for one or two missing prisoners, perhaps three, unless the camp happened to be rich in ghosts.

A ghost was a prisoner within the camp who did not appear on the Germans' nominal roll. All well organized camps collected ghosts when the occasion arose, which, normally, was when an escape took place. If twenty men got out of a tunnel, another three or four would go into hiding inside the camp. Thus, when the escape was discovered, and the Germans made their count, it would appear that twenty-three or twenty-four had got out, instead of the true figure of twenty.

These individuals became ghosts. They had a safe hiding place to retreat to when the appell parade occurred and elaborate precautions were taken to ensure that they were not surprised by any snap appell at an unusual time. They slept in their hiding place. A camp with a good supply of ghosts could fake the appell count with ease, simply by putting the right number of ghosts in the appell line-up. Of course the system had its numerical limitations. But its value to small parties of escapers, and the majority of successful break-outs were achieved by one or two prisoners only, was immense.

'I think the army may have a few ghosts here,' said Charles, 'but they can't help us for this scheme. Not unless the ghosts are holed up in the gymnasium, which they obviously aren't or they would have pissed off long ago.'

'No,' I agreed. 'Ghosts won't help us in this case. We've got to think of something else.'

And think we did. I spent hours establishing that it was impossible for me, a small man, to hide myself under Fessler's Polish greatcoat. I tried hanging upside down from his shoulders with my feet tied together with a rope which bore down on his neck. I tried hanging from his neck the right way up. Even though Fes was a very big man and his Polish greatcoat was an immense shapeless coverall, it did not work. As he lurched along with me suspended under his coat, he looked so enormously fat that the guards would certainly have been suspicious. We had to throw that idea away.

We then tried to get the guards used to the idea of one of our party carrying with him a sack full of our gymnastic gear—medicine balls, boxing gloves, rubber soled shoes, towels, anything we could think of. The result was negative. No sacks through the gate, which put paid to my plan of being carried out in a sack.

I had almost discarded the gymnasium plan when I made a most surprising find. I had been looking all round the Arab Quarter for a safe hiding place for my various precious but illicit belongings, saws, files, various maps and odd articles of civilian clothing which I had acquired. I decided to dismantle the enormous circular table in the Arab Quarter to see if the massive central leg, which was probably hollow, could not be used as a hiding place. There was no lack of helpers and we had the table top removed very quickly. The central leg was, in fact, hollow but already packed with contraband of a previous occupation. We hauled out a large four-pronged grappling iron with some thirty metres of rope attached to it. Ideal for getting down into the moat or for getting out of it on the other side, if the grappling iron could be positioned.

I immediately claimed the find as my own and there was no dispute but a series of claims for second and third rights. The rope, when we examined it, was found to be useless. I was of the opinion that it must have lain hidden inside the table leg since the Franco-Prussian war. It was rotten and moth-eaten and would not have supported a marmoset.

When the table had been reassembled, Charles and I took a walk round the battlements. Charles's thoughts coincided exactly with my own.

'God damn it,' he said, 'we can do it. We have to get a new rope, of course. We're down in the moat during the morning exercise period. Someone in the gymnasium party has the rope and grapple on the outside wall of the moat. Divert the sentries. Lower the rope. Then up we go. We join the boys in the gym and then hide up. It's perfect.'

At certain hours the moat was open to all prisoners who wanted to use it for exercise. Descent to the moat was from the castle itself and one did not go past the guards, so there was no check on the number of prisoners going down or coming up. While the moat was open to prisoners there was also the usual small party in the gymnasium. It would not be difficult for a prisoner, sitting on the outside wall of the moat by the gym, to fix the grappling iron and surreptitiously lower the rope down to the bottom of the moat. As for getting the rope across the drawbridge, that should be simple. Any big man could wind the rope round and round his body and cover up with that multi-purpose garment, the Polish greatcoat.

'We had better register this with the escape committee, straight away. And we'll ask them to provide a new rope. They've probably got one or, if not, they can get one made by all their willing slaves.'

'No.' I firmly vetoed the idea. 'Let's leave the escape committee out of it until we're absolutely ready to go. They are too damned bureaucratic and interfering for my liking. They may make all sorts of difficulties and conditions. We'll work the whole scheme out to the last detail and we'll tell them the day before we go.'

'But the rope,' argued Charles, 'where do we get the rope if we don't tell the committee?'

'Leave the rope to me,' I said, 'I'll find us one.'

'When?' he asked disbelievingly.

'This afternoon. Come with me and you'll see.'

I had taken an intense dislike to the authoritative escape committee, which dated from the occasion when Tony and I registered with them our intention to jump off the train during the journey from Spangenberg to our next camp. This move, the grapevine had it, was certain and not very far away in the future.

The procedure we were made to go through to obtain the committee's fiat was farcical.

First, one had to pass a medical. This meant running up three flights of a spiral staircase to the doctor's office, timed against a stopwatch. When the man said go, I took off like a rocket and arrived at the tape completely out of breath, my ankle hurting like hell. The doctor, obeying the rules, grabbed my wrist and counted, looking at his watch. After thirty seconds he dropped my wrist and put his stethoscope to my heart. Then he looked me in the face, for a long ten seconds.

'You can't go in this condition,' he said.

'Why not, doctor?' I questioned him. 'Is there anything wrong with my pulse rate?'

'Sub-normal, if anything,' he answered 'and your lungs are perfectly sound. Running up the stairs didn't affect you. But with that burnt face, where can you go?'

'My dear doctor,' I said with slow emphasis, 'I will be very grateful if you'll write a medical report on my present physical state, as you find it, for this stupid escape committee. But please spare them and me any remarks which lie outside your own terms of reference.'

There was an embarrassed silence for maybe half a minute. Then the doctor smiled.

'OK,' he said, 'I'm passing you as fit.'

He had not looked at my right leg.

Eventually Tony and I received official notification that we were fit enough to escape from the train and that we had been allotted a period of seven days when we had priority for our attempt. This apparently meant that if we found ourselves on a train during that period we had the committee's gracious permission to escape. But nobody else did.

I was so angered by this bureaucratic stupidity that I went to see Digger Larkin.

I told Digger exactly what I thought, mixing no metaphors and using only the shortest of adjectives. First, I objected to the medical examination, which I thought was entirely *ultra vires* and unjustifiable. I cited the army prisoners from Crete we had met in the Lower Camp.

'Digger,' I said, 'you know very well that not one of those men was physically fit to escape, according to the standards of the committee here. So what were they supposed to do? Dismiss their guards? Give their parole? And when the slightest hint of an opportunity to get out occurred, while they were, for instance, still in Greece, with a friendly population, do you think they hesitated, just because they had dysentery? Many of them escaped, sick and weak as they were. Compared to them we are all Olympic champions.'

Digger, calm and unruffled as ever, gave me the official line. The opportunities were rare and had to go to those best equipped to take advantage of them.

'You know that's a lot of balls, Digger. And so is this business of allocating a time period to various individuals for the train escape. Getting off the train depends entirely on the determination and ingenuity of an individual in an unknown set of circumstances. You can't select the individual ahead of time or legislate for unpredictable circumstances.'

'But, Tommy, we are only trying to be fair.'

'Well, don't try so damned hard or you'll inhibit escape. Look at the practical side. When we travel from here to the new camp, we'll be in six or seven different compartments in the train—if we're not in cattle trucks. There'll be no communication between compartments. So what are we supposed to do?—the ones who have not got permission to escape. Go to sleep? For the whole journey? Suppose I cut a hole in the floor in my compartment, but it's not my week to escape, what do I do? Call a meeting of the escape committee?'

'Now, let me explain . . .'

'Digger, I don't want explanations. I just want to tell you this. On the next train ride I am going to do my damnedest to get out, permission or no permission. Anybody who wants to can follow me. As far as priorities go, it can only be done one way. The first one ready to go gets the first crack. I can assure you that down at our level there aren't going to be any arguments.'

'Tommy, please let's take this a little calmly. This escape committee here is only doing its job. If they didn't control escape activity, there would be clashes of interest and interference between uncoordinated escape attempts. How would you like it if you'd planned to do a Woody across the power lines tomorrow night and found three other parties trying to do the same thing?'

'My dear Digger,' I answered, 'the trouble with the escape committee here is that they have no operational troops. They are only administrators. Nobody is going to get out of this bloody castle, unless one of our party pulls off a miracle. The committee has got all the time in the world for over-administring, simply because there's never any action.'

'So what do you want, Tommy?'

'A little logic and no obstruction. On the train you are going to be the SBO.* The committee's authority stops short at the castle gate. I want your permission to get off the train, if I can, in whatever circumstances. I can promise you that I won't interfere with anybody else's attempt, but will give maximum cooperation.'

'You obstinate Pommie bastard,' said Digger, in the friendliest of tones, 'I'm going to have to give you one of my last cigarettes while I think this over.'

We smoked in silence. The enjoyment of tobacco was too rare a pleasure to be disturbed by argument.

'OK, Tommy,' said Digger, putting out his cigarette with great care, 'if you can get off the train, go right ahead. If you want any backing, let me know, I'll do all I can.'

'I want some food,' I answered.

'Until some parcels arrive, there isn't any. You know that. But there is supposed to be a consignment on its way from Dulag. I don't run the escape committee, as you know. But I'll certainly tell them to put some provisions aside for anybody who wants to escape from the train.'

And with that I had to be content.

Four

EARLY after our arrival at Spangenberg I had made friends with an army major who taught me one of the most useful accomplishments I could have acquired as a prisoner of war. Frank could pick any lock he was confronted with and I had spent long afternoons with him learning this skill. By the time I left Spangenberg I was criminally proficient.

Frank was a thorough and most conscientious teacher. First he taught me the basic mechanics of the mortice lock and the padlock and I spent hours taking locks apart, re-assembling them and mak-

* Senior British Officer.

ing keys to fit them. He showed me how to make a master key which would open a whole series of locks of a particular type. I also learned that ninety per cent of all door locks I would encounter in Germany would be of the mortice type and that they could be opened simply and quickly with a piece of bent wire.

When Frank was quite satisfied that I thoroughly understood the mechanics of locks, I started an intense practical course under his guidance which consisted of un-locking and re-locking every door in the castle we could safely work on. We did this with a lockpick which I had manufactured myself. The beauty of a lockpick is that it is a crude tool which can be made in ten minutes in practically any circumstances. All that is needed is a stout piece of iron wire some seven inches long and with a diameter of about an eighth of an inch. At one end, the last three quarters of an inch is bent to slightly less than a right angle. At the other end a simple handle is made rather like the handle on the common sardine tin opener.

The working end of the lockpick has to be flattened by hammering. Two stones will do the job if no hammer is available and, if perfection is wanted, the working end of the lockpick is heated to red heat and re-tempered by plunging into water. A little filing against any rough surface and there is a tool to open many doors.

At Spangenberg, I must have made a half dozen lockpicks in a range of sizes which I kept in a safe hiding place. My favourite one, which I always carried on me, had a very short shaft and was small enough to be palmed during the searches which were a routine occurrence.

One of the many locked rooms on which I had practised my skill under Frank's instructions was sort of a builder's storeroom, stacked with the normal run of a mason's equipment. There were bags of cement, buckets and trowels, wooden poles for scaffolding, planks, barrows, spades and shovels. I had remembered this while talking to Charles.

Neither Frank nor I had ever stolen German equipment from any of the many locked rooms we had opened. To us prisoners everything was tempting, but Frank's principle was that if you did not need a particular item immediately and for a particular purpose, you left it where it was. This avoided making the Germans suspicious and, anyway, you could always come back and steal it when it was required.

Thinking back to the builder's storeroom, I was certain that I would find a length of serviceable rope there. I did not remember having seen any but, if there was any rope stored in the castle, I was sure that it would be in that room. That afternoon I collected all my lockpicks from their hiding place and went back to the builder's storeroom, with Charles to act as lookout. It was a long journey. First we climbed the winding staircase which gave access to our own Arab Quarter, going on up to the top floor. There I opened a locked door and, having re-locked it behind me, we proceeded through a whole series of inter-connecting rooms which were full of school desks. I never fathomed why. These rooms flanked the courtyard on the top floor of the castle. Then there was another locked door to be negotiated and another spiral staircase leading us down again to the level of the courtyard. Almost underneath the staircase was the door to the storeroom. Of course, normal access to this storeroom was from the courtyard, but this door was always kept locked and we would not have dared to make our illegal entry that way.

I opened the storeroom, after about a minute's fiddling, and locked the door behind us. Charles had not said a word during the whole journey but I could see that he was completely flabbergasted at my proficiency. For my part, I was delighted with my own performance; it was the first time I had tried out my skill without Frank's supervision.

It did not take us three minutes to find the rope we needed. There were five or six coils to pick from and we untied the likeliest to measure its length and test its strength. It was perfect, roughly fifty metres long and strong enough to carry ten of us. We decided to leave it where it was and to pick it up on the eve of our escape. It could not be in a safer place. We went back to the Arab Quarter by the same route, careful to lock all doors behind us and leave no trace of our passage.

Suddenly our escape plans had taken on an alarming quality of reality. From being a possible solution to an apparently insoluble problem, they had changed into a planned operation which, like it or not, we would have to go through with. We were almost past the point of no return and nervously excited.

We could do nothing but immerse ourselves in the manifold preparations which had to be made. Most of our maps were already traced and covered nearly the whole of Germany. But where were we going? I wanted to go South to Switzerland. Charles wanted to go north to the Baltic. I had rough maps of the Schaffhausen crossing and a very clear idea of a way into Switzerland up the Inn valley from Landeck in Austria.

We had not said a word to anybody, but our furtive activities, plus the fact that we had first call on the rope and grapple, told their own story. All the Arab Quarter knew something was cooking. Often we asked advice, frequently it was thrust upon us unasked.

Woody, the power line rider, was as original and positive as ever. And he gave us furiously to think, so attractive were his ideas.

'Switzerland?' he jeered. 'You two Pommies will never walk that far. You're taking too many chances and Tommy is lame anyway. Stettin? A lot of balls. Even if you got to the Baltic coast, and that's further away than Switzerland, you'd probably drown trying to sail to Sweden. Stick to your own trade. Fly home.'

If ever Woody got out, his plans were simple. He was going to make straight for the nearest airfield, steal an aeroplane and fly back to England. Nothing could have been more appropriate for an escaping RAF officer. Nor was this plan as crazy as his scheme to ride across the moat on a wooden trolley attached to the power cables. He was extremely well prepared and had a great fund of knowledge on the subject. He had authentic cockpit layouts of a number of German aircraft—the Junkers 86, 87 and 88 as well as the Heinkel III. He knew his cockpit drills by heart and was confident that if he ever got inside any one of these aircraft he could get it safely off the ground and back to England—provided there was enough fuel in the tanks and he did not get shot down approaching the English coast.

Woody got out his own escape maps and showed us the exact location of all the airfields in our area. There was quite a choice within a radius of three days march. Woody could also tell us which type of aircraft we could expect to find at each airfield. How he collected all this information, I have no idea, but it was his one passion and interest.

He had also worked out how to cut and modify a RAF uniform to look passably like a Luftwaffe uniform—and it was not at all a difficult modification. The slight change in colour tone required was achieved by a liberal dusting with chalk powder and as long as no German got friendly enough to clap you on the back, thus raising a cloud of dust, there was no reason to suppose that the disguise could not be successful. Woody's idea was that, in such a uniform, he would not be conspicuous on a German airfield in the early hours of first light and would have time to select a suitable aeroplane before jumping in, starting up and taking off for Blighty.

The simplicity and directness of Woody's method of returning home was very tempting, but left us with the irrational feeling that it was all too easy. Nevertheless, I spent many hours learning the cockpit drill of the commonest of the German aircraft, and also carefully plotted the location of military airfields on my maps.

As for other methods of travel, stealing a car was out of the question. Cars were few enough in Germany and petrol was strictly rationed. There would be an immediate hue and cry and one could not expect to get very far. Stealing a bicycle was a much better idea, but bicycles were not easily come by and were preciously guarded possessions. There were records of escaping prisoners covering fantastic distances on racing bicycles, dressed appropriately in the typical shorts and singlet of the professional racing bicyclists. However, this required some organization, for one would look pretty silly wandering around the vicinity of a prison camp dressed as a racing cyclist looking for a bicycle.

Finally, there was the most attractive of all methods—going to the nearest railway station and buying a ticket. This method, of course, involved taking all the risks of moving openly among the German population. It meant that one had to have enough knowledge of German to be able to ask and answer questions without arousing suspicion. It meant also that one's clothes had to be good enough to pass muster in a crowd. It meant that one had to have an identity and the documentation to go with it, good enough to satisfy any of the many German policemen or military controls one would encounter.

The difficulties inherent in train travel were, for us at Spangenberg, too many to overcome. Few of us spoke German, although we were studying it industriously. We had practically no German money, which was essential to buy a railway ticket. We had no civilian clothes and no idea of the kind of documentation which we should have to carry. At that early stage of our incarceration, and most of us had been prisoners for not more than two months, we had not studied the possibility of forging identification documents.

Charles and I postponed our decision about where to aim for and concentrated on the problem of how to climb out of the moat in broad daylight, without being shot.

For the next three days we studied the movements of all the sentries who had a view of the moat at the point where we planned to make our climb. We drew meticulous diagrams and calculated where the blind spots lay. We timed the sentries on their individual beats and tried to establish a pattern.

Our conclusion was that our plan had a fair chance of success. There were two sentries whose attention would have to be diverted elsewhere during the critical minutes when we were climbing the rope. The success of our attempt depended absolutely upon these two diversions. They had to be spectacular enough to absorb the sentries' attention for a few minutes, but natural enough not to arouse the suspicion that their attention was being deliberately distracted. It was a nice problem and we decided to get the most imaginative brains in the camp working on its solution.

One important factor we could not assess was how long the diversions would have to last. Neither Charles nor I had had much experience of climbing ropes and had no idea of whether it would take thirty seconds or five minutes to climb out of the seventy foot moat.

We calculated that we needed at least another three days to get ourselves ready. We had to prepare our clothes and our packs, complete our maps and get hold of enough concentrated high energy foods to keep us going for at least two weeks. It was obvious that we now had to go to the committee and seek their help. We decided to go and talk to them the next day and went back to planning our diversions for the sentries.

The diversion which would be staged in the bottom of the moat, we could produce from our own resources in the Arab Quarter. Oliver Philpot volunteered to direct the show. He proposed a boxing match, with gloves, seconds, referee and all the trimmings. The two contestants, who again would be volunteers from our RAF party, would beat the hell out of one another in the most spectacular way.

After due consideration and detailed discussion, we turned the plan down. Nobody was fit enough to keep up the pretence of an energetic boxing match for more than sixty seconds. As soon as the aggressivity of the boxers flagged, the sentry's attention would wander.

The next suggestion was to stage a game of rugby in the moat. This was an excellent idea in that the Germans do not understand the game and are always fascinated by its apparent violence. To hold the sentry's attention fixed during the vital minutes of the climb, a scrum could be organized against the moat wall, right beneath the sentry. This could be a sort of Eton wall game scrum, with everybody piling in and jumping on top, creating a mêlée which could be continued as long as was necessary. Provided there was plenty of action and noise, the sentry's attention was bound to be concentrated on the strange behaviour of the mad English in the moat below.

The diversion on the Gymnasium side of the moat would have to be arranged by the army, as it would be the turn of one of their parties to use the gym. I had no doubt at all that they could organize an effective spectacle for the second sentry. Details could be worked out in the morning, after talking to the committee.

But our moat scheme finished exactly there. The next morning, at dawn, the RAF contingent was moved out of the castle.

Free as a Running Fox

The RAF party was moved from Spangenberg castle on 28 April 1942. It was a rude awakening for us that morning. Just before dawn, about forty German soldiers burst into the Arab Quarter. We were all asleep and they achieved complete surprise. We were turned out of our beds and given thirty minutes to pack our belongings, with a German guard standing alongside each one of us.

Although we had known that this move was imminent, we had seriously underestimated our captors and their tactics were completely successful.

Our guards gave us no opportunity to get near the various ingenious hiding places where our precious contraband was kept. We packed our belongings listlessly, having to submit every garment and item to a search before it was stowed away in our kit bags or in the cardboard boxes we used for these occasions. A number of desperate attempts were made to divert the attention of the guards while precious material was retrieved, but nearly all failed.

We were then lined up along one side of the barrack room, together with our baggage, while the Germans searched the room. Mattresses were emptied of their straw fillings, beds dismantled, floorboards pulled up and every piece of furniture thoroughly inspected. The pile of booty discovered grew bigger and bigger. Maps, compasses, tools of every kind, articles of civilian clothing, half-made haversacks, the variety was astonishing. Our losses were enormous and the Germans delighted with their haul.

My collection of lockpicks was discovered and created a small sensation, but they could not be directly attributed to me. From the remarks of the Abwehr officer to whom they were triumphantly presented, I learned that the German slang for a lockpick was 'Deitrich' and that it was a criminal offence to carry one. I fingered the one I had in my pocket, wrapped in my handkerchief.

On the whole I had lost little of value. Like many others, I had completed my basic arrangements for the move when the rumours started to become insistent. The two cardboard boxes, which served me as small suitcases, were both loaded with valuable items. This was a method of concealment which the Abwehr, at that time, had not discovered.

The cardboard boxes were the containers in which Red Cross provisions were packed. Their construction was simple, two outer layers of thin cardboard with, in between them, a filling of stiff corrugated paper. These three components, glued together, made a strong, tough container. They were ideal for hiding flat items. One carefully separated the outer layer of cardboard from the corrugated filling underneath, cut away the filling to the exact shape of the article being hidden and re-glued the outer layer into place. In the lining of my boxes I had concealed a hacksaw blade, a collection of traced maps, some notes on the Junkers 87 and 88 cockpits and a small amount of German money. In the bottom of the shaft of one of my walking sticks I had a three-cornered file. In the hem of my handkerchief I had a twenty mark note. None of this material had been discovered.

Communally, however, we took a beating. I saw one searcher with a handful of original Air Ministry maps, printed on rice paper, especially for prisoners-of-war. With growing fury I realized that I had never had access to those maps. I edged closer to the table where the booty was stacked until I was near enough to identify them. I recognized one as being a large scale plan of the docks at Stettin, something I had been searching for, but had never found.

Again, I smelled the dead hand of the escape committee. All those maps should have been made available to anybody who showed an interest. They could have been copied and returned to the jealous guardianship of the committee. Now it was too late and heaven only knew when such accurate maps might again come our way.

I wondered whether something could not be done, even now, to retrieve the situation. It looked impossible, but it was worth a try. I moved over towards Marcus Marsh who was, I thought, the right man for the occasion. Marcus never needed explanations. He was always aware of the realities of any particular situation. While at Spangenberg he had taken on the job of rations officer, or something like it, and spent all his day in the kitchens trying to ensure that we got the maximum value from the little food we received.

All day he was in contact with the Germans and, with his natural authority, he could handle them as firmly as he handled his horses back at Newmarket. He knew every one of the German staff and I suspected, indeed I very much hoped, that he had a hold over more than one of them as a result of having bribed them.

'Marcus,' I whispered, 'we've got to have those maps back.' I indicated the pile on the table.

Marcus nodded.

'Might be done,' he said. 'You got any ideas?'

'Got any friends among these goons?' I countered.

'Not that friendly.'

There was a pause for thought.

'Let's try it this way, Marcus. When we leave here, you stay until last. Try and get yourself a guard you know, who isn't a suspicious type, to stay with you and help you with your luggage.'

Marcus always had twice as much to carry as anybody else.

'Edge up to the table, in reach of those maps,' I continued, 'and just wait until I create some sort of a diversion to distract your guard. Then grab them if you can.'

The guards started to herd us out of the Arab Quarter. Marcus appeared to be having great difficulties with his luggage and was dragging a heavy suitcase nearer to the table where the maps were.

I had a quick whispered conversation with Barney Runnacles. He gave me the simple German phrase I wanted.

In the corridor outside our barrack room, I let everybody push past me. I was using two sticks and moving, apparently, with great difficulty. I stopped at the top of the staircase, where I could see the exit from the Arab Quarter. When I judged that the last prisoner and guard had left—except for Marcus, who I knew could hold on for minutes—I put on my act.

'My watch, my watch,' I screamed in German. 'I left it on my bed.'

I propelled myself back down the corridor to the door of the Arab Quarter, making great leaps between my two sticks, and repeating my lament at the top of my voice.

I was going the wrong way to escape, so nobody tried to shoot me. The guards were caught on the wrong foot and nobody followed me immediately. I bounded into the Arab Quarter, still screaming my German sentence.

Crossing the room in four or five great leaps, I arrived at my bunk, still yelling. The guard who had remained with Marcus was watching me in open-mouthed astonishment. Five seconds later the Abwehr officer and a Feldwebel burst into the barrack room in pursuit.

I showed them my watch, which I held in the palm of my right hand. It had, of course, been on my left wrist when I left the room.

'Thank God, I've found it,' I said.

There was no need to talk German to these Abwehr types, their English was excellent, even if they did not admit it.

'It's a waterproof Rolex and cost me fifty pounds.'

Marcus was already on his way out of the door, with a German guard carrying his suitcase. There were still maps on the table but, it seemed to me, the pile was much smaller.

I caught Marcus's eye as he went out into the corridor. He gave me an imperceptible nod. We'd pulled it off.

I was meek, mild and polite with the Abwehr and rejoined the other prisoners strapping my Rolex back onto my wrist. I quickly resumed my part as a grand blessé, with my two sticks, my limp and burnt face, and rode to the station on the baggage cart.

I arrived a few minutes after the others and was escorted into a large waiting room, where all our party was already assembled. There was an unusual, depressing silence, which boded ill. Normally forty prisoners make more noise than a cage of monkeys.

The reason was immediately obvious. There was to be another search. At one end of the room there were benches set in a long row. Behind them were Abwehr men. It looked just like the customs hall at Dover.

I moved over towards Marcus.

'I grabbed one handful,' he said, 'and got most of the maps. They are here.'

He opened his battledress top to show me.

'Do you want them now?' he asked, looking at the reception committee at the end of the room.

'We'll never get them past those boys,' I said. 'They are real trained Abwehr. I'll go through the search now. You look around the place and see if you can't hide them somewhere where I can pick them up after I've been through.'

'I'll see what I can do.'

I had little doubt at all that Marcus would find a solution to the problem.

The search was really thorough. I was stripped naked, everything in my boxes and kitbag was dumped on the bench in front of me and each individual item was minutely examined. But I lost nothing.

My Red Cross boxes were not ripped apart, they had not yet discovered that particular deception. My walking stick, with the file in it, I had left standing against the wall where I could pick it up later. My handkerchief, with the twenty mark note and the lockpick, I kept in my hand.

My eyes were still giving considerable trouble. They continually filled with tears and mucus and I dabbed them and cleaned them with my handkerchief every few minutes. This action was so natural and so necessary that nobody suspected it. I even put my carefully crumpled handkerchief on the bench in front of the examiners while I stripped for them. But I retrieved it immediately afterwards and, from then on, kept making use of it.

When I was dressed again and had my kitbag and cardboard boxes repacked, I joined the others. Those prisoners who had been searched were separated from the ones who were still awaiting the ordeal.

Marcus was sitting on the floor against the back wall of the room. He had a sly smile on his face. Next to him, against the wall, was a wooden wastepaper basket. Marcus looked fixedly at the wastepaper basket and then back to me. I got the message.

I too went and sat down against the back wall, as close to the centre as the guard, who was keeping the two parties of prisoners apart, would let me. Marcus got up and made his way towards the benches.

The wastepaper basket was about ten feet away and in forbidden territory.

I again untied the string securing my cardboard boxes and dumped the contents of each of them in a heap on the floor beside me. Then I started to repack, slowly and methodically. The guard was watching me, which was how I wanted it.

What I needed was rubbish, a big pile of rubbish. It was a difficult problem as I was not carrying anything I really wished to throw away. However, there were my letters, some pieces of newspaper in which my shaving tackle was wrapped and a note book, from which I could tear some pages. There was also a bar of chocolate with a red wrapping on the outside and silver paper inside. That would make for good litter, but it was my only reserve of food.

I was in no hurry, because the search would be continuing for hours. Gradually, I accumulated an untidy heap of torn up paper on one side of me—the side away from the wastepaper basket. As a finishing touch I decided to sacrifice the chocolate. I ate it with slow relish and scattered the silver paper artistically over the heap. Everything else was repacked and my cardboard boxes retied.

The guard had lost interest in me, but he had registered what I was doing. I now needed help and looked to see who was among those who had already been searched. I caught the eye of Charles Hall and he came over and sat down.

'I need your help, Charles. Go back and collect all your luggage and be ready to come over here when I give you the nod. When you come back, stay standing up and dump your luggage to the right of me, just here. And bring somebody else with you.'

'Roger.'

Charles strolled back to join the others.

When the guard approached me again, I beckoned to him. I pointed to the wastepaper basket on my left and to the untidy mess on my right. My meaning was obvious.

The guard hesitated. It was easy enough to read his thoughts. Should he demean himself by bringing me the wastepaper basket, or should he let me go into forbidden territory to get it?

He jerked his head towards the wastepaper basket, indicating that I could go and fetch it.

As I came back with it, I nodded at Charles who came over dragging his kitbag and carrying his boxes. He was followed by Tony Barber. I put the wastepaper basket beside the heap of rubbish and sat down again. I started to transfer the rubbish to the basket. The guard watched me for a while, but then got bored again and walked away.

With Charles and Tony standing talking in front of me and the accumulated heap of our assorted baggage, I now had a good screen between me and the Abwehr narks at the end of the room. It was the moment to get the maps back.

'Charles,' I said, 'lean your kitbag against the wall here and, at the same time, kick over the basket so that it falls towards me.'

Charles did just that and most of the rubbish spilled on to the floor at my side. Within seconds I had located the crumpled ball of ricepaper maps and put them into my trouser pocket. I swept the rubbish back into the basket and the operation was over. Inconspicuously we all moved back into the crowd, leaving the wastepaper basket in splendid isolation against the wall.

While this was happening, I had been conscious of Marcus's voice, shouting angry protests at the search bench. I realized that he had been following our ploy with the wastepaper basket and was doing all he could to focus the attention of the Abwehr on himself.

Tony was in a cheerful mood and eager to start the train journey.

'We're travelling in cattle trucks,' he announced. 'I've seen them waiting there at the platform. We could not really hope for a better chance. Those floor boards may be thick, but we have plenty of time. We're bound to be travelling all night, even if we leave here by noon, which, at our present rate of progress isn't very likely. I've got my saw. What about you?'

'I've got a hacksaw blade. I've also got a file and the best idea might be to make another saw out of one of our issue knives. It's got a good handle and it's strong.'

The Germans issued each prisoner with a soup bowl, a mug, a knife, fork and spoon. We carried them everywhere we went. The knives were blunt, but large and well made.

'Well,' said Tony, 'let's make sure we're first into our cattle truck and grab ourselves some floor space at one end—the front end, I should say—in one corner and more or less over the axle.'

'Can I join you?' asked Charles. 'We'll make it an all PRU job.'

'If you don't mind being third out through the hole,' answered Tony, 'you're welcome. But being third out may not give you much of a chance, especially if the train has started moving.'

Charles insisted on coming.

'Maybe there'll be time for all of us to get out while the train is still stationary, you never know.'

'What about food?' Tony was raising the critical question. 'I hear that the committee have got some. Can't we get hold of it now?'

'You try,' I countered. 'The only answer I can get is that it will be given to us on the train. Apparently we just have to be good boys and leave all the arrangements to the committee.'

'Hell,' said Tony, 'I hope they don't make a cock of it. Somehow, they don't inspire me with confidence. Did you see those maps the Germans found? Those shouldn't have been lost like that.'

'Don't worry. Marcus got most of them back. They're now in my pocket. They were in the wastepaper basket here.'

'Good God,' Tony was incredulous, 'is that what you were after? But how did they end up among the rubbish?'

I told him the whole story.

Marcus came to join us.

'You get them?' It was more a statement than a question.

I nodded and grinned.

'When you sort them out,' Marcus went on, 'you'll find a collection of dirty mark notes in the middle of the bundle. About a hundred marks in all. Let me have them back when you get a chance.'

'It will be safest to do it on the train.'

Marcus agreed.

Two

WHEN the search was finally over, we were all assembled on the station platform and the roll was called. The Germans identified each of us individually against photographs and the identity discs with which they had issued us. They were being very careful. The purpose of the check was, presumably, to ensure that none of our party had swapped identities with any of the army prisoners.

When this was over, the German officer in charge of the party, with the senior interpreter and the Abwehr officer in close attendance, walked up and down our lines making an apparently random selection of individuals. Those selected were made to assemble in another group. I was among those picked out and segregated. Neither Tony nor Charles were chosen.

The interpreter then informed our group that we would be travelling in comfort in third class carriages, while the rest of the party would be accommodated in a cattle truck. We had been selected, he said, because we were senior officers, or elderly, or sick or wounded. The German Reich, he emphasized, always treated prisoners of war with the maximum correctness and consideration, we should be grateful and not create trouble during the long journey ahead of us. Any prisoner who attempted to escape would be shot. The guards had strict orders.

I looked over at Tony and Charles in the other group. But there was nothing I could do to join them. I had been playing the part of the grand blessé too convincingly and it would have been ludicrous to try and persuade the Germans that I preferred travelling in a cattle truck.

The train eventually pulled out of the station. I was sitting on a hard wooden bench with eight other prisoners and one German guard, armed with a rifle and a pistol, sharing the compartment. The guard sat in the outside corner seat, his back to the engine. My place was diagonally opposite to him, on the inside of the train, facing the engine. The windows of the compartment were closed and firmly wired in that position from the outside.

In front of me was a lavatory which had two doors, one from my compartment and the other giving access to the adjoining compartment. This next compartment was a mirror image of ours and had the same complement of one guard and eight prisoners.

In a third compartment, which did not in any way connect with ours as the carriage had no corridors, was another small party of prisoners, including the SBO, adjutant and other staff, together with the German officers and NCOs in charge of us.

After we had been journeying for a while and everybody had settled down, I asked the guard if I could use the lavatory. He said not to shut the door, to remember that his rifle was loaded and that he had orders to shoot any prisoner attempting to escape. But he remained relaxed and made no effort to accompany me.

The lavatory had its own window, this time of frosted glass, and it was solidly fixed in the shut position by some arrangement outside the window. It was obvious that if I could get this window open, escaping from the train was going to be no problem.

I heaved down with all my weight on the handle at the top of the window and was delighted to find that it yielded for a tiny fraction of an inch, which gave me a gap just sufficient to slide a knife blade through and explore the system the Germans had used to close it. It seemed to be primitive enough—a tough piece of wire anchored above the window by a large nail hammered into the carriage side and bent over and, at the other end, by another nail hammered into the wooden frame of the window. The way out was so simple, it seemed unbelievable.

My inspection of the lavatory had not taken two minutes and I came back into the compartment buttoning up my trousers for the sake of the German guard. From now on it was essential to keep him happy and unsuspicious. It was also necessary to prevent anyone else from making any bungling attempts which would interfere with my plans. I still had a lot of difficult work to do on the window before I could get it to open easily when the time came and still look firmly secure both from the inside and the outside.

There was only one way of ensuring that I got no interference and that was to announce my intentions, which I did immediately.

Marcus Marsh was sitting next to me and I whispered to him that I was going out through the lavatory window as soon as it was dark and asked him to pass the word around. I added that I would welcome any one person who wanted to come with me, but that I thought two was the limit, if we were to have a hope of getting away undetected. I also asked for food, especially concentrated foods, like chocolate, raisins and sugar.

The word got round the compartment fairly fast. We did not, in fact, have to be particularly cautious because it was obvious that, unless he was a very cunning fellow and a remarkably good actor, our guard spoke not a word of any language but his own. Nevertheless we whispered, probably because the atmosphere had become conspiratorial.

Everybody in turn looked at me as they got the message but I saw no response in anybody's eyes. I had rather expected somebody to signify that they would like to come along, but at that early stage I was not particularly concerned as my mind was working out methods to get the window fixed. And there were still five or six hours of daylight.

Marcus reminded me of the stolen maps, which I had completely forgotten. I got them out of my pocket and put them inside the cardboard box which I held on my knees. I sorted out

Marcus's Deutschmarks and slipped them into his hand. Surreptitiously he counted them.

'Here, Tommy,' he said, nudging my elbow, 'take these. There are fifty marks. If you don't get away, let me have them back.'

'Thanks a lot, Marcus. They'll be very useful. If you don't mind I'll go through these maps later. First I want to get started on the lavatory window. There'll be lots of time to waste before it gets dark.'

I had glanced very briefly at the crumpled maps and realized that they represented a real treasure. I wanted to go through them calmly and in detail.

I spent the next half-an-hour retrieving my tools from their hiding places and secreting them in various pockets. I also took my German knife, which looked as if it might be the most useful tool of all of them.

It was time to get to work.

I asked the guard if I could go and visit the next compartment, passing through the lavatory, to talk to my friends there and borrow some cigarettes. The guard agreed but said I was to leave both lavatory doors open. This was no handicap as the guard could not see what was happening in the lavatory from where he sat.

I did not go through to the next compartment, but spent five minutes in the lavatory working on the window. I discovered that I could reach the nail above the window with my German knife and, after much struggling to obtain the right leverage, I managed to move it. If the extruding part of the nail, which was bent upwards, could be rotated through ninety degrees, the retaining wire could be slipped off and there would be, as far as I could judge, no obstacle to letting the window down. Even if the wire could not be dislodged, I could cut through it with my hacksaw blade in a matter of seconds.

As soon as I was satisfied that I could move the nail, I returned it to its vertical position with the wire in place and intact. I then went back to the compartment and gave the guard one of my few precious cigarettes.

From where he sat, Marcus could see what I was doing in the lavatory and give me warning if our guard got restive or suspicious. He was a natural conspirator and I knew that I could rely on him completely to cover all my moves.

When I sat down again beside him, I asked him to go through to the next compartment and tell them what was going on.

'Tell them there is still room for one more on this job,' I reminded Marcus, 'and get them to start a regular exchange of visits with us.'

I wanted both guards to get used to a casual exchange of prisoners between the two compartments because, in this way, if I did manage to get out of the window, my absence would not be immediately noticed.

During the long afternoon of that tedious train journey, a regular interchange of visits between the compartments gradually became an accepted move by the two guards. But nobody offered to come with me through the window.

On my third visit to the lavatory I worked on the nail until it would move freely through ninety degrees and back again, without the retaining wire becoming detached. I calculated that that was as much preparation as was needed. I was quite confident that, when the moment came, I could rotate the nail through 180 degrees and slip the wire off. Then all I had to do was to pull down the window and get out.

I was concentrating all my attention on the delicate task of getting the nail back into its original position, when there was a great crash from the compartment.

I whipped round and saw Marcus bending down to retrieve a Red Cross box which had apparently fallen off the rack. The look he gave me was a warning of immediate danger and I hurriedly jammed the window fully shut and stowed my tools in my pockets.

I whipped down my trousers and squatted on the lavatory seat. A few seconds later, the guard appeared in the doorway. He was embarrassed to find me so occupied and retreated.

'Später, später,' he muttered as he turned his back.

'Ich bin fertig,' I called after him, as I pulled the plug. I redressed quickly and left the lavatory free for the guard. I should have thought of it, the poor bastard had not relieved himself in four hours.

After that scene, it was obvious that I would have to stay out of the lavatory for some time. I settled down to examine the stolen maps and to complete all my preparations for a getaway.

I studied the maps one by one, well covered by the open top of my Red Cross box, which lay on my knees. There were eleven maps in all. For my own use I selected a large scale plan of the docks of Stettin and another of the docks at Danzig. The Schaffhausen crossing was also covered in minute detail, and I put it aside. At that point in time, I had no idea which way I would be heading after getting off the train.

There were smaller scale maps of Poland and Czechoslovakia, and of Austria showing its borders with Italy, Switzerland and Germany, and of the south-west corner of Germany showing the whole Swiss border. There was a map of northern Germany, including the Dutch and Danish frontiers.

I did not want to be greedy so I added two more maps to my stock. One of central Germany, which would cover the area we were travelling through, and the one showing the Swiss–German border.

The rest I gave to Marcus, not doubting that he could get them through the search which was to be expected on arrival at the new camp.

There was still a long wait until dark and my other preparations were soon made. I had no civilian clothes, but was wearing an airman's uniform and quite a smart airman's greatcoat which, with the brass buttons replaced, would pass muster. At least it was better than my Polish greatcoat, which was packed in my kit bag. I decided that as soon as I was off the train I would cut off the brass buttons and replace them with buttons made of wood, which I would whittle from whatever suitable bit of wood I found. I had a needle and cotton.

I stowed my maps and my compass in my pockets and decided to take only the lockpick of my collection of tools as well as a strong penknife. The rest I handed over to Marcus to get through if he could.

My major preoccupation now was food. I had none at all. I discussed the situation with Marcus. He confirmed that there were Red Cross parcels travelling with us on the train, but he had no idea who had charge of them, or where they were. He offered a slight ray of hope.

'I've got the feeling,' he said, 'that we are bound to make a stop soon. We've been going steadily for four hours now and the engine is bound to run out of water or coal or whatever they burn. You can find out where the parcels are at the next stop.'

'Let's hope so,' I replied, 'because there isn't much time. It will be dark in two hours.'

Marcus was right. Less than an hour later, the train stopped at a wayside station and we were allowed off. We were served with hot soup which was most acceptable, if not very nourishing. I went looking for the escape committee and eventually ran one of them to earth. I came straight to the point.

'The food,' I demanded, 'the parcels, where are they? I'm getting out as soon as it is dark and I've got to have my escape rations now, at this stop.'

'Don't kid yourself,' he answered, 'you won't get off the train. We're too well guarded.'

I was getting angry.

'Where are those parcels?' I insisted with slow emphasis and sub-dued fury.

He suddenly became apologetic.

'Well, you see, what happened was this. The Germans transported them to the station for us and there they were put in a separate truck with all the other stores. We can't get at them unless the Germans decide to give them out.'

'Really far-sighted organization on your part,' I said sarcastically. 'What do I do now? Go and ask the Germans for some food because I want to escape?'

'Now listen, Tommy, there is no need to lose your temper.'

But I had turned my back and gone to look for Tony.

Tony's news was half good. They had started cutting the floor-boards but these were thicker and harder than he had expected and the saw kept breaking. Nevertheless, he hoped to have made a hole big enough to get out of before morning.

'Why don't you join us and bring your saw?' Tony invited.

'I'm sorry Tony, but I've got my way out all ready. I'm getting off as soon as it's dark. See if you can get the Leutnant to let you swap with somebody in our carriage. So far, nobody has offered to come with me.'

But Tony felt that he could not abandon his hole in the cattle truck floor and the others who were working with him. I preferred my lavatory window, so we continued our journey in different sections of the train.

Before leaving Tony I gave him my walking stick, the one with the file in it.

'You can cut a new saw with the file,' I said. 'If you don't get out, try and get it through the search at the new camp. It's the most useful tool we have.'

He took the walking stick.

'Good luck,' he said. 'Where are you going to aim for?'

'I've just no idea, it depends where I get off the train.'

When the train got moving again it was late in the evening and the light was fading fast. I was getting more and more tense as darkness approached and I was still very angry about the food fiasco. I sensed that my nervousness and rebellious mood were embarrassing to my companions and disturbing their peace.

I asked every fit man in the compartment, directly, whether he wanted to come with me. I got no takers.

This depressed me. In the first place, I wanted company. Secondly, I began to think that they were right and I was wrong. Even if I got safely away from the train, I needed a whole series of miracles to have any hope of reaching and crossing a frontier, with no food and no civilian clothes. Looked at calmly and logically, it was probably wiser to sit back on one's wooden bench in a third class carriage and hope that a more suitable opportunity would occur some day in the future.

But I could not see it that way. For me, the fact of escaping, even if to nowhere, was a notable victory over my captors. Getting one up on them gave me enough personal satisfaction to make my imprisonment bearable for a long time to come, even if I was recaptured.

I did not even bother to canvass the second compartment. If anybody wanted to escape, he would at least have the energy and initiative to come and tell me.

It was obvious that I was going to have no companion, but I still needed food. I started asking direct questions of each prisoner in turn. Had he any chocolate, raisins, sugar, glucose—anything? I was asking for precious things, rarely seen and jealously hoarded. Heads were shaken and nothing was produced. And my provisions for the great journey into the unknown consisted of a complete loaf of black bread about a foot long and three inches square— the ration for the compartment—and a one pound tin of Lyle's golden syrup. Two more cumbersome articles could not have been imagined. I considered them in despair as I wondered how I was going to carry them when I wriggled my way through the small window of the lavatory. Again I cursed the obstinacy and inefficiency of the escape committee.

It was now beginning to get really dark and I had the old familiar feeling in my stomach that comes with excitement and fear. Marcus was going to help me out of the window and then close it after me, attempting to push the nail and wire back to their original positions. Marcus had studied the mechanics of the operation and felt sure that, with his knife, he could close the window again so that it looked normal at a casual glance.

When it was fully dark, I turned to Marcus.

'I'm going out at the next stop, whenever that is. As soon as the train starts slowing down, I'll go into the lavatory and get the window ready. You follow me casually just when the train stops.'

'Roger,' he answered. 'Get somebody to come through here from the other compartment, we want a little to-ing and fro-ing.'

The train clattered on through the night. The countryside was completely black and there was no moon. The curtains of the compartment were closely drawn to prevent the faint light of a single bulb in the ceiling being visible outside. There was a noticeable tendency for most of my companions to settle down to sleep and, indeed, I was feeling very sleepy myself. I hoped I would not have to wait too long for the next stop because it was getting more and more difficult to dragoon anybody into making an occasional visit to the other compartment. And it was essential to keep the guard used to this movement and unsuspicious of it.

It must have been about two hours after dark when I felt the brakes go on. Quite definitely the train was slowing down. I waited tensely for a long minute. The deceleration became more pronounced. We were going to stop. I touched Marcus's knee and, as casually as I could, strolled into the lavatory. I had the tin of treacle and the loaf tucked into the top of my tunic, so that my hands were free.

The train was now going very slowly and I started to work feverishly on the window, afraid that I had left it too late. I found I was sweating slightly, although the night was cold. I jerked the window down as hard as I could and got a half-inch gap through which I could work on the nail. The nail rotated easily through the first ninety degrees and I then changed my leverage to work it round to the vertical. I got it down another thirty degrees and found that I could push the wire loop away from the nail—and the window was free.

Marcus was standing right behind me now. The train was barely moving. The brakes went on again and it juddered to a complete halt. Looking through the slit at the top of the window I judged that we had stopped at a signal way out in the country. There was no station, no buildings, no lights, no danger. I nodded to Marcus, pulled the window down cautiously and poked my head out to have a look around.

There was a man standing on the track, less than three yards away, clearly visible in the light from the firebox of the engine. I shut the window fast but quietly. He had his back to me and had not seen anything. Obviously it was the engine driver or his mate and I could not get out of the window while he was standing there.

I explained the situation to Marcus.

'I'll have to wait until we get started again, then when the fireman climbs back into the cab, I'll get out as fast as I can.'

At that moment the train started again, in a series of jerks. I waited while I counted ten to let the fireman get back on board, then pulled down the window. All clear, but we were gathering speed. Hurrying desperately, I leant backwards through the window, reaching upwards on the outside to find a grip for my hands. I got a good hold and then started easing my bottom and legs out through the window. Marcus was shoving and it was a considerable struggle, which, although it may only have lasted seconds, seemed much too long to me, with the train accelerating every second. My loaf of bread jammed and Marcus grabbed it saying he would throw it out after me. Suddenly my feet were out and I was dangling by my hands on the side of the train. I found a purchase for my feet and lowered my handhold to the window sill. I then found a lower platform for my feet and turned to face forwards, hanging on with one hand. The train was now moving frighteningly fast and there was no time to be lost. I pushed off outwards into space with all the force of my legs and one arm, hit the ground with stupefying violence and rolled, falling forward. My elbows and forearms took the brunt of the fall, but as they were well protected by my greatcoat, I did not get hurt. I got a last glimpse of Marcus framed in the window.

I lay absolutely still on the ground, with my head between my arms until the whole length of the train had passed and then, looking up very cautiously, watched its red tail light receding into the darkness.

I stared at the tail light for long minutes, until it had disappeared. Then I listened to the receding noise of the engine. As long as it made that regular chugging, it meant that my escape had not been discovered. And the noise did not stop. It just faded into the distance. I had made a clean getaway.

I was unwilling to move, although I knew I should get as far away from the railway as I could, as soon as possible. The effect of adrenalin which had been pumping into my bloodstream while I was getting through the window had completely worn off. I felt a lassitude, a sense of depression and a sudden complete loss of confidence in myself. I wanted to smoke a cigarette, but dared not.

My eyes had now become adjusted to the dark and I tried to take stock of my immediate surroundings. The first thing I saw was a black object not more than six inches from my nose. I felt it and discovered it was an iron staunchion, made from a piece of rail, stuck vertically into the ground. I thanked my guardian angel for my perfect timing. A tenth of a second later and I would have smashed my head on that unfriendly piece of iron.

I pulled myself together and started searching for the loaf that Marcus had thrown after me, crawling on my hands and knees in the pitch dark. The loaf should have been a little way ahead of me and, perhaps, a little further away from the lines. I felt around for ten minutes, but could not find it and was forced to decide that I would have to abandon my loaf and get away from the area. This depressed me even more. Now I had only a tin of treacle and I would have to eat it with a knife.

Three

I GOT to my feet, still undecided which way to go. For the first time, I looked behind me. Less than a quarter of a mile away there was a station, dimly lit but clearly identifiable as such, with four platforms and extensive sidings.

Crouching down, I ran across the tracks to the embankment on the north side. Just over the top of the embankment was a wood and I dived into it.

The unsuspected proximity of the station, which meant policemen and railway guards, had unnerved me although there was no logical reason to suppose that my presence in the area was suspected or that I was in any way visible from the station. The night was far too dark.

Controlling my irrational panic, I stopped running and sat down behind a bush.

Lighting a cigarette, I inhaled deeply while considering my next move.

The truth was that I did not know exactly where I was. The last pinpoint I had been able to make from the train was when we passed through Erfurt, about an hour before jumping. After that, I had not been able to get any further check as to where we were.

Allowing that the train had been moving between twenty-five and thirty-five miles an hour, I formed a rough idea of my position, within broad limits.

'Where do I go from here?' I asked the question aloud. With no food but a tin of treacle I could not hope to reach any frontier on foot. Train travel was out of the question, my clothes were not good enough and I had no documents. I would certainly be picked up at the first station I approached. My only hope seemed to be the long shot—to make for the nearest airfield and steal an aeroplane.

Without looking at my maps, I knew that Merseburg and Halle lay north-east of me, possibly within three or four nights march. There were airfields close to both these towns. I had seen them more than once when on photographic missions and Woody had marked their approximate locations on my maps.

This plan appeared to be my best bet. If, on my way, I picked up any food, by finding or stealing, I could always keep going north towards Stettin and try to stow away on a Swedish ship.

Before moving off I checked my possessions and re-stowed them comfortably in various pockets. I had the usual collar stud compass, a lockpick, a penknife, a German table knife, a ball of string, a needle and thread, a Gillette razor and three new blades, a cake of soap wrapped in a small piece of towelling, a comb, a tooth-brush, a spare pair of socks and half a dozen clean handkerchiefs. It was a habit with me always to carry a lot of handkerchiefs because my eyes were still troublesome.

In addition, there was my collection of maps, all my notes on the starting drills and cockpit layout of various German aircraft and seventy Reichmarks.

My provisions consisted of a well sealed bottle full of drinking water, nearly a pint of it, and, of course, a bright green round tin containing one pound nett weight of Lyle's Golden Syrup.

Perhaps most important of all, I had a freshly started pack of cigarettes of which there was eighteen left.

The treacle tin would not fit into any of my pockets and I would have dearly liked to discard it, there and then. But that was out of the question. I was going to need all the energy I could get and a pound of molasses, I felt, represented a lot of energy. Working mostly by feel, I tied some string securely around it and made a long loop which I could slip over my head and one shoulder. This got the tin out of the way although it would have looked most odd to anyone I might meet. As I had no intention of meeting anybody, this point did not bother me.

My watch showed that it was already twenty-five minutes since I had jumped off the train and I was still within fifty yards of the point where I had landed.

'Get moving,' I said to myself, 'and stop dithering.'

All the energy, the enthusiasm, the determination to escape which had been keeping me going during my few months of imprisonment seemed to have evaporated. I felt lost and abandoned in the depths of a wilderness of darkness. I wished with all my heart that Tony had been with me, or anybody at all, so that we could at least have talked and drawn courage from each other.

I skirted round the wood I had been in and, after crossing a few fields, crawling through hedges and stumbling through ditches, came to an asphalted road. According to my compass, the road headed roughly north-east, which was the direction I wanted. I set out at a brisk march. My watch said 9.10 p.m. It would not be light before 5 a.m. and I was confident I could cover a lot of distance in eight hours.

As I walked, my morale improved and I began to enjoy myself.

I had escaped. I was free. Free to roam around in the dark in the middle of Thüringen or Saxony, or wherever I was. Free to hide in woods or ditches all day. Free to freeze and starve. Free to run until I was caught. Free as a fox.

But the realization that I was a fugitive, that every man's hand was against me, that my chances of evading re-capture were minimal, did not depress me. I had won a battle in escaping from the train. I had upheld the honour of our small party and of the RAF. I had made trouble for the Germans. The longer I stayed free, the more trouble I would give them.

I wondered how long Marcus would be able to disguise my absence. I had formed a fairly negative opinion of most of the characters I had left behind in the two third class compartments, but not of Marcus. I knew that he would drive them to move from one compartment to the next to cover my absence for as long as possible. In fact, as I heard long afterwards, the Germans did not discover I was missing until hours later when the train made another stop and the prisoners were allowed off, given some soup and counted.

I laughed happily thinking of the panic and consternation of the Germans when they finally discovered they had lost a prisoner, in spite of all their precautions. As I marched, I talked aloud to myself, planning what to do if I reached an airfield. Then I recited the starting procedure of the Junkers 52, the 87 and 88. Occasionally when I felt I was miles from any human being or habitation, I sang songs in time with my marching.

My ankle was giving no trouble and I walked easily, with hardly a limp. As long as I kept exercising it, it did not hurt. It was only when I stopped to rest that the pain began.

After about two hours steady progress on the same road, in nearly pitch darkness and through absolutely empty countryside, I came to a village. I was reluctant to walk straight through it, for fear that I would be seen and stopped. But I was even more reluctant to try and circumnavigate it in the dark. This would have meant negotiating an unknown number of hedges and ditches and I would not have had any idea, when I found a road again, that it was the right one. I had grown to like the one I was on. It was heading in more or less the right direction and was comparatively straight. So I plucked up courage and walked directly through the village. Every house was closed and dark; not a soul was abroad. At the fountain in the middle of the village I had a long drink and filled my water bottle. Then I walked on and out of the village. Not a dog had barked.

This gave me great encouragement and that night I walked right through the middle of four other villages without ever seeing a soul. I reckoned that by dawn I would have covered a good twenty-five miles. But if I had had to make a detour around all the villages on my route this distance would have been cut by half. Occasionally, I came across signposts which I read with the help of matches, for I had no torch. But I never found a name I recognized.

As the sky began to lighten in the east, I started to worry about finding myself a good hiding place in which to spend the day. In the dark it was impossible to select or assess the suitability of any hiding place, but the lighter it got, the more urgent the problem became. Gradually it became possible to distinguish the outlines of woods and trees against the sky and the nature of the countryside. The terrain was gentle and undulating without any steep hills. It was very much an agricultural region with large tracts of plough and few woods. I guessed that in this area the local inhabitants went early to bed and were up and about by dawn. It was urgent to get off the road and hide myself. In vain I looked for a haystack, the traditional warm hiding place for the runaway, but there was none in sight.

It was now dangerously light and already I was beginning to feel conspicuous. I saw a wood on the horizon, about two miles from the road and turned off towards it. In the corner of a ploughed field I came across a pile of turnips, or they may have been beet. I selected the largest one and went on to the wood.

The wood was of conifers, disappointingly sparse and affording little cover. On the far side of the wood, away from the road, I found a large dry ditch, where I would not be visible unless somebody walked right alongside it. In the deserted countryside, this seemed unlikely.

I sat down in the bottom of the ditch, where the leaves were still covered with frost, and had my first meal—slices of raw turnip spread with treacle. It was revolting and I could not force myself even to finish the first slice. So I ate treacle with my knife until

I was nauseated, thinking all the while of that delicious loaf of black German bread lying somewhere on the railway tracks.

Five minutes later I was fast asleep in the bottom of the ditch. I must have slept two hours before I awoke shivering and frozen to the marrow. Any further sleep was out of the question, it was too cold. After some violent exercises to get my circulation back, I ate some more treacle and lit a cigarette. It was still only 8 a.m. I had another ten or eleven hours to spend in that ditch. I very much doubted if I could endure it, unless I could sleep or occupy myself in some activity.

I got out my maps and started to study them. It was the first time I had looked at them since leaving the train.

Assuming the train was between twenty-five and thirty-five miles out of Erfurt when I jumped and that I had covered twenty miles during the night, my position now had to be in the area of Naumberg or Weissenfels, but some distance to the north.

It was not easy to identify with any degree of certainty the road I was on. Its heading was rather south of north-east, roughly parallel to the railway, but a considerable distance from it. Eventually it should lead me to Merseburg which was little more than twenty miles from Naumberg.

As I had not seen any signposts indicating Naumberg at any of the crossroads I had passed during the night, I concluded that I had still some distance to go before Naumberg lay abeam of me, to the south. There was a small town named Eckartsberga marked on the map which, I thought, must be in the close vicinity. From Eckartsberga to Merseburg was twenty-five miles in a straight line, possibly thirty-five by my road.

'I can do it easily in two nights' march.' I was again talking to myself. 'On the third day I can pinpoint the airfield exactly by watching the aircraft taking off and landing. On the third night I can get inside the airfield in darkness and look around. It would help if there was some moonlight. By dawn, or soon after, I should have selected my aeroplane and be ready to go. Then due south to Munich, there won't be any fighters down there, and turn right for Lake Constance. I can't possibly miss Lake Constance. Slap it down right alongside the lake on the Swiss side.'

At least it was a plan of action. Something to go for and give my country walk a purpose.

But would I last three more days? I looked distastefully at my tin of treacle. Did it still contain the energy I needed to walk all night and freeze all day for another seventy-two hours? I was not very confident.

The situation was so ludicrous, I laughed aloud. A stackful of Red Cross parcels on the train with us, full of compact, high energy foods like chocolate, raisins, glucose, Horlicks tablets and those damned organizers could not even arrange for me to have two sixpenny chocolate bars.

'Smug, complacent, lazy, inefficient, little-minded bureaucrats.' I addressed the nearest fir tree with venom. 'If they had let me have the food I asked for, when I asked for it, I would have a real chance, instead of having to go through a sort of survival course in full reality. I wonder if I am supposed to trap rabbits and dig for edible roots?'

Never again, I swore, would I leave anything to any so-called committee.

Just for the hell of it, I measured the distances to Germany's borders. Switzerland lay 280 miles to the south-west, France 280 miles to the west, Stettin was a mere 220 miles to the north. Well, that was my own fault. I should have escaped while I was still in France. Eckartsberga was the wrong place to choose as a starting point.

About midday the clouds cleared and the sun shone warmly. I left my ditch and settled comfortably with my back against a tree where I had a commanding view of the countryside and the full benefit of the sunshine. I occupied myself by cutting the RAF brass buttons from my greatcoat and, with my penknife, whittling wooden toggles to replace them. These toggles I sewed on to my coat with needle and thread, using the ball of Red Cross string I had in my pocket to make, at least I thought so, elaborate frogging on the coat.

My hands were too cold to attempt any more sewing, although there were all my tunic buttons still to be dealt with. So I got out my cockpit drills for the German aircraft and started studying the Ju 52, 87 and 88, the most likely aircraft at any German field. But I could not concentrate and anyway I knew them all by heart. Last minute cramming would not help. If I got inside an aeroplane, I was quite confident that, given five minutes peace to study the controls, I could get it started and off the ground. And then on to Switzerland, hedge hopping, never more than a few feet above the ground or the highest obstacle on my path. Steer 200° on the compass and I was bound to see Nurnberg, Munich or Lake Constance. The navigation problems did not worry me.

I went off into a daydream about a remarkable escape from Germany in a Junkers 52. No, I changed the dream, a 52 would not do, I would never get all three engines started. Better an 88. That was really fast; furthermore it landed very nicely with its wheels up, on an even keel and with no damage to the pilot. I had seen some which had been forced down in England. All I needed was a big pasture, just over the Swiss border. Preferably with no cows.

There was no point in attempting a North Sea crossing and running the gauntlet of our own fighters and flak, not to mention the German fighters who would certainly have been alerted.

After two happy hours of warmth, the clouds rolled in again from the north-east and the temperature dropped immediately. I went back to the ditch and slept at once. I was so tired that all that could keep me awake was the cold. While I was warm, I could sleep for ever.

When I woke again it was nearly 4 p.m. Again I was frozen and shivering and I exercised to stimulate the circulation.

I ate more treacle.

I smoked another cigarette.

What to do next, to kill the hours before dark?

My maps and papers had to be hidden. So I opened the lining of my tunic and stowed them all in appropriate places. I kept out 30 Reichmarks and hid away two twenty marks notes. My lockpick went into the thick collar of my jacket. I completed the concealment with some fancy work with needle and thread. Now I had nothing suspicious in my pockets to be found in a perfunctory search, except for a packet of Players, with thirteen cigarettes. My matches were German.

It was nearly seven o'clock before it was fully dark and I felt safe enough to leave my hiding place. It had not been a good one and I hoped to find a better one next day.

When I tried to walk, I found that the effect of the cold and the previous night's exercise had been to seize up my ankle. It was solid. None of the joints would move. I could only hobble.

I made painfully slow progress back to my road. Once on the asphalt, however, the going was easier and, although limping, I was able to move at a fair pace. After about an hour's marching, with the increased circulation of my bloodstream, the ankle loosened up and I found I could walk almost normally.

Unlike the night before, the sky was not permanently obscured by cloud. Occasionally I could see great areas of star-studded sky and there was promise in the east of a moon to come.

When I came to the first inhabited area, it was still only 9 o'clock. I was pretty sure that this must be Eckartsberga.

It was much too early to walk through it because there were bound to be plenty of people still about. Rather than face the hazards of walking all round it, I retreated behind a hedge and rested.

The moonlight was getting brighter as the moon gained altitude in the eastern sky.

I ate some more treacle. The tin was now less than half full.

I smoked another cigarette. Twelve left.

I massaged my ankle to keep it warm and to prevent it from solidifying again.

Nervously, I waited until 10.15 p.m.

Then I walked straight through Eckartsberga without seeing a soul.

For the rest of the night I plodded on, talking to myself but singing very little. I did not have the breath to spare. It was forced progress, my will driving my legs. I felt hungry, lightheaded and very tired. By midnight there was a brilliant half moon in the sky which, to my night-accustomed eyes, illuminated the whole countryside.

It was about 3 a.m. when I realized I was approaching a rather bigger town than I had hitherto passed through. I thought it might be Laucha and hoped to find confirmation. Keeping close to the houses on the south side of the road, where the moon shadows were deepest, I walked quickly and quietly. When I came to the central square, there was a choice to be made. Only my road led into the square but at the far end I had to turn left or right.

Flipping a mental coin, I aimed for the right hand corner of the square. Now I was fully exposed to the moonlight and felt uncomfortably conspicuous. But at 3 a.m., who would be looking out for an escaped RAF officer? At the corner of the square I saw a sign on the wall opposite indicating the road to Weissenfels. I knew that the road indicated by the sign was the wrong one for me. I had to leave the square by the left-hand corner, cross a river and I would be directly on the road to Merseburg.

I was about to cross the road when I heard a distant noise of footsteps. I retreated into the shadows and listened intently. Two sets of footsteps, I thought, nearly in step. It could only be policemen.

Moving quickly round the corner, I surveyed the square. In the middle was a gargantuan equestrian statue. Behind it a church. On my side of the square, clearly visible in the moonlight, was a Gasthaus, an old coaching inn.

The gates to the stable yard were wide open and about thirty yards to my left. I slipped into the yard and hid behind one of the massive wooden gates. I could see the square through the gap between the gate and the gate post.

After three or four minutes, the policemen rounded the corner into the square. They walked straight past the entrance to the inn yard. I listened until the sound of their footsteps on the cobbles died away.

As I still had to cross the top end of the square in bright moonlight, to find the road to Merseburg, I decided to wait another five minutes on my watch in case the policemen came back.

The inn yard was flooded by moonlight and I studied it. On the right were the stables and on the left what appeared to be the kitchen, with a row of refuse bins outside the door. Above the kitchen and at the bottom end of the yard were bedrooms, all dark and curtained. It would be heaven, I thought, to be up there in bed covered by one of those fluffy white eiderdowns which the Germans use.

When five minutes was up I left the yard and crossed the square rapidly. Almost immediately the road turned to the right and I saw a sign for Merseburg. I crossed the river bridge and was soon in open country again.

I was tired, mortally tired. Both my legs ached, the good one as much as the damaged one. I needed to rest.

When I found some dark shadows under a clump of roadside trees, I lay down supine. For ten minutes I just breathed deeply and tried to relax. Then I went through my routine.

I ate treacle with my knife.

I smoked a cigarette. Eleven left.

As I smoked I tried to assess my situation in realistic terms. The conclusion I came to was that I was, very nearly, at the end of my tether. Unless I ate abundantly and slept well, I could not get through another 24 hours. The thought of freezing in a damp ditch all next day and marching all through the following night was a nightmare which I could not face. And even if I forced myself to do so, flogging the last ounce of energy out of my body, would I then be able to face the very complicated process of stealing a German aeroplane?

I smoked another cigarette. Ten left.

I had to eat, that was the first priority. An idea had been forming in my sub-conscious and now I let it surface and examined it.

The Gasthaus on the square. The kitchen would be stacked with food. The door would present no problem. I would go back, steal food, hide up, eat and sleep. With my belly full, I could reassess my situation more realistically.

I stubbed out my cigarette, not bothering to save the butt. There were more important things in my mind than second-run cigarettes. Painfully I got to my feet and turned back towards the town.

Four

I WALKED rapidly but furtively. My character had changed. I was no longer an escaped prisoner of war, impudently defying the Germans and protected by the Geneva convention, I was just a common criminal intent on larceny. In less than ten minutes I had reached the square and was surveying it from the deep shadows at the north-east corner. It was still bathed in moonlight and completely deserted. There was no sign or sound of the policemen. I hoped they had completed their last patrol and would not be back.

I moved round the north edge of the square, keeping in the shadow, until I had to cross the road to reach the inn yard. Twenty seconds later, I was outside the kitchen door. My lockpick was already in my hand.

For a few seconds I stood still in the moonlight, breathing deeply and wiping the sweat from my hands on my greatcoat. I was feeling hot, but at the same time I was shivering.

Now my lockpick was engaged. I could feel the force of the spring and had a good contact with the bolt of the lock. With infinite caution I lifted up the spring as I rotated the lockpick. There was the slightest of clicks. The lock was free. Pressing down the outside handle, I opened the door and closed it quietly behind me.

The kitchen was illuminated by moonlight coming through the uncurtained windows. On my right, directly under the window was a sink with draining boards each side. A massive table stood in the middle of the room. Against the right hand wall was an immense stove. On my left were swinging doors which led into the restaurant, or so I supposed. Directly in front of me the whole wall, except for a closed door, was lined with low cupboards, surmounted by shelves which reached to the ceiling. Just on the left of the cooking stove was another closed door. This door I identified as being the entrance to the larder. From the yard I had seen a small, square, typical larder window, just to the right of the kitchen windows.

It had taken perhaps thirty seconds for my eyes to re-adjust themselves to the changed intensity of light and to survey the whole scene. I had been standing stock still. Then I moved over to the stove.

Inside an enormous black pot there were potatoes boiled in their skins. Masses of them. I ate one immediately, skin and all, while looking around for some receptacle to carry my booty. Hanging up behind the door, I found a voluminous shopping satchel, made of ersatz leather. I crammed this half full of potatoes, perhaps thirty of them.

I tried the handle of the larder door. Locked. A good sign, I thought, there must be something inside worth locking up.

The lock was easy and I had the larder door open in seconds.

The spring was a strong one and threw back the bolt with a frightening noise which I thought would waken the whole household. I stood motionless, listening intently, but there was no reaction from upstairs and I opened the larder door.

Inside the larder it was really dark as practically no light came through the small window. I lit a match and gazed in wonderment at the treasures it revealed. When the match went out I went silently into the kitchen to look for a big sharp knife. I found it immediately, stuck in its slot at the end of the kitchen table.

Back in the larder I located the ham I had seen by matchlight and sliced a dozen thick slabs from it. Next I took two enormous sausages and a sealed packet of ersatz butter.

I risked another match to look over the wine shelves. In its brief glare I identified the long necked bottles of what I hoped might be Moselle wine, although I cared little. I took three bottles.

A minute later I was ready to leave. I had one bottle of wine and all the food in the satchel and a bottle in each of my greatcoat pockets.

Closing the larder door I left it unlocked. From the yard I relocked the kitchen door after me. This, I hoped, would give the impression that it was an inside job. One might suppose that one of the hotel guests, feeling hungry during the night, had gone down to the kitchen, found the larder door open, eaten thirty potatoes, ten pounds of ham, four pounds of sausage and drunk three bottles of wine.

With acute pleasure, which was mostly anticipation of the Lucullan feast I was about to make, I formed a clear mental picture of this imaginary guest. He was probably a commercial traveller. Perhaps his line was the very wines I had stolen. He was not particularly tall, nevertheless he was a big man, with jowls and a fat neck. He weighed about 220 pounds and his enormous belly was retained by a wide leather belt. The belt was of real leather. The ersatz imitation manufactured in wartime Germany would not have stood the strain.

My mouth watered in sympathy as, with the imaginary scapegoat for my crime, I savoured the gargantuan meal he had so much enjoyed.

It was not a very credible story, but something on those lines might enter the mind of the good inn-keeper, when he discovered the theft, and keep him from calling the police immediately.

Standing in the moonlight outside the kitchen door of the Gasthaus while I manipulated the lockpick, I needed all my self-control. I wanted to run and run. To hide. To disappear.

At last the door was locked and with my satchel under my arm and the wine bottles in my pockets I walked straight across the square. The whole operation had taken nine minutes.

It was not until I was well clear of the town that I began to unwind. Really, I thought, it had been a nice coup. Maybe I was in the wrong profession. I was so hungry and in such a hurry to eat that I had to force myself to keep walking. My legs had no strength and the hill I was now climbing seemed endless.

Exactly an hour after leaving the Gasthaus, I started looking for a hiding place. The terrain on my left climbed steeply away from the road and was thickly wooded. The moon was now behind me, in the western sky, still bathing the scenery with its cold light. In the east the first flush of dawn was just visible. Leaving the road, I climbed the hill on my left and soon found myself in a thick wood of deciduous trees. As I penetrated deeper into the wood the undergrowth grew thicker. Determined to be safe from police searches and casual eyes, I kept going uphill, eventually taking to my hands and knees to crawl between thickly growing brushwood. I stopped in the middle of a nearly impenetrable patch of undergrowth, which I had only been able to reach by crawling painfully on my stomach.

All around me were bushes of brushwood over six feet tall and, among the brushwood, high trees. Only a ferret could find me there.

With my penknife I started to cut down the brushwood in a rough circle. It was a long laborious job, but I wanted a long, enjoyable rest. I laid the brushwood down all over my cleared circle so that it formed a thick bed, insulating me from the still frozen earth. There was more brushwood to cover me.

When my bed was ready, I burrowed into it and opened the satchel. Slicing two huge potatoes in half, I filled each with butter and a thick slice of ham. Then I opened a bottle of wine. My penknife had one of those corkscrew attachments, which, to my surprise, was most efficient.

Never had food tasted better or wine been more welcome. The wine seemed to penetrate to my toes and fingertips and I felt a warm glow pervade my whole being. I continued drinking and soon started to feel light headed. That was what I wanted. If I could get blind drunk I could sleep for twelve hours.

After drinking rather more than half the bottle, I recorked it and put it aside. Using the satchel as a pillow I lay back enjoying a lassitude and sense of contentment greater than I had felt in many months. The war, my imprisonment, my plans for the morrow were all forgotten. I was just a happy man with a full stomach and a comfortable bed beneath him.

I would have liked to smoke, but that dry brushwood was really dangerous. A spark, a dropped match or cigarette and there would have been a raging inferno within seconds.

Almost immediately I fell into a deep, dreamless sleep. It was one o'clock in the afternoon when the sun on my face woke me. I had slept for nearly eight hours.

My first thought was of lunch, a magnificent gourmet lunch, eaten slowly and with relish, each course accompanied by the best wine from my cellar.

I crawled out of my brushwood bed and went for a walk, stamping my feet and swinging my arms to restore my circulation. On the edge of the wood, with a clear view of the valley below, I smoked a cigarette and tried to identify landmarks. There were no aeroplanes to be seen in the sky and nothing to indicate the existence of an airfield anywhere in the vicinity. I calculated that I was looking south towards Weissenfels and that Merseburg was out of sight, hidden by the corner of the wood.

My plans were simple and pleasant to make. First, an enormous lunch at which I would consume as much as possible. Enough wine to make me thoroughly sleepy. Three hours siesta and then off towards Merseburg. Stop walking at 4 a.m. and concentrate on finding another safe, warm lying-up place. The following day, I could again eat well and would be on the top of my form for the difficult challenge of stealing an aircraft.

As I made my way back to my brushwood den, I composed the menu for lunch. Later I wrote it down feeling that so remarkable a gastronomic occasion was worth recording.

Saucisson Surprise à la Boche
STEINWEIN 39
Jambon Volé en Pleine Nuit
TEUFELSKELLER 38
Pommes de Terre à l'Allemand
Faux Beurre à la Mode des Krauts
Sirop Doré à l'Anglais au Couteau

Like a busy chef I immersed myself in the preparations for a lunch. The sausage was carefully sliced and laid out on the table-cloth, which was my greatcoat. I cut in half and buttered a dozen potatoes, using up all the ersatz butter that was left. The ham was arranged artistically in overlapping slices. I uncorked another bottle of wine.

With the hors d'oeuvres I would be drinking Steinwein, there was nearly half a bottle left over from breakfast. The main course would be accompanied by a bottle of Teufelskeller. Both were white Rhine wines and already well chilled in my woodland cellar.

I ate slowly, savouring every mouthful. The sausage was spiced and delicious, it needed long draughts of Steinwein to wash it down. The ham and potato was my meal for the week and I consumed it steadily, without any diminishment of appetite. When all twelve potatoes and all the ham was gone, I was gorged as a Strasbourg goose. The bottle of Teufelskeller was more than three quarters finished.

Le Sirop Doré à l'Anglais, I politely refused. I was sorry to have to skip coffee and cognac too, but it was not offered.

Making my way to the edge of the wood, I basked happily replete in the warm sun, looking forward to my siesta and wondering if I could possibly force myself to wake up again at seven o'clock.

Again I slept soundly and undisturbed. My subconscious, however, was still vigilant and I was suddenly wide awake at exactly 7 o'clock. It was nearly dark and the moon had not yet risen. To revive myself, I finished the rest of the Teufelskeller.

Before leaving my hide-out I collected every scrap of evidence of my crime and removed all traces of my presence except for the cut brushwood. I stowed the empty bottles in the satchel where there was still a good supply of potatoes and one complete sausage, as well as a remnant.

Back on the road again, I moved slowly, waiting for my ankle to thaw. There was plenty of time. By morning I had to be somewhere in sight of the airfield at Merseburg, well concealed and, I fervently hoped, comfortable. All the real action would take place the following night. According to my calculations I had little more than 15 miles to go.

Since leaving the train I had not washed or shaved. It seemed to be a good idea to rectify this omission. I decided that during the night I would look for a fast running stream where I might clean up.

The nature of the terrain had changed. The road was no longer level but climbed and descended between wooded hills. It was no longer straight but curved frequently to follow a contour or a river bed. At intervals there were small bridges which carried the road over fast running streams.

As I walked on I began to worry more and more about being caught with the evidence of the previous night's crime still on me. Breaking and entering was not permitted by the Geneva Convention and, there was no doubt that, if caught and convicted, I could be sentenced to a term of civil imprisonment which might be very different and much more unpleasant than life in a prisoner-of-war camp. It would be stupid to take unnecessary risks.

At the next bridge I left the road and walked upstream along the bank of a swift torrent.

The terrain was uneven with big boulders and outcrops of rock. Trees came down to the edge of the stream. Although the moon was still low in the sky, there was enough light to distinguish these obstacles and to find a path through them. Eventually I came to a wide expanse of pasture, surrounded on three sides by tall trees and, on the fourth side, bordered by the stream. Here I was out of sight and hearing from the road and there was no sign of any human habitation.

The first thing to do was to bury the evidence. Just inside the wood, I dug a hole in soft earth. In the hole I placed the satchel, two empty wine bottles and a not yet empty treacle tin. The potatoes were not incriminating, everybody in Germany lived on potatoes and it was even plausible that I had brought them with me from Spangenberg. The last bottle of Teufelskeller was different. That was damning evidence. The sausage too was dangerous.

I just could not bring myself to bury an excellent bottle of Riesling and a delicious sausage. It did not make sense. After all, I had not encountered anybody yet on my march, and, if I went cautiously, I should be able to continue to avoid meeting any locals, whether policemen or peasants.

I counted the potatoes. There were thirteen of them. The bottle of Teufelskeller, I decided ruthlessly, would have to be buried. But not the wine. I emptied my water bottle onto the grass and refilled it carefully with wine. This left the wine bottle about one quarter full. With my penknife I sliced the remaining sausage into thirteen slices and inserted each slice into a potato. Then I ate three potatoes with their sausage filling and finished the wine in the bottle. The bottle went into the hole. I refilled the hole with earth and tamped it well down. Over the site I brushed back dead leaves and mulch. No visible evidence.

By the side of the stream I found a flat rock from which I could comfortably perform my ablutions. First I washed my feet and threw my old socks far into mid-stream. The water was icy cold but its after effect was most invigorating. Rapidly I stripped completely and immersed myself in the water. The cold left me breathless and gasping. I thought my heart had stopped.

Grabbing the cake of soap, I rapidly lathered my face, neck, armpits and crutch. Then again under the water. This time the shock was less, but the cold was beginning to penetrate to the marrow of my bones. Leaping onto the bank, I snatched up my towel and ran, entirely naked, across the pasture, towards the woods. My piece of towel was little more than a foot square, but it sufficed to get me approximately dry. I ran back again to where I had left my clothes and dressed hurriedly.

The clean socks felt marvellous and there was a warm glow all over my epidermis, which completely revived me in body and spirit. When I was again fully dressed, I lathered my face and shaved. I was well practised in shaving without seeing my face in a mirror.

The cold dip had revived my hunger and I devoured two potatoes, gulping them down with long draughts of wine from my water bottle.

I felt too clean and healthy to smoke.

As I made my way back to the road, I was again eager and confident. In each greatcoat pocket I had four sausage filled potatoes and I still had about half a bottle of wine. Starvation was a long way off. Stealing an aeroplane no longer seemed to be so crazy a plan. All I needed was a little luck the day after tomorrow, when I would be inside the airfield. And it looked as if luck was running my way.

I was, perhaps, fifty yards from the road when I saw the lights. Twin headlights, approaching from the direction of Merseburg. In wartime Germany, an automobile meant one of two things: high-ranking military or the police. If it was the police, it would probably be the Gestapo. The local country police had no motor cars at their disposition. Since leaving the train, I had not once seen a car, either in motion or parked.

I fell flat on my face and watched. The car was moving slowly. It seemed to me that its occupants must be looking for somebody and that somebody might be me.

There was no possibility at all that I could be seen from the car and I watched it until it had disappeared.

It was a very bad sign and probably meant that my presence in the area was known. This was a quite logical deduction, as the Spangenberg guards on the train would have been able to guess fairly accurately where I had jumped off. By now, a general warning would have gone out to all police stations. If, in addition, my inn-keeper had reported the theft, any search would now be centred on this area.

The immediate question to answer was whether the road I had been following was now safe. If that police car came from Merseburg, would it use the same road to return to base? I thought not. On the way back to Merseburg, the police might well take the road which ran through Bad Bibra, not far to the north, so as to extend the area of their search.

I took to the road again and walked fast.

Five

THE night before the moon had been a friend. Tonight it was an enemy. If there were police patrols on the road they would certainly see me before I saw them. Any policeman standing in the deep shadows cast by the moon would be invisible to me.

By abandoning the road and moving cross-country, this danger could be avoided. But the terrain was too difficult. I was still in the hills and to follow a rough compass course away from the road would have meant crossing unfordable streams and forcing a path through thick forest. It was the road or nothing.

I walked nervously, keeping to the shadows whenever possible. All my senses were keyed up and I was ready to dive into the ditch at the slightest indication of danger. As time passed and I made distance, I gradually persuaded myself that there was no police watch on the road. The test would come at the next town or village big enough to have its own police station.

The road had started to descend again and the going was easier. Not that I was tired. On the contrary, I felt full of energy and ready to walk all night. Without incident except for barking dogs, I passed through two hamlets, each no more than a group of farmhouses and barns. But I knew that there must be trouble ahead. As I got nearer to Merseburg and the river, the density of the population was bound to increase and it could not be long before I came to a village big enough to have its own policeman. I was quite certain he would have been warned to look out for me.

The moment came shortly before eleven o'clock. I could see a massed group of houses ahead, including a church and other large buildings.

'Do I chance my luck again?' I wondered, 'and walk straight through? Or is this where I make a tactical detour?'

I moved off the road to think about it and to take a rest. I was not hungry, but I drank some wine wishing that it had been water instead. I lit a cigarette and counted my stock. Only eight left. I would have to remember to buy another pack as soon as I landed in Switzerland.

This thought cheered me and I decided that, having got so close to my target, it would be stupid to take unnecessary risks. I would make the detour. It was still early in the night and there was not far to go.

My little collar stud compass was quite useless for taking bearings, so I evolved a very simple plan. I would walk due north on the Pole Star for half an hour, then north-east for half an hour, steering by my compass and the Pole Star, finally I could regain the road by heading between south-east and south. It would cost me at least an hour and a half in time, but I could afford it.

Half an hour later I was still less than a mile from the point where I had left the main road. I had encountered every kind of obstacle, the most difficult being deep-irrigation ditches which were nearly too broad to jump. There had also been wide tracts of ploughed land, which I had tried to avoid. Walking across plough is one of the slowest and most painful exercises I know. Besides, I wanted to keep my trousers clean.

Almost exactly at the point where I should have turned northeast, I came to a river. It was not a mighty river like the Elbe or the Danube, but nobody would have dared insult it by calling it a stream. It flowed calmly but fast and, to me, it looked deep. At least deep enough to come up to my neck, whether my feet were on the bottom or not. The far bank was a good forty feet away. I made the obvious deduction that the river flowed through the town I was trying to avoid, where there would be the only bridge for miles around.

I could swim across, of course, but that would mean pneumonia, unless I stripped, made a bundle of my clothes and held them clear of the water. Johnny Weissmuller might have done it, but it was beyond me.

There was no easy way of overcoming the obstacle. Either I went back to the town and crossed the bridge, braving the policemen, or I walked upstream until I came to another bridge. I decided to walk upstream.

Fortunately, there was a well beaten path along the river bank. I set out at a really fast pace, hoping to make up time. After an hour's march, I had found no way to cross the river and was nearly despairing.

'Another fifteen minutes,' I said aloud, 'then I am going back to the town. I should have played my luck and kept straight on, instead of making this bloody silly detour.'

A few minutes later, I saw the railway bridge. There was no mistaking its massive girder work. I climbed the railway embankment and crossed the river. I noted that it was a single line track.

From the top of the railway embankment I had an extensive view of the moonlit countryside, and I stopped to plan my next move. There was no longer any purpose in trying to return to the road I had been following.

Retreating under the railway bridge I had a quick look at my map, in the light of successive matches. It was largely a wasted effort. I could distinguish very little detail in the matchlight and had only a rough idea of where I was. Of one thing I was certain. I must be within ten miles of Merseburg. The railway, I presumed, was a minor branch line which would eventually lead to Merseburg, either directly or after joining the main line. I would walk along the tracks for another four or five miles and then hide up for the day. Wherever I was, I should be in a position to see the airfield, or at least the aircraft making use of it.

For a single-line track, there was a lot of space on top of the embankment. I found I could walk comfortably and rapidly at the side of the rails, clear of the ends of the wooden sleepers, without meeting any obstructions. Although I felt very conspicuous in the bright moonlight, I suppressed my uneasiness feeling certain that, at that hour, nobody would be observing the railway embankment.

Certainly the embankment offered me the fastest and most direct route across the countryside. The frequent irrigation ditches, which all ran in a south-easterly direction, passed through culverts under the embankment. Each one of those ditches would have presented me with a different, individual problem, if I had been walking through the fields. In an hour's march along the railway, I could cover between four and five miles. Had I still been moving cross-country, I would have been lucky to average two miles an hour.

The growing assurance that I was nearing my goal was immensely encouraging. Less than twenty-four hours ago, before pulling off the Gasthaus job, my morale had been way down near absolute zero.

Now it was soaring up towards the dangerous zone of over-confidence. I felt buoyant and energetic, confident that I would find a solution to any problem which lay ahead. I was even optimistic about my chances of stealing an aeroplane.

I had been following the railway for nearly three hours, when I saw the ideal hiding place for the following day. Just to the north of the track was a small, isolated hill, standing out above the flat country around it. It was well wooded and looked as though it

might offer good cover. From that hill I should be able to get a
clear view of the country for miles around and thus locate my
airfield.

As soon as I was abreast of the hill, I left the railway.

A quarter of an hour later, I had climbed to the top of the hill
and was looking for a place to sleep.

If there was anything wrong with the wood, it was that it was
too well kept. There was no brushwood at all and underfoot was
spongy turf and grass. It seemed more like a park. There was no
really safe place to hide, but still, there were a lot of trees. It
would have to do. It was too late to find another. Besides, the view
all round was magnificent. I could not have picked a better observation post.

Before sleeping, I ate four potatoes with sausage and drank spar-
ingly of my water. I had finished the wine and refilled my bottle
at the river. The water tasted muddy. My bed was a shallow depression in leaf mould near the summit. I was asleep before the
moon set.

A violent rainstorm woke me at about 9 o'clock. Somehow, I
had never taken rain into my calculations and wondered what to
do. I could either lie where I was, getting wetter and wetter, or
try and shelter behind a big tree. In either case, I concluded, I
would end up equally soaked. I lay where I was.

When the rain had stopped, some half hour later, the sun came
out, but there was no warmth in it. Without moving from my leaf
mould bed, I ate another potato. Three left. I was very cold but
did not have the will power to do anything about it. I had no desire to stir, to think or act.

At first, I did not recognize the noise, I was too deep in my
frozen torpor. When I suddenly realized that it was an aeroplane,
passing low and close. I came back to reality with an abrupt tran-
sition. I scurried, half crouching, to a point where I had a clear
view, just in time to see a Fiesler Storch disappearing from sight.
My identification was positive, there was no mistaking the high
wing, the long struts and the ungainly undercarriage.

I looked round to see where the Storch might have come from.
Almost immediately I located the airfield. I could see two aircraft

in the circuit and another, a Ju 52, which had just taken off. It was between three and four miles away.

For half an hour I studied my line of approach to the airfield, noting all the obstacles I would have to surmount and getting a clear mental picture of the pattern of irrigation ditches. With my collar-stud compass, I took a very approximate bearing.

The airfield was a busy one. On the side farthest from me were three big hangars, with their doors wide open and many aircraft parked on the tarmac outside. At various points round the perimeter of the field were small groups of dispersed aircraft. At that distance, I could not identify the types of aircraft, nor could I see any sign of a security fence. I wished I had a pair of binoculars. With their aid I could almost have selected my getaway aircraft from among those dispersed around the edge of the field.

The Fiesler Storch came into view again. It was flying along the railway line, slowly and with not more than 200 feet of altitude, heading south-west. I watched it until it disappeared into the distance.

'A Fiesler Storch, a Fiesler Storch,' I found myself repeating. 'Maybe that's the best solution.'

Certainly, it was an attractive idea, and had a great deal in its favour. It was the only German aircraft I had any experience of and I knew its controls and starting system. One great advantage about the Storch was that it could be started from inside the cockpit, without any external help. It was extremely slow, but, on the other hand, it needed a bare hundred yards of clear space to get airborne and could land on a pocket handkerchief. My biggest doubt was for its range. I was by no means confident that, even with full tanks, it could fly from Merseburg to Switzerland. But of one thing I was certain. If, in the early light of dawn, I found myself beside a Fiesler Storch parked in an isolated position the temptation to take a chance on its range would be nearly irresistible. It was such an easy aircraft to steal.

When I was quite sure that I could find my way to the airfield blindfolded, I went back to my leaf mould bed. I needed as much sleep as I could get. I was sorry, now, that I had finished the wine. It would have helped to keep out the cold.

Six

THE first thing I saw when I awoke was a man standing less than ten feet away, looking down at me. He had his finger to his lips as if to warn me from crying out. But I was so paralysed by his sudden apparition that I was speechless.

For a full minute we looked warily at each other in absolute silence. His boots, I noticed, were broken and caked in mud. The bottoms of his trousers were secured by untidy puttees. He wore a shapeless, half-length coat with a bright coloured patch on the left sleeve. He had a peaked cap pulled well down over his eyes.

'Good God,' I thought with a sudden surge of new hope, 'he's not a German. He's some sort of a prisoner, like me.'

I beckoned to him to get down out of sight and to come closer. He was much too visible standing. He came and crouched near me, taking cover behind a tree. He did not inspire me with any confidence but, at the same time, I realized that I, too, must look like a walking scarecrow. He had probably guessed from my appearance that I was a fugitive.

'Ich bin Pole,' he said, touching the bright patch on his sleeve.

So he was a Polish prisoner-of-war. But what was he doing here? Had he escaped too?

As if in answer to my unspoken questions, the Pole pointed to the field below the wood where I saw there was a pair of horses hitched to a plough. He made it clear that that was his team and that he was employed as a farm labourer.

'Englischer Flieger,' I said, to break the ice.

The atmosphere changed at once from one of uneasy suspicion to one of immense friendliness. The Pole grinned all over his face, showing brilliantly white teeth and shook my hand vigorously. He was delighted. In an excited whisper he started a long speech. I could understand less than half of what he was saying but it was easy to guess his meaning. He was talking about our bombing raids on Germany which were growing steadily in intensity. He wanted more and more bombs. It was hurting the Germans, he said. Their war industries were being destroyed. Deutschland would soon be kaputt.

His intense hatred for the Germans gave a vicious emphasis to his words.

'Are you a bomber pilot?'

There was a macabre expectancy in his voice. I knew that had I answered affirmatively, he would have embraced me immediately.

'Nein,' I answered almost apologetically. 'Spitfeuer.' I had never thought that I would ever feel ashamed that I had not personally blasted any Germans to eternity.

'Ah, Spitfeuer, Spitfeuer,' he repeated. He was getting over his disappointment that I had not actually bombed any German city. A Spitfire was good enough. It had the reputation throughout Europe of being the most lethal fighter in the air. It had defeated the Luftwaffe during the Battle of Britain.

To my relief, the excitable Pole had calmed down. From a capacious pocket he extracted an enormous sandwich, which was thinly spread with jam. Opening the sandwich, he offered half to me. It was of white bread, cut from a large cottage loaf. I imagined it must have been baked on the farm. Since arriving in Germany, I had never seen anything but hard, sour, black bread, which was never fresh and never stale.

I refused the bread because I was not hungry and still had some potatoes left. I suspected that Polish prisoners in Germany were kept on very short rations. The gaunt look of my new companion confirmed this. I did not offer him a potato because I still had an uneasy conscience about them. I did not want anybody, even a friendly Pole, to know that I had them.

But my new friend was so insistent that there was no way of refusing his slice of bread. In the end, I compromised by accepting the slice, breaking it in two and handing half back to him.

We both ate our half slices with enjoyment. In sign language, he indicated that he had to go back to his ploughing. Then, taking hold of my left wrist and pointing to my watch, he made it clear that he would come back and meet me in the wood at eight o'clock that night. When he was sure that I fully understood this, he shook hands again and made off down the hill towards his horses. About twenty yards away, he turned back towards me.

'Deutschland kaputt,' he said in a stage whisper, grinning happily.

'Deutschland kaputt,' I whispered back, giving him the V-sign.

A wave of his hand and he had gone from my field of vision.

The unexpected encounter had greatly disturbed me and I began to wonder if my plans were still valid. Lighting a cigarette, I tried to make a calmly factual assessment of the situation.

From every point of view, the friendly Pole was a great embarrassment to me. I did not need his help and could not confide in him. But it was far more than a matter of embarrassment. If the Pole got into my act, he would introduce an element of danger, much more for himself than for me, which I had, at all costs, to avoid.

In those early days of the war, when Hitler was still arrogant and triumphant, the status of the Poles was pitiable. The Aryan master race, having conquered and occupied Poland, treated its inhabitants with less regard than cattle. Poland was worse than a subject nation, it had been reduced to a slave nation. The value of a Polish prisoner was equivalent to the value of the work he could do. He was not an individual, not even a human being and had neither rights nor protection. A Pole who rebelled or transgressed any of the Nazi laws had no value and was disposed of without ceremony.

My planned adventure for that night was not for any Polish prisoner. If he were caught inside a German military airfield, he would be shot out of hand or just clubbed to death by the sentries who found him. Nobody would worry, nobody could protest, the Polish nation no longer existed.

I knew this because there were many hundreds of Poles in the RAF who had somehow escaped from their homeland and come to England to fight with us. Often, in peaceful country pubs in England, it had been difficult to believe their stories. The atrocities they told of were too great. It was impossible for us to conceive the stark terror and blind hatred which Hitler's hatchet men inspired. The Gestapo and the SS were organizations we had heard about, but our comfortable imaginations could not present to us the horror of being at the mercy of these ruthless automatons whose minds were empty of all human feelings, of all compassion. As they would subsequently plead in their own defence, when finally tried for their crimes, they obeyed orders blindly. Their orders were to exterminate all those who the maniac leader of the Aryan master race had decreed to be unfit to live as slaves.

These stories came back to me as I thought about my new friend. They were easier to believe now.

He was a lucky man to be a slave labourer on a German farm. If he stayed where he was, there was even the hope that one day he might return to his home and find his family again. If he became involved with me, in the slightest way, he would be putting himself back into the realm of terror, into the hands of the Gestapo and the SS.

We were both fighting the same enemy, but we were each fighting a different war. I was just an amateur, playing the game according to Queensberry. Mine was a gentleman's war. The Geneva Convention gave me licence to escape. Even breaking into a military airfield was not a serious crime, as long as I was not accused of sabotage. Within certain limits, the Germans would punish me, but I was not, at any time, risking the death penalty.

For the Pole, however, there were no Queensberry rules and no referees. My presence could not protect him. If he was caught by the German inside a military airfield, his life would be forfeit. The fact that he knew of my presence in the area was already dangerous for him.

There was only one decision I could make. I would leave the hill and look for another hiding place. At all costs, I must not let the Pole find me again. As soon as the light began to fade, I would go back to the railway embankment and hide in one of the culverts. I would wait there until two or three o'clock in the morning and then make my way to the airfield. If there was any moon at all, I might be able to locate and examine the aircraft I wanted before dawn.

I crawled between the trees to a point from which I had a clear view of the airfield and the railway embankment. Because of my changed plans, a new route had to be studied.

There was a long straight irrigation ditch which ran directly from the railway to close to the airfield. It crossed under the railway about two miles further down the line, to the east. That would be the ideal route for me. If I went straight back to the railway the way I had come, at the point where it passed closest to the hill, I would have to cross five other irrigation ditches before coming to the one I had selected. If they were too wide to jump, I could cross them by climbing up the embankment.

Visually, I went over my route again and again, until I had every detail of it fixed in my mind. It was a simple route and I would not need to refer to a map again. I decided that I would not walk along the railway itself, in case it was guarded, but would cross underneath it at the first culvert and keep close to the embankment, possibly in deep shadow, on the far side from the airfield.

There had been a few brief showers during the morning, but now there was low cloud coming fast over the hill. I was beginning to be cold again.

I ate two more potatoes and smoked another cigarette. My watch read a quarter to three. I made up my mind to leave the hill in the middle of the next heavy rainstorm. It would be unlikely that anybody would see me and, under the railway culvert, I would at least be sheltered. I was anxious to get away from my hiding place, now that it had been discovered. The last thing I wanted was to meet my Polish friend again. In the fields below the hill, I could not see any sign of the Pole or his horses and presumed that the weather was unfavourable for ploughing and that he had gone back to the farm. Certainly, it was no day for a picnic in the woods.

About two miles to the north, there was a solitary man with a shotgun, walking across a field, a dog following him. He would be looking for rabbits, I imagined. I hoped he would not come in my direction, or I would have to retreat to the railway. But there was no reason to suppose that he would make for my wood. There was absolutely nothing to shoot. I watched him unconcernedly. He could not see me and did not seem to present any threat. As soon as it started raining again, he would go home. I went back to studying the airfield.

It must have been ten minutes later, when, out of mere curiosity, I again turned my head to look for the man with the shotgun. He was still visible, but nearer now, and he had company. Spread across three fields, at intervals of something over a hundred yards, I counted twelve men. All had shotguns and most had dogs at heel. The line of guns was advancing towards the hill at a steady walk, with the left flank advancing faster, so as to cover the eastern side of the hill.

My stomach was a tight knot. I was feeling sick. They were coming for me. They were going to walk straight up the hill and through the wood. I had to leave, and in a hurry. Back to the railway, through the culvert and then run. East or west, I asked myself? West, I thought, away from Merseburg, back towards the forests. The line of guns would take at least twenty-five minutes to reach the top of the hill, maybe even longer. By that time I could be far away and out of the trap.

Already, I was crawling on my belly through the trees, making south, in the direction of the railway. As soon as I had the summit of the hill between me and the hunters, I got to my feet. Hiding behind a tree, I surveyed the quickest route to the nearest culvert under the embankment. I intended to run all the way, at about the speed of an Olympic quarter miler.

But my retreat in that direction was cut off. On the top of the embankment were three more men also armed with shotguns and looking towards me. They, too, were well spaced so that they covered any line of descent from the hill.

The sour realization that this was the end of my escapade was difficult to take. But I knew that my road stopped there. There was going to be no dawn adventure in a Fiesler Storch, or in a Ju 87. I would not be buying my next pack of cigarettes in Switzerland. Indeed, I would not be smoking for many days to come. The men who were surrounding the hill knew I was hidden there. They were going to flush me out like a frightened pheasant. If I broke cover and ran, those guns would open fire. I thought of Watlington Hill and the frightened pheasants running before the line of beaters.

I had only one problem now. How to surrender with dignity and how to avoid having my uniform ruined by a few barrels of buckshot.

How had I been located, I wondered? It had to be my Polish friend. There was no other reasonable explanation. Not that I thought he had deliberately given me away; I was certain he had not. I had read his character differently. But, if his foreman or his boss had seen him leave his horses and enter the wood and had seen me too, then everything fell into place. If the Pole had been asked who it was he met in the wood, he could either lie and, quite literally, risk his neck by so doing, or he could tell the truth and say that there was a runaway English airman hidden there. He did not really have a choice. Once the Germans knew he had had contact with somebody in the wood, he had to report my presence. He would have been crazy not to do so. His life was at stake. Mine was not.

Rapidly, I reviewed my situation. Except for one map, which I buried quickly under the soil, all my other documents were sewn into the lining of my jacket. They probably would not be found, and, even if they were, they were normal contraband for a recaptured prisoner-of-war. The lockpick and the twenty Mark notes could stay in my handkerchief. I transferred them to a new handkerchief and disposed of the old one. I had two potatoes, with sausage filling, in my pockets. I would eat those before the guns arrived. Otherwise there was nothing to worry about.

The three men on the railway embankment appeared not to have seen me and I crawled back to the other side of the hill. The line of guns was now about a mile away and, I judged, should reach me in not more than fifteen minutes. I ate the last two potatoes and buried their skins. Then I turned out both pockets of my greatcoat to get rid of all the crumbs. When I was absolutely sure I was clean of all incriminating evidence, I looked back at the guns.

They were less than half a mile away, advancing steadily in a well maintained formation. It was time to go.

I got to my feet and walked without stealth, or any effort at concealment, through the trees towards the guns. Just before I reached the last of the trees, an excited shout, repeated up and down the line, indicated that I had been seen. I kept walking, very slowly, for another twenty yards until I was in open country and plainly visible. Very deliberately I surveyed the whole line of armed farmers, looking from the extreme left of the line to the last man on the right flank and then back again.

I lit a cigarette and sat down. The line had stopped advancing and was frozen. Every man was looking at me. The dogs, I was relieved to see, were under control and mostly at heel. In any case, I reassured myself, gun dogs do not attack men, however ragged.

I settled back comfortably on one elbow and waited. In a few minutes it would all be over. How strange, I reflected, this would be the second time I had surrendered lying down.

Seven

I WAS in the centre of a circle of shotguns. Each man was about ten yards from me, his gun held in two hands and pointed. Fingers, I noticed, were on triggers. Safety catches were off.

There had been a remarkable lack of shouting, indeed, the silence was grimly menacing. Everyone knew what he was doing. For these farmers, killing a rat or a mad dog did not need shouted orders.

I kept my eyes fixed on the man immediately in front of me. He gave me the impression of being the leader of the group.

He screamed four or five words at me. Although I had not understood, the gesture he made with his gun was unmistakable. I got carefully to my feet and raised my hands high above my head. I saw the guns move as I moved.

I wished everybody would relax. Double-barrelled shotguns are dangerous weapons. I had always been taught that they should never be pointed at people, even when unloaded. These guns were all loaded and I had the feeling that nobody was going to worry much if a finger twitched and a gun went off.

The head man approached me, his gun now resting under his left armpit and over his forearm. It was pointing towards the ground. The other guns had not shifted.

With a slap of his right hand, he knocked my dark glasses from my face. They fell on the grass about four feet away. I was in the habit of wearing dark glasses to hide my burnt face and protect my eyes from wind and cold, to which they were most sensitive.

He stared at me for long seconds and I sensed that all the others were also staring. My burnt face always made an initial impression. It seemed to be the moment to make some contribution to the scenario.

'Ich bin Englischer Offizier.'

I said it flatly, without expression.

'Kriegsgefangener,'* I added.

The man gestured to one of his companions, who stepped forward from the circle, picked up my glasses and handed them to the leader. He returned them to me and I put them back on my face. They were unbroken. I was wondering whether I should put my hands back above my head, or whether that stage of the proceedings was over. I compromised by finding a more comfortable, mid-way position. The tension was beginning to diminish and the more it relaxed the happier I felt.

The head farmer, for it was now obvious they were all local farmers, handed his gun to a companion and started to search me. Everything I had was taken from me and examined. Even the contents of my water bottle were tasted. The packet of Players cigarettes was handed from one farmer to the other. Each of whom fingered a cigarette and smelled the tobacco.

The tension had largely disappeared and the mood of my captors was changing. They were no longer grim men hunting a dangerous criminal, they were beginning to be pleased with themselves. They were chatting freely, exchanging comments about the various items which had been found on me. My Rolex watch was much admired.

My handkerchief, with the money inside it, had remained in my right hand and I occasionally dabbed at my eyes. Nobody thought of looking at it.

Everybody wanted to have a close look at the brass buttons on my tunic. The stuff of the tunic was fingered; it was coarse, rough material, being an airman's tunic and not an officer's.

'What rank are you?' The question was asked with some suspicion.

'Major,' I answered loudly.

There was a buzz of comment, to which I listened with interest. Many were disbelieving; I was too young to be a major. Another argued that with these pilots promotion came early.

The remark was significant. They appeared to know that I was in the air force. Was it the uniform, I wondered, or had they been told they were looking for an airman?

The general effect of my announcement, however, was to make

* Prisoner of war.

my captors even more proud of themselves. They had made an important capture. A major, no less.

I felt that it was up to me to play my part. These yokels with their dangerous twelve-bores formed a most important audience. I ought to give them what they expected. Their idea of a major would be, I suspected, an arrogant and authoritative man, not a meek scarecrow with his hands above his head. I had to make a quick metamorphosis. Pity I had no monocle.

I addressed the leader of the group.

'Meine Uhr, bitte.'

I tried to sound assured and to reproduce that unpleasant intonation of Teutonic arrogance reserved for addressing inferiors. I was asking for my watch.

I held out my left hand to receive the watch at the same time lowering my right arm to my side.

It was a critical moment. Would the farmer yield and give the Herr Major back his watch, or would he re-assert his own, unchallengeable authority? He only had to raise his gun. As we looked each other in the eyes, I wondered what he was thinking.

He handed back my watch. My battle was won. It just needed the coup de grâce.

'Meine Zigaretten, bitte.'

He handed me the pack of Players. There had been four left. I looked inside. There were still four cigarettes and there, too, was my precious cigarette holder. I fitted a cigarette into the holder and put it into my mouth.

I waited.

The Herr Major needed a light.

Would anybody be stupid enough to fall for this one.

Two men in the circle were fumbling in their pockets, but the leader himself lit my cigarette for me. It was all over. My status was established. I had surrendered with dignity.

I had a strong desire to kick the head farmer in the stomach; I had not forgiven him that slap across the face. Instead, I offered him a cigarette. He refused politely. He was not a smoker. He wanted one of the brass buttons from my tunic.

I cut off all four buttons and gave them to him, indicating that he should distribute them among my captors as he thought fit.

From that moment all was plain sailing. The farmers were happy. They were bringing in a real, live major. I was happy because the major in question was still alive.

The march to the local village took little more than half an hour. We headed in a north-westerly direction, between the hill and the airfield. No guns were pointed at me, nobody was hustling me. Conversation between my captors was animated and excited. Occasionally I would be asked a question, but I had given up trying to decipher the local accent and merely gestured with my hands that I had not understood.

I noticed that the safety catches of the shotguns, now slung by their straps over individual shoulders, were on. This was not carelessness. If I had made a run for it, I would have been blasted to pulp before I had gone twenty-five yards. It was obvious that all these boys could handle a gun and hit a moving target the size of a partridge nine times out of ten. They were not worried that I could get away.

Our entrance into the village soon transformed itself into a triumphal procession. Every living inhabitant had turned out for the occasion. Our rather casual grouping had changed into a more precise formation, with me in the middle and the farmers evenly spaced all round me. Guns were again pointed at me but I was no longer worried, it was purely to impress the onlookers. Even the farmers knew that I realized this.

In the middle of the village square was the reception committee. There was one policeman and two civilians, dressed formally in dark suits, surrounded by an expectant audience. It was obvious that my arrival was awaited. The policeman was wearing a green uniform, with a greatcoat which ended somewhere between his calves and ankles. On his head he had that fantastic helmet worn by the Schupo. His right hand was on the butt of the automatic at his belt. He was a small man.

Although I did not understand the speeches, I appreciated them. If not the guest of honour, I was, at least, the reason for the ceremony. It was heartening to note the pride and self-congratulation with which every speaker told of the day's events. Never had the village had a greater day. I felt that, if only I had learnt a little more German, I would have liked to have made a speech myself.

The ceremony ended with me being formally handed over by the farmers to the authority of the law, amid loud applause.

The policeman's gun was now in his hand. He looked nervous and his nervousness communicated itself to me. I sensed that it was important for me to lower the tension.

'Major Calnan,' I said, bowing slightly, hoping that I had achieved just that condescensious angle of inclination permitted to a major when addressing one of lower rank.

'—— Schmidt,' he barked. His heels clicked together. I had not understood what his rank was but put him down as some kind of a superior sergeant. He had not softened but at least we had established a military relationship.

He gestured to me to precede him. Just off the square, giving right on to the street, was the village lock-up. He opened the door and waved me in with his automatic. Immediately I was inside, the iron door clanged shut behind me and I heard the key turn in the lock.

The stench was overwhelming.

Before the war I had wandered all around Europe, travelling third class by train and stopping whenever the wooden seats got too hard. I used to put up in the cheapest hotels and hostels I could find. On these journeys I had, of necessity, used many public urinals in Paris, Marseilles, Naples, Budapest, Syracuse, Tunis, Malta, Belgrade and London. I could not remember any lavatory which smelled as strong as that cell.

After a moment's inspection, the reason for the stench became clear. It was not a public urinal, but a private one, reserved for the local drunks who got locked up. One corner of the walls had once been tarred over and, at floor level, there was a tube through the masonry leading out to the street gutter.

Otherwise the cell was just a hole in the wall. The only window was in the iron door and this was small and barred. The only furniture was a leather covered bench, upholstered with horsehair, which was bristling through the leather at many points. The cell was dark, illuminated only by the light which filtered through the window in the door. In the ceiling was a single electric light bulb, but it had not been turned on and the switch was outside.

I sat down on the bench, which was supported by two chains attached to the wall. I wanted to lie supine and rest for a while, but that leather was so grimy and filthy that I could not bring myself to do so. I wondered how long I would have to spend in that malodorous place.

Maybe, I thought, it did not depend entirely on Mr Schmidt. Perhaps I could take my own decision.

I got out my lockpick and started to work on the lock. It was again a mortice lock, but big and heavy. If I had had a choice of tools from my complete collection of lockpicks, I would have chosen the biggest and had the door open in a few minutes. The tool I was using was small and the leverage it could exert was minimal. But I had time to waste and continued probing.

The secret of lockpicking is to be able to translate the tactile sensations one receives through the instrument in one's hands, into a clear mental picture of the mechanics of the lock in question. The principle of the mortice lock is simple. A low grade steel spring, not a coil spring but a thin flat section of stressed metal, retains the bolt firmly fixed in the open or shut position. This spring is lifted by turning the key in the lock. The key itself, in order to rotate and so lift the spring, has to operate a number of wards, all of different patterns, which is why keys to mortice locks have such complicated shapes.

A lockpick evades the protecting wards and goes to work on the spring itself.

I soon located the spring of the lock but found that I had little leverage to lift it sufficiently clear of the bolt to let me start trying to move the latter from the closed to open position. I kept trying, all the while getting a clearer mental picture of the mechanical problem I was trying to solve. I now knew that the door could be opened. The only question was whether my small lockpick could exert enough leverage.

Having nothing better to do, I kept trying. Nearly every time I got the spring lifted, I failed to get enough purchase on the bolt and, invariably, the spring clicked back into its slot.

After half an hour and some twenty attempts, I was perspiring freely. I took off my greatcoat and went back to work. I had the impression that the slight manipulation of its parts which I was causing, was having a lubricating effect on the lock. A number of times I got the spring lifted, but could not get a good purchase on the bolt without releasing the spring.

Suddenly, it happened. I had the spring raised and the bolt had moved under the torsional pressure of the lockpick. The lock was half open.

I stopped there and returned to the bench to think. Using my greatcoat as a pillow, I lay down on that greasy leather surface, trying to close my mind to the lice and bed bugs which infested the upholstery.

So I could open the cell door. That was fine, I was no longer a prisoner, but could leave when I pleased. I could, for instance, now step out into the village street, walk past the police station in broad daylight and into the main gates of the local airfield. For a few seconds I tried to imagine the scene at the gate.

'Where do you think you're going?'

This from the guards.

'I just came to collect a Fiesler Storch. I'm flying it to Switzerland.'

'OK, bud. Report to the duty pilot.'

It might have been as easy as that. One slight difficulty was that I had not enough German to say my own lines, even if I had written them myself.

It was no good day dreaming. I would have to wait until after dark. Then I might have a chance of getting out of the village unseen and finding my way into the airfield. But I would have to watch my timing.

The best plan I could conceive was to leave the cell about two hours before dawn, hoping that would give me just sufficient time to find my getaway plane and take off as soon as I could barely see the far side of the field. Now I needed luck, all I could get.

Eight

SCHMIDT came for me just after seven o'clock. When he opened the cell door I saw that he was supported by four of his farmer friends, with their inevitable shotguns.

It was a short journey; back to the village square and into Schmidt's office. The room was ugly, with dirty walls. The furniture consisted of a tidy desk, with no evidence of any backlog of paperwork. There were three hardbacked chairs along one wall and another chair, with armrests, behind Schmidt's desk. A window gave onto the square.

All this I took in at my first glance, but all my attention was focused on an enormous terracotta stove which reached from the floor nearly to the ceiling. It was going full blast and giving out heat, hot heat, welcome heat. Heat which I had not enjoyed in months.

Schmidt sat down behind his desk. I pulled a chair from against the wall and sat opposite him. Then I took off my greatcoat. This heat had to be absorbed. Schmidt was talking, but I was not listening. I was just basking, soaking in the warmth.

From the drawers of his desk, Schmidt had produced various forms and a strange black box. I watched with interest while he opened the box. It contained a complete, do-it-yourself finger printing kit. From the way he read the instructions on the outside of the box, I guessed that he seldom bothered to finger print his drunks when he put them away in that filthy cell.

For a moment I thought of objecting, pulling my rank, protesting. But I gave up the idea. If he really wanted my fingerprints he could always take them forcibly with the help of the four yokels who were standing behind me.

The messy business was soon over and my thumb prints recorded in the little square reserved for the purpose on no less than five sets of forms. It was encouraging to note that British bureaucracy yielded nothing to the German system. Although I had never before been fingerprinted, I was sure that in any police station in England, copies in quintuplicate would have been the minimum. We might win the war yet.

My hands were now filthy. The black ink had a penetrating and pervasive quality.

'Waschen,' I said.

'Später,' answered Schmidt shortly.

This was one German word with which I was thoroughly familiar, both in its formal meaning and what it really implied. It has a signification rather like mañana for the Spaniards in that it postpones action for an indefinite period.

I got to my feet.

'Sofort waschen,' I repeated. 'Mit Seife.'

The German words were coming to me without difficulty. I had insisted that I would wash immediately and with soap.

Schmidt gave in. He realized that he needed my cooperation to complete his forms. He led me down a dark corridor to a wash room where there was a basin. While two farmers guarded me, he disappeared again to fetch soap and a towel.

I locked myself in. The two farmers stood in the corridor outside. The wash room had no window and the only way out was through the door.

I turned on the taps. From one came hot water. It was unbelievable. Hot water from a tap was something I had given up for the duration.

The opportunity was too wonderful to let slip. I rapidly stripped to the waist and had a luxurious wash. The farmers banged on the door.

'Augenblick,'* I answered. I hardly knew what the word meant, but it had been addressed to me dozens of times by various Germans, when they meant me to wait another fifteen minutes for something I urgently needed. I was delighted to get my own back in their own language.

When I finally emerged from the lavatory, I felt thoroughly clean and refreshed. Everybody else was in a bad temper.

Back in the office the good Schmidt launched himself into a long harangue. At that stage of my imprisonment my knowledge of German was not small, but it was highly uncoordinated. I knew a large number of regular and irregular verbs which I could decline by heart, exactly as they were presented in my grammar. I had learnt an even greater number of those strange nouns which grammars always seem to select for the student. But above all I had a thorough knowledge of all the basic words which governed the life of a kriegie, such as Los, Raus, Appell, Abort, Brot, Kartoffeln, Englische Flieger, Spitfeuer and Deutschland kaputt.

In spite of this not unconsiderable knowledge of his language, I just was not able to follow the gist of his remarks. I discarded the idea of trying French or Italian on him, both of which I could speak reasonably fluently. In the first place, I doubted whether he

* Immediately.

knew a word of either language. In the second place, it was all his problem and not mine.

When he had run out of breath, Schmidt handed me a printed form, already decorated with my thumbprints. I understood that, somehow, he and I had to get this form completed. This needed thought and I decided to change the subject.

'Ich bin hungrig,' I said.

This may not have been the most idiomatic way of telling him I wanted to eat, but he still got the message. He protested volubly at first, but the finality with which I pushed aside his precious forms soon convinced him.

Dear old Schmidt. He was a good guy for a policeman. He surrendered without blowing his top and we all went across the village square to the local hostelry. The four farmers sat in a corner, their guns leaning against the wall, and ordered beer. The policeman and I took a table for two, close to the stove.

The policeman ordered fried eggs and potatoes. My mouth was already watering and at that moment I could have completed any forms he produced.

He seemed to sense this and he handed me the forms. I studied them listlessly while he gave me a running commentary on each of the items. Occasionally this was a help. I came to the conclusion that at least ninety per cent of the questions he could answer himself, from his own knowledge. These were items such as where had I been captured, the colour of my hair, eyes, particular marks, fingerprints, etc. But there were a few vital questions which only I could answer. And I remembered very well the so-often repeated briefings I had had. Reveal your name, rank and number, nothing else. At Dulag Luft I had also given my age and religion. This may have been a mistake but it now meant that I had two cards up my sleeve.

I handed the pen and forms back to Schmidt, indicating that he should act as scribe. Slowly and carefully I dictated to him. When he had recorded my full name, rank and number I stopped and shook my head to indicate that I was going no further.

Schmidt immediately went into a tantrum. Watching him carefully and listening to the tone of his voice rather than the words, which were coming out far too fast for me, I began to be convinced that he was afraid. That he was literally afraid of not getting his precious form fully and duly completed, so that he could submit his brilliant report on how he, single handed and with the greatest bravery, had captured the dangerous fugitive, the English terror flieger. I began to realize just how badly Schmidt needed to have the form completed in all detail.

It was a first hand example of how the German bureaucratic machinery worked. Failure to complete a form on Schmidt's part was probably a completely inexcusable piece of incompetence, worse even than failing to capture an escaped prisoner or letting the prisoner escape again.

This could be Schmidt's greatest moment. He had his prisoner, all he needed was the fully completed form in order to turn in a perfect copy-book file on the subject and then confidently sit back and await promotion.

This was how I read the situation and I decided to play the hand accordingly.

'Schmidt,' I said, dropping the Herr which I had hitherto allowed him, 'Ich bin Major, Sie wissen das, nicht?'

The effect on Schmidt was electric. He sat to attention and his heels clicked together under the table.

'Jawohl, Herr Major.' The response was entirely automatic, a conditioned reflex. The Germans are trained that way.

I looked him straight in the eye, trying to get that steely glint in my own eyes which, to any good major, should be mere child's-play.

'Erst essen, dann sprechen,' I said.

First eat, then talk. Trying the while to look like James Cagney.

Poor old Schmidt, he was a good loser. The fried eggs and chips were in front of me within five minutes, during which interval I did not say a word. I finished them in less than two minutes, eating rather faster than top class majors are expected to. I asked Schmidt for a cigarette, which he gave me and lit for me.

'Jetzt sprechen,' I said, meaning, now we'll talk.

It was a long and painful process, that of getting across to him what I wanted to say. But the fact that he was very anxious to understand helped greatly and, from the depths of my memory, I was managing to drag up a lot of German words I had forgotten I knew.

The gist of my message, had it been said in English, was this.

'My dear Schmidt, I am a prisoner of war, protected by the Geneva Convention. All the information that international law requires me to give you, is already on the form. I cannot give you any more information. I also refuse to argue the matter with anyone except an officer of a rank senior to mine, that is no less than an Oberst Leutnant.'

The punch was in the last line. An Oberst Leutnant, in Germany, ranks just above the Archangel Gabriel. Not only would access to an Oberst Leutnant be difficult for Schmidt, but it was the last thing he desired. This had to be his own personal triumph and he just did not need even the merest Leutnant to help him. He was now beginning to realize that he badly needed my co-operation.

I took advantage of the pause for thought to ask Schmidt for a glass of wine. He looked at me long and steadily. Then he ordered the wine—a bottle. It was now entirely evident that we had reached an understanding, that we had, so to speak, drawn up the heads of agreement. All that was left to do was to fill in the detail of the clauses.

After the wine had arrived and been poured, Schmidt again put the form in front of me. I was now on dangerous territory. Every question which remained unanswered lay outside my strict limits of name, rank and number. I had been warned so many times that to exceed these limits, even for a seemingly trivial question, was a disastrous mistake, as well as being a factual breach of security.

So it was with some trepidation that I looked at the blanks in the form. Names of father and mother and of both paternal grand-parents.

It was a nasty dilemma. On the one hand there was the certainty of another plate of eggs and chips; on the other hand the danger of compromising the security of England and her allies by revealing the Christian names of my paternal grandmother. It was not entirely crystal clear to me why, if I said that my grandmother's names had been Mary Jane, the British Empire would be in peril. As my grandmother had died many years before I was born, I had never known what her Christian names were.

But a briefing was a briefing. I had to play the rules and to hell with the second plate of eggs and chips. Mine not to reason why.

I pushed the form back to Schmidt. Almost, it hurt me to do so. I was afraid he was going to burst into tears. Instead, he snatched my wine glass from my hand, just as I was raising it to my mouth. The wine went all over the tablecloth. The four farmers at the corner table jumped to their feet.

A small splash of wine had ended up on one of the forms. Anxiously Schmidt dabbed it with his napkin and poured salt over the stain. I felt very sorry for him.

I made him take up the pen again and gave him all I had left, my age and my religion. Another two blank spaces completed.

My wine glass was re-filled and I swallowed it in one gulp, holding the glass out for more. Schmidt poured again.

I knew well that the game was nearly over. I had no more ploys left. But the thought of that stinking cell, where I would have to spend the night, gave me new strength. I would keep the game alive as long as possible. I was in no hurry.

At that moment the German army arrived. They consisted of two soldiers and a Feldwebel. They had come for me.

Schmidt and the Army exchanged salutes. I listened with great attention and gathered that I was to be taken to Weissenfels that night, by the soldiers. Although it put paid to my somewhat unreal intention of unlocking my cell door and still getting into the local airfield, I was immensely relieved. It was all over. I could relax.

Nine

THE cells in the military barracks at Weissenfels were at least clean. There was the usual two tier wooden bunk, with straw-filled mattresses. I was given two blankets. Five minutes after the cell door had been locked behind me I was asleep, completely exhausted. It must have been past midnight.

For the next twenty-four hours, I only got off my bunk when nature called. To go to the lavatory, which was at the end of a long corridor of cells, I had to bang on the door to attract a sentry's attention. The sentry always arrived immediately.

Meals were brought into my cell. Not a great deal to eat, but

as much as I needed. I was happy just to sleep and be comparatively warm. I was not even thinking.

On my third day in the cells at Weissenfels, I began to take an
interest in my surroundings. I had no reading matter and no cigarettes. I became aware that time was passing very very slowly.
The graffiti on the walls of the cell were the first thing to attract
my attention. There were no pornographic drawings; I imagined
that that would have doubled the length of any prisoner's stay.
But there were plenty of writings.

My first impression was that some long suffering character by
the name of Dicken had been a very regular guest in that cell.
Almost every inscription on the walls seemed to have been signed
by the unfortunate Dicken. The Beetle Bailey of the German
Army, it seemed.

'3 Tage Dicken.'

It was clearly printed all over the whitewashed walls.

'10 Tage Dicken.'

The poor fellow had been sentenced to ten days in the cells,
instead of the usual three.

I began to be very curious about the wretched Dicken. He
seemed to spend all his time in the cooler.

Many of the inscriptions were dated and I was thus able, having
nothing better to do, to start collecting some statistical data on
how many days my friend Dicken had spent in the cells in any
one year.

It added up to a frightening total. More than one hundred
days in that very cell during 1941 and well on the way to breaking
his own previous record during 1942. And I had only examined
half the inscriptions on the wall.

How could he stand it, I wondered. Could discipline in the
German Army really be so strict? Surely, it was non-productive to
jail a soldier so often.

It was not until I found the two lines of verse, carefully printed
beneath the window, that the mystery was explained.

'Halbe Stunde ficken
Drei Tage Dicken.'

Dicken, it was now clear, was not an individual but army slang
for a spell in the cooler. Ficken is very close to its Anglo-Saxon

equivalent. Halbe Stunde means half-an-hour. Drei Tage means three days.

The rhyme, which I now found repeated more than once, was the lament of the soldier who had dallied too long in the local brothel and got back to camp after his pass had expired.

Having completed my studies of these erudite graffiti and successfully solved the mystery of Dicken, I began to be bored.

Nobody in authority had come to see me. There had been no interrogation. I was just a man lost in a cell. I wondered whether I should start to stir things up, but decided against it. Even if the rations were minimal and I was beginning to get very hungry again, at least it was a pleasant rest. I would wait, I thought, twenty-four hours before starting to raise hell. Meanwhile I got to know the guards, practised my German on them and borrowed the occasional cigarette.

I also ascertained that I could open the cell door with my lock-pick. The door still remained bolted on the outside, but I was beginning to see a possible method of overcoming even this little difficulty.

I did not really want to escape, just then. I doubted that it was possible. I preferred to re-join my companions in the new camp, recuperate and make much more careful preparations before trying again. But if it came to raising hell merely to draw attention to myself and get somebody in authority to come and see me, then it might well be worth trying out my theories about opening the cell door.

During my regular visits to the lavatory I had carefully studied the geography of the cell block. It was a simple layout with a narrow central corridor and cells leading off on each side. The corridor was something over fifty feet long. On one side there were eight cells, on the other seven. The symmetry was balanced by the lavatory. At one end of the corridor was a blank wall, the end of the building. At the other end was an iron door with an eye level grill in it. The door was kept locked. Beyond the door there was a sentry on duty. Beyond the sentry, down a short corridor, was the guard room.

All the cells appeared to be occupied by German soldiers. Whenever I walked down the corridor, disembodied eyes would be visible through the little peepholes in the cell doors. I was an object of great interest to these unfortunate goons and I never sensed any hostility. At my appearance with my guard, they would yell, catcall and make every kind of comment, but the tone and tenor seemed to be not unfriendly to me. Birds of a feather, it seemed, have their own code of camaraderie.

Each time I returned to my cell, I studied the outside of the cell door with the greatest attention. It was of wood, but appeared to be most solid. In addition to a mortice lock, it was secured on the outside by a simple iron bolt. This was a strong, flat piece of iron, about one and a half inches wide, which moved into an appropriate iron clamp, fixed to the frame of the door, when the cell was locked. The handle for the bolt was simply made. At one end, the flat iron bar had been bent through a right angle and jutted out from the surface of the door for some two inches, thus providing a handle. I had noted that the bolt moved backwards and forwards with ease through well oiled iron clamps.

Immediately above the cell door, just below the ceiling, was a hole in the wall, about nine inches square which opened on to the corridor outside. Fitted in the top of this rectangular opening there was an electric light bulb which was all the illumination provided inside the cell. The distance from the hole above the cell door to the bolt outside was about four feet, much too far for the bolt to be reached with one's hand.

But suppose I extended my reach? All I really needed was a broomstick handle. I could slip it through the square hole and push back the bolt with it. Nothing could be simpler, the only snag was that there was no broom handle lying around my cell.

It was obvious that I could easily get my arm far enough through the hole above the door that, from the elbow down, my arm would be free outside the cell.

I took one of the slats from my bed; it was about two feet three inches long. Holding it in my hand, I calculated that with it I could extend my reach to over three feet. Unfortunately, this still left me at least a foot above my target.

I needed at least another two feet of reach. Nevertheless, I felt I was getting closer and an exact, if highly complicated plan was beginning to form in my mind.

First I needed string. The ball of string which I had in my pockets when leaving the train—it seems years ago—had been confiscated by the farmers, handed over to Schmidt who, in turn, had consigned it to my German Army escorts. It had not been returned to me. Nor had my penknife.

On the other hand, the straw filled mattress on my bed had a coarse fabric cover and, in the jail, I had been issued with a knife, fork, spoon, mug and soup bowl.

I started to rip thin long strips from the edges of the mattress cover. Singly, they were not strong, but when plaited and knotted together in triplicate, they passed the tests I applied. I prepared about 20 feet of triple plaited material. It had an attractive blue and white chequer pattern.

From the two tier bunk I selected the narrowest, thinnest and lightest bed slat. With the German knife I slotted it carefully so that it would be firmly held at one end by the string I had prepared. Then I made my measurements.

When the bed slat had been lowered through the hole, it had finally to be manoeuvred into a position in which it was flat against the outside of the cell door, with one edge resting against the handle of the outside bolt.

To move the bolt, I intended to pull the bed slat in the appropriate direction by means of two other strings attached just above and just below its point of contact with the bolt handle. These strings had, in some way, to reach me from the bed slat through the peephole in the cell door.

My first essential task was to establish the exact position of the bolt. From inside the cell, there was no indication at all, neither screws, nor nails, nor holes filled in with putty. The only sure way I could achieve my aim was by unlocking the cell door.

This was not a difficult task and took less than five minutes manipulation with my picklock. By applying all the weight of my body to the inside of the door, I was able to estimate, within a few inches, where the door was held closed by the outside bolt. On the inside of the door I made two marks which indicated the area within which the bolt had to be.

Next I measured the distance between the bottom of the rectangular hole and the position of the bolt. With this data, I was able to decide the exact point where I should knot the string suspending the bed slat so that, in the vertical sense, it extended from well above to well below the handle of the bolt. I was then able to notch the bed slat in two other points which would eventually be just above and just below the handle of the bolt, and firmly to attach two more strings at these points. If I could only get those two strings back into the cell through the peephole, I knew I was in business.

It was too dangerous to make any trial runs. I would have to wait until night and then go through the drill, hoping it would work first time. Soon after midnight, when the guard changed, promised to be the best time.

The evening meal was served about six o'clock. It consisted of a mug full of peppermint tea. For solids one was expected to have saved some bread and margarine from the morning's issue. After drinking the tea and eating the one slice of bread I had saved, I went straight to bed. I willed myself to wake up at midnight and then slept. I was still tired.

I awoke exactly at midnight and lay huddled under my two thin blankets, fully clothed as usual, reluctant to move. My courage had evaporated, my initiative had gone. After a quarter of an hour, I had talked myself out of bed. The electric light bulb in its square hole over the cell door illuminated the cell brilliantly.

Within a few minutes I was ready. To the bed slat, I had attached all the strings. The one which suspended it was carefully knotted at the exact point which would indicate to me that the slat had reached the position I wanted. The other two strings, which I somehow hoped to recover through the peephole, were each about eight feet long, more than enough to work with.

I jammed my German table knife through the peephole so that it projected about three inches beyond the outside of the cell door. Taking infinite caution to avoid making the slightest noise, I moved the two tier bunk up to the cell door. Climbing up to the top bunk, with the bed slat and its various strings, I went to work.

First I unscrewed the electric light bulb and put it carefully aside. There was still enough light coming through the hole to enable me to see what I was doing. Then I fed through the two long strips with which I hoped to be able to force the bed slat up against the handle of the bolt, and eventually move it to the open position. With my arm right through the hole in the wall, I paid out the two strings so that they would fall beyond the peephole and be caught by the projecting knife blade. Fixing everything so that it would not move, I climbed off the bed again and went to work on the peephole.

With my lockpick I drew both strings in through the tiny circular hole. The one which was attached to the lower end of the bed slat, I left hanging in a long loop outside the door. It was essential that, when I lowered the bed slat into position, this string should be below the handle of the bolt. The second string I drew as tight as I dared and attached to the bunk.

Back on the top bunk. I eased the bed slat out through the hole, taking great care not to disturb the strings. Very carefully I lowered it down, until the knot in the string indicated that it was in the right position. I tied the string firmly to the bed. Now, if I was lucky, I should be able to draw the bedslat up against the handle of the bolt.

Through the peephole, I started to draw the strings tight, inching them in with the gentlest of pressure. I felt the bed slat move into place against the bolt handle. Gently but firmly, I started to pull both strings together. They got tauter and tauter, but nothing moved. I slacked off the strings and tried a sharp jerk. The bolt moved. Keeping a steady pressure I pulled it the full length of its travel.

Before leaving the cell, I removed all traces of the method I had used. I put the bed slat back in position and hid the strings among the straw inside the mattress, having cut them up into small pieces. I screwed back the electric light bulb and returned the bunk to its normal position.

I did not know whether I was going to be able to escape from the cell block. Nevertheless I donned my greatcoat and put my few possessions in my pockets. I was ready to go.

There was no trouble with the lock, it opened easily and quickly. Stepping out into the well lit corridor, I closed the cell door behind me, without re-locking it. Crouched down and moving on tip-toe, I approached the iron door at the end of the corridor. I peeped through the grill. Not three feet away was a sentry. He was sitting behind a small table to one side of the corridor and was dozing. Beyond, through another door, was the guard-room. It was well lit and I could hear voices. There was no escape that way.

I retreated to the lavatory. Here the only window was high in the wall and fitted with iron bars. They looked to me to be as solid and impregnable as the bars on the window of my cell. It would take a week's work with a hacksaw blade to cut through them. Just to be sure I was not overlooking anything, I climbed on to the wash basin and examined the bars closely. There was not a hope.

Sitting on the lavatory seat, I reviewed a hopeless situation. There no longer seemed to be any point in creating a ruckus and drawing attention to myself. It would lead to endless trouble and the Germans might well discover the system I had used to get out of my cell. It would be a serious mistake to give them this knowledge, which might be so valuable on some future occasion. The only thing to do was to go back to my cell and lock myself in again. Of course, I would not be able to replace the bolt. My system of strings and bed slat was uni-directional.

I was thinking of the consequences of this when I suddenly saw the solution to the problem.

I went back to my cell and took off my greatcoat and shoes. In stockinged feet I went back to the corridor. With infinite caution and stealth, I slid back the bolt on the cell next to mine, leaving it in the open position. It had made no noise. I did the same on every cell door. Then I went back to my own cell and locked myself in, happy with the night's work. Suspicion was now diverted from me. But there were still the makings of a fine pandemonium in the morning.

I slept well, determined to wake up at the first sign of commotion in the corridor outside.

It was soon after six o'clock in the morning when the first prisoner started hammering on his cell door and yelling to be taken to the abort. This, I thought contentedly, should be when it all starts.

A small circular plywood cover kept the judas closed from the outside, but this was easy to shift. I arranged the judas cover to give me a discreet, narrow angle of vision. I saw the guard pass along the corridor, still sleepy and grumbling to himself. The cell where he stopped was on the other side of the corridor two doors up from me. I could watch the guard clearly. He was doing everything automatically and it was not until he put his hand on the bolt to open it that he suddenly froze.

He swore obscenely and turned slowly round. In less than a second he had seen that every cell had its bolt withdrawn.

'Feldwebel!' he yelled, 'komm schnell. Hier ist etwas los.'

He kept yelling.

There was the sound of heavy boots pounding down the corridor from the guardroom. I retired quickly to bed and pulled up the covers.

The panic and the shouting increased as each minute passed. More and more Germans arrived. I started banging on my door.

The cover over the judas was pushed aside and a malevolent eye glared through.

'Später,' said a harsh voice and then told me, with considerable venom, to shut up.

I got dressed, calculating that the Kommandant would be visiting me soon. Outside the cell the guard's story was told again and again, each time a more senior officer arrived. By now I had moved the judas cover to one side and was watching proceedings without any attempt at concealment.

The arrival of the commanding officer was announced by a sudden dead silence. As he came into the crowded cell corridor, everybody else made way for him. My field of vision was suddenly blocked by a broad back in field grey.

The Kommandant started giving orders.

'Everybody outside,' he ordered, 'except you, you and you.'

Boots started pounding the corridor floor. When I got another view from my peephole the only people left were the Kommandant and his adjutant, the Feldwebel of the guards and one other officer.

The Feldwebel told the story again, standing rigidly to attention.

'Wo ist der Engländer?' asked the Kommandant.

The Feldwebel indicated my cell.

'Get all the other prisoners into the exercise yard. Search their cells from top to bottom.'

'Jawohl, Herr Oberst.'

The Feldwebel rushed off to carry out his orders. My cell door was opened and the Kommandant with his adjutant walked in. I got up from my bed and greeted them.

'Good morning, colonel,' I said. I noted that he was in fact only a lieutenant colonel. He was a man of perhaps fifty years of age, slightly running to fat. On his cheeks were the traditional duelling scars. A monocle hung round his neck on a black ribbon. His uniform was spotless, his boots brilliantly burnished. He was the very picture of a proper German colonel.

'Good morning, major,' he answered in English which he could only have perfected at Oxford. 'I hope you slept well last night?'

'Like a log, colonel, like a log. Nothing disturbed me. Even when I am hungry, I always sleep well.'

'Are you complaining about the rations?'

'Certainly I am. And about the accommodation. The Geneva Convention does not permit you to imprison an officer of my rank together with German soldiers. I demand to be sent immediately to a proper prisoner-of-war camp.'

The Kommandant screwed his monocle into his left eye and the ghost of a grin appeared on his face.

'I can assure you that I will be very glad to be rid of you. You are a dangerous man, major. If all goes well for you, you could be on your way to the Luftwaffe camp by noon. If all goes well.' There was a nasty emphasis on his last sentence.

'Let's not exaggerate, colonel,' I answered. 'I am an escaped prisoner of war, as you know. You also know that it is my duty to escape. My attempt to escape represents no danger to Germany. I have not harmed anybody and would not. It is quite unfair to describe me as a dangerous man.'

'I am not entirely convinced of that, my dear major. There is a poor innkeeper not far from here who complains of having been robbed of enough food to feed an army and enough wine to float a battleship. You would not know anything of that, I suppose?'

'Not a thing, colonel, I assure you. I don't even know what you're talking about.'

'Never mind, major. The Gestapo are working on it. I am confident they will come up with the right answer. The criminal will certainly be caught and severely punished. I should think he will be lucky if he gets less than five years.'

'Your laws must be very severe, colonel. By the way, I must congratulate you most sincerely on your excellent command of our language.'

'I wonder why you are trying to change the subject, major? Does it embarrass you?'

'The only thing which embarrasses me, colonel, is having to share a lavatory with a lot of criminal Gefreiters.* What really does annoy me is that if you were a prisoner of war in England, you would be treated like a colonel, with all the privileges due to your rank. You would have a comfortable room and . . .'

'That's quite enough, major,' he interrupted brusquely. 'Try to understand that I am not here to indulge in light-hearted banter with you. I suspect, indeed I am damned sure, that you, somehow, got out of your cell last night and started to open all the other cell doors, at least to the extent of opening the bolts. I know every one of the soldiers who are here in the cooler. Admittedly they are, each one of them, unreliable and stupid. Most of them are regular inmates here. But not one of them has the ability, the initiative, the courage or the desire to do what was done last night.

'You did it.' He pointed an accusing finger.

'Did what, colonel? I really have not followed you.'

'Perhaps you have, perhaps you have not. Anyway, I think you are responsible. You will now be taken from this cell and searched very, very thoroughly. If we find what I am looking for, then you, my dear major, are going to take the consequences.'

I grinned at him with a show of confidence I did not feel. I took my handkerchief from my pocket and, removing my dark glasses, cleaned my eyes of the usual accumulation of mucus and tears. I felt the lockpick in the hem of the handkerchief. That was what they would be looking for.

'I will be really happy to leave Weissenfels,' I said. 'It's a thoroughly depressing place. Your hospitality has been well below standard.'

The Kommandant ignored me and barked out a series of orders in German. A minute later the two guards appeared and escorted me into the guard room. There I was stripped and all my clothes searched. They soon found everything which I had hidden in the lining of my tunic, maps, money and cockpit drills of German aircraft. Each item was passed to the Kommandant who examined it and looked more confident and self-satisfied. But my handker-

* German soldiers first class.

chief trick still worked. I kept it in my hand and with it my lock-pick.

When I was again fully dressed, I turned to the Kommandant.

'If you have quite finished with me, colonel, I would be glad to leave here and rejoin the Luftwaffe.'

'I wish them luck, major. You will be leaving by the 12.40 train. You should be in Sagan tonight. Your guards will be my men.

'My orders to them will be very strict indeed. I now know that you are a very clever man as well as being dangerous, as I said before. If you make any mistake of judgement, they will shoot you. Is this understood?'

'I believe every word you say, colonel. I promise I'll be good. Would it be possible for me to get a decent breakfast in this establishment of yours?'

'Do you promise to be good?'

'Yes, I promise.'

'Then you will get an excellent breakfast. I will see to it. Goodbye, major.'

'Goodbye, colonel.'

We looked at one another for two seconds. We might have shaken hands, but, in the circumstances and in front of that audience of army goons, it would not have been politic. We both understood this.

The colonel gave his orders and I was taken back to my cell. Half an hour later my breakfast was served. It consisted of two boiled eggs, two slices of cold fat bacon, two gherkins, four slices of bread and a hunk of ersatz butter.

My breakfast was over in two minutes flat. As I wiped my mouth clean, I felt grateful to the colonel for his generosity and manners. It was obvious that he knew perfectly well what I had done. It was equally obvious that he was very glad to be rid of me. The breakfast had been a nice parting gift and I appreciated it.

I had not the slightest intention of trying to escape during the train journey to Sagan. I wanted home and home was the nearest prison camp.

Stalag Luft III

THE next ten days I spent in solitary confinement in the prison block at Stalag Luft III. This was the much vaunted new prison camp, constructed on Göring's orders to accommodate the rapidly growing number of allied air force prisoners. It was located near the town of Sagan, in the depths of Silesia. The Luftwaffe was inordinately proud of the place, claiming that it was the last word in prison-camp design, entirely escape-proof and equipped with every possible amenity. They were sadly wrong on both counts.

The prison block lay outside the barbed wire compound which housed the prisoners. It lay in an adjoining compound, equally securely enclosed by barbed wire, known to the Germans as the Vorlager. There were few other buildings in the Vorlager and no prisoners except for a small group of Russians. The nearest building to the prison was the sickquarters.

My cell was clean and comfortable. It offered me solitude and privacy which was exactly what I needed most after living for three months in distastefully close physical proximity to my forty companions in the Arab Quarter at Spangenberg.

Everything in the cell was new and unused. The whitewashed walls were unmarked, the cement floor still smelled damp, the two-tier bunk, the table and stool were of newly-planed pinewood; above all, the mattresses on the bed were fresh and virgin. I was the first inhabitant of the cell.

The German food ration, which was all I was given, left me hungry. But after four months of imprisonment my stomach had contracted and hunger was no longer a physical pain inside me. It was an ever present frustration which I had learned to accept. Tobacco was the best antidote for it and I had soon arranged for the German prison guards to supply me with cigarettes, by promising them two for every one they gave me, when eventually I received a supply.

For an hour each day I was allowed into the prison yard for exercise. The rest of the time I lay on my bed thinking and dreaming. Mostly I thought back over my escape from the train, re-examining and analysing every little episode. I was furious with myself that I had, so to speak, wasted an escape. Getting away from my captors was difficult enough. Getting back to England promised to be much more difficult. I was determined that, the next time, I would be much better equipped for the second phase of the operation.

The mistakes I had made were obvious. Setting out on foot with no food had overloaded the odds against me. Next time, committee or no committee, I would carry sufficient food to last the duration of my planned journey. But never again would I attempt to walk to the German frontier. It was too much of a test of endurance and I was not fit enough for it.

When I next got out, I would travel by train. I would walk no further than to the nearest railway station where I would buy a ticket to Danzig or Kiel or Cologne. I would be suitably dressed, have some German money, speak a little of the language and have some documentation as a foreign worker. There were tens of thousands of foreigners employed in Germany, mostly French or Italian, who were allowed to use the trains. With luck I could be on the frontier within 24 hours of getting away and would not need to carry more than a sandwich with me.

I discarded the 'fly-yourself-home' scheme as too optimistic and uncertain. It should figure, I concluded, only as an emergency plan of action when the main aim could not be achieved.

My mind kept returning to the scene in the railway carriage before I had made my exit through the window. There had been sixteen prisoners in the two compartments. More than half of them were not fit and active enough to jump from a train. But the others could have made it. And yet they had not even considered coming with me. No one had asked a single question or examined the lavatory window to assess their chances. They had just sat there in an embarrassed silence, looking fish-eyed and disapproving. It had been disconcerting and discouraging. I had even wondered, momentarily, whether I was not making a mistake, whether they were not right and I wrong.

We all had a duty to escape but this, when examined carefully, was a very imprecise instruction. If it meant that one's duty was to return to one's unit, in order to go on fighting the war, it did not necessarily mean that one had to jump out of a train window in the dark, in the middle of Germany. One could quite logically argue that such a course of action was much more likely to result in a broken neck than anything else.

Viewing the episode in retrospect, I was glad that nobody had decided to come with me because the second man out would probably have been badly hurt. The train was moving very fast by the time I was clear. So their judgement had not been far wrong.

When I analysed my own motives for attempting to escape I realized that, although I was strongly conscious of my duty, this was largely dominated by an intense personal desire to escape. I desperately wanted to get home, to take up life again where I had left it.

Partly, this was ambition. The air force was my whole life. I had known no other since I went to Cranwell as a cadet at the age of seventeen and a half. It was also my whole future and imprisonment would effectively ruin my chances of a successful career. Officers who spent a war inside a prison camp did not get promoted. To me escape was not only overridingly important, it was equally urgent. I had to get back quickly.

There was also a strong element of rebellion in my reactions. I disliked and resented being pushed around by my captors and having to obey unreasonable orders because pointed guns insisted. If there was a way to escape from these intolerable conditions, I intended to take it.

I understood that every individual saw his problem differently and that at one end of the scale were those prisoners for whom capture had been a final act and who were content to accept it as such. They were glad to be, at least, alive. For them the war was truly over.

At Spangenberg I had also come to realize that to devote all my mental and physical energy to the problem of escape had a very beneficial, therapeutic effect. The difficulties and variations of the problem were so challenging that I was always fully occupied. This was the surest way to avoid that gradual deterioration of morale and character, the results of which were quite evident among the longer term prisoners who had nothing to do but wait for the end of the war. Confinement was destructive unless one countered its ill-effects.

My first escape had taught me a lot, mainly that I needed much more experience and first hand knowledge of how to travel in Germany. I was now certain that getting out of a prison camp was the simplest part of the operation and that I could achieve it again. The problem I had to study more deeply was how to get out of Germany.

On my fifth day in the cells, a kitbag was delivered to me containing a complete change of clothing, a hundred cigarettes and two books. There was a note from Marcus welcoming me back to the fold and adding that he had kept a bed for me.

My first concern was to repay my cigarette debts to the prison guards. By now I knew most of them well and had selected the one I thought to be most susceptible to bribery. I repaid him his cigarettes at the rate of three to one and let him know that I had a good stock of them. English cigarettes then had a high market value and were in demand. The German cigarette was a sweet and unsatisfying substitute.

I started cautiously by asking him to bring me a notebook and a pencil. The price, after a lot of bargaining, was seven cigarettes. It was delivered next day.

I knew the guard's name and, on the first page of the notebook, I printed a short message in German.

'THIS NOTEBOOK WAS PROVIDED BY OBER GEFREITER HANS SCHULTZ FOR THE PRICE OF SEVEN ENGLISH CIGARETTES.'

A day later I told Schultz I wanted a railway timetable and as much information as he could collect on the passes required by a civilian to travel by train.

'Why do you want this?' he asked, alarmed.

'I'm going to escape again and I want to travel by train.'

'I cannot help you. It is forbidden.'

I showed him the front page of my notebook.

He went chalk white in the face and tried to snatch the book from me.

'Don't be silly, Schultz,' I said. 'If you take the notebook, I can write the same thing on the wall.'

I tore out the page and put a match to it. Schultz watched it burn with growing relief.

'Here are twenty cigarettes,' I said giving him a fresh pack. 'Bring me that timetable tomorrow and the information about passes. Find out also how far a civilian can travel without a pass.'

Next morning Schultz was back with the timetable. He also gave me a lot of confused and somewhat contradictory information about the passes a civilian might be asked for at the railway station. I gathered, however, that a foreign worker going home on leave would require an Urlaubserlaubnis, issued by the police. Another requirement, for a duty journey, might be a Reiseschein. On the other hand, a journey of under 200 kilometres probably would not require any passes. I did not know how reliable Schultz's information might be, but at least it was a starting point for my researches and the railway timetable was a quite invaluable document. I was very pleased with myself and determined to get a lot more information out of Schultz.

Schultz made no appearance the next day, nor the day after. When I enquired about him from the other guards they told me he was sick and had been excused duty for five days. Obviously, I had frightened him a little too much.

I left the prison without seeing him again, but with my precious timetable under my belt. Marcus, kind and reliable as ever, had kept a bed for me in the end room of block 62. At that time there were only eight of us in the room, all from Spangenberg. It was a great improvement on the Arab Quarter.

At first, the new camp looked impregnable. It was no more than a rectangle of desert which had once been a pine forest. All the trees had been cut down and the area surrounded by a formidable double fence of barbed wire. High sentry towers, set in the fence, dominated all the approaches to the wire with machine guns. Nowhere was there any shade or cover. It was hot, airless and depressing.

In theory, tunnelling was a possibility, in that the soil was very suitable. But all the buildings from beneath which a tunnel would have to start were located so far from the fence that a large scale enterprise, taking very many months, would have been necessary. I was too impatient to contemplate such a long term plan and very pessimistic about the probability of being able to hide the existence of a tunnel-in-progress for more than a short time.

The main gate was very well guarded and all vehicles leaving the camp were rigorously searched. Many attempts were made to get through the gate hidden on a cart or truck, but they all ended in inglorious failure and a spell in the cooler. I was beginning to feel trapped.

The Germans had never stopped boasting that the camp was escape-proof and subconsciously we were beginning to believe them. But their unbearable complacency was entirely destroyed on mid-summer's day of 1942 when Bill Goldfinch, Henry Lamond and Jack Best made one of the most remarkable escapes of the whole war. This achievement, so unexpected but so welcome, delighted and excited us. Our morale took an enormous upward bound and we started to jeer at the Germans about their escape-proof camp.

There was something very mysterious about the method the three had used to get out. Nobody could understand it; there was some Houdini-like trick concealed somewhere.

The facts were clear enough, made quite obvious when the Germans dug up the tunnel. From start to exit, it must have been nearly 150 feet long and it had been bored through the sand only a foot below the surface. The quite unexplainable aspect of the whole achievement was that it had been completed in two days by three men.

Anybody with even the smallest experience of tunnelling knew that a 150 foot tunnel certainly took a month to construct and more usually three months. Furthermore, the tunnel working force would have consisted of at least twenty men. 150 feet in two days was impossible. I had to find out what the trick was.

I sought out a knowledgeable prisoner who lived in the same barrack as Bill Goldfinch and the others.

'How did they do it?' I asked.

'They did a mole, old boy.'

I remained unenlightened.

'What the hell's a mole?' I persisted.

'I don't really know. It seems that it's a new method of blitz tunnelling.'

'It certainly is that,' I answered. 'Tell me, who helped them with the job? Who knows something about it?'

'Why don't you talk to Bill Searcey? He was working with them.'

'Thanks, I'll do that.'

I tracked down Bill Searcey, a friendly Australian whom I knew only slightly. He was glad to tell me the story and soon I had put together the incredible theory of the mole.

The original idea had been Bill Goldfinch's. He and Henry Lamond had registered it with the escape committee at Stalag Luft I at Barth, but were moved to Sagan before they could put it into practice.

The theory of the mole was entirely revolutionary and quite frightening. The classic concept that a tunnel was an underground passage which led from point A inside to point B outside the prison, was discarded. The mole was a tunnel which was not a passage. It started at point A and proceeded towards point B, but it was filled in behind the diggers as they advanced.

Thus the tunnellers dug sand from in front of them and packed it into the tunnel behind them, sealing themselves in. They made progress towards their goal in a small section of tunnel which was always moving forward with them. For most of the time the mole had neither entrance nor exit.

It took a little time to digest this new idea and to examine all its implications. The new possibilities it offered were startling and I spent hours with Tony Barber trying to find a way in which we could apply the mole technique to the local situation. It seemed to me that it had everything in its favour. It was quick; by its very nature it had to be. There was a strict limit to the time the molers could spend sealed underground. It was simple; it had no refinements such as shafts, shoring, hauling equipment or air lines. After the initial one third of the tunnel had been dug, no more spoil was removed from the tunnel. It was mainly this factor which, by eliminating all the labour and effort of spoil dispersal, enabled the mole to be pushed through at such unbelievable speed. This absence of spoil also eliminated the greatest risk there was of detection by the Germans.

If the principle of the mole had been only theory, Tony and I might have argued about it for months or taken a purely academic interest in it. But Jack Best and company had proved that it worked.

They completed the first fifty feet of their tunnel while pretending to dig a new soakaway behind the wash house. They disposed of all their tunnel spoil in the soakaway pit, leaving the tunnel clear for its first fifty feet. This took them from lunch time until the evening roll call. Immediately after the roll call, all three crawled into the tunnel and started digging from the face and packing the sand in the entrance to the tunnel. Bill Searcey, apparently working on the soakaway, carefully sealed the tunnel mouth from the outside. That evening the three molers reached the seventy-five feet mark, which was about halfway, and Bill Searcey flooded the soakaway with water, effectively covering the entrance and completely sealing off their retreat. That night they were too tired to do anything but sleep and to combat the cold, which was intense below ground, huddled as close together as possible. A few tiny air holes driven through the roof of the tunnel gave them sufficient air.

Throughout the next day they dug incessantly, taking spells at the face. By dark they had moled another seventy-five feet and were ready to break. It was the shortest night of the year.

Exhausted and completely impregnated with sand, they emerged from their hole in the ground and got safely away. They made directly for the nearest German airfield.

My chance came just ten days later and it was the Germans who set it up for me. They started to dig a trench just inside the tripwire which was a single strand of wire, set about a foot from the ground, running all round the camp about twenty feet from the main fence. The guards had orders to shoot without warning at anybody who crossed it.

The obvious purpose of this ditch was to intercept any shallow tunnels in being and to discourage new ones. The ditch was being dug in sections at various strategic points around the perimeter. As I watched the work, which progressed very rapidly, an embryo of an idea formed in my mind and I went in search of Tony.

We rejoined the growing crowd of prisoners who were watching the Germans at work. Watching others work is a universally popular pastime. For us prisoners it was a rare pleasure. The crowd was in a boisterous mood and the German working force was the butt of every kind of taunt and jibe.

'What do you think of that, Tony?' I pointed to the ditch.

'It puts a stop to any more moles,' answered Tony.

'I don't think so. What about a mole from the bottom of the ditch itself? Only sixty feet to dig. We could get out tonight.'

'But how do we get into the ditch, Tommy?'

'We jump. Covered by diversions. What do you say?'

'Let's try.'

Two minutes later we had registered our plan with the escape committee. Jimmy Buckley was always easy to find. He listened in silence.

'When do you want to go?' he asked when I had finished outlining the plan.

'Tonight,' I answered, 'right after the evening roll call.'

'Good God,' he exclaimed, 'you are in a hurry.'

I refrained from explaining that it was six months to the day since I had been shot down and that I thought this a sufficiently good reason for leaving immediately. I knew I was being emotional rather than practical.

'These diversions take time to organize,' continued Jimmy. 'You need three, one for each sentry tower, and they will have to be convincing. Make it tomorrow night and I'll have everything on the top line.'

We agreed. 1 July seemed a good date.

'There's one other small thing,' said Jimmy. 'You'll have to take a third man with you.'

I looked at him aghast.

'Out of the question,' I answered. 'This is a two-man mole and there's no room for anybody else. He'll take up too much space. We have to be moling by dark and we don't want to dig more than twenty feet before sealing in. If we take a third man we'll have to dig another six to ten feet before sealing. It doesn't make sense.'

Jimmy was calm and unruffled as ever.

'I'm afraid you haven't much choice. If you don't take him he gets first go. He registered five minutes before you did, as a solo effort.'

'Sixty feet solo? He's out of his mind. Who is he?'

Neither Tony nor I knew him. We had no alternative but to accept him.

'OK we'll take him with us,' I said with bad grace.

'Right. What else do you need?'

'German money and some concentrated food.'

'Can do. Will fifty marks be enough? I haven't got much.'

'Try and push it up a bit, we're travelling by train.'

'Oh, are you?'

Jimmy was immediately interested. A long discussion developed during which we exchanged all the information we had each collected on the subject. I agreed to give him my railway timetable before leaving. It was apparently the only one there was inside the camp.

Dealing with Jimmy Buckley had been a pleasure. He had arrived at Sagan from Stalag Luft I at Barth and had immediately taken over responsibility for the escape organization. There could not have been a better man for the job. He had had the same responsibilities at Barth and there were few people who knew more about the game. It was a welcome change to deal with an expert and an enthusiast. My well-entrenched hostility towards escape committees started to evaporate rapidly.

The following evening, immediately after the roll-call, the complex plan for our escape started rolling. Tony and I were walking round the circuit, each in a different group of friends to give us cover. I was about 500 metres ahead of Tony, which was the equivalent of half a circuit. As I passed under the first sentry tower, I saw the diversion party was already assembled and about to go into its act. I strolled casually along the path by the tripwire looking out for Jimmy Buckley who was controlling the whole operation.

Jimmy was easy to locate. He was sitting on a tree stump reading a book. I knew that from his position he could see the three other controllers who were watching the reaction of each of the sentries to the diversions. If Jimmy got the all clear from all three controllers he would give me the signal to go by raising his hand to his face and stroking his beard.

I was nearly abreast of Jimmy and close to the point where I wanted to get into the ditch. He was still reading his book. I had resigned myself to another full circuit when, out of the corner of my eye, I saw his hand go to his face. Immediately I jumped.

There was nothing acrobatic about it. I only had to clear the tripwire and a lateral distance of some four feet. I hit the bottom of the ditch with a soundless crash. There were no shots, no shouting. I had not been seen.

I started to cut sand with a small digging tool. I made the entrance to the tunnel some two feet from the bottom of the ditch which meant that there was six feet of sand above me.

Half an hour later only my feet were projecting from the tunnel entrance. The floor of the tunnel sloped sharply upwards. I wanted to reach the pine-root layer, a foot below ground level, after about ten feet of forward progress. We did not dare to seal in behind us until we were close to the surface. It lessened our fears of being trapped by a fall, as we could always dig out, and it made it easy to bore air holes through the roof.

There was no sign of my two companions, so I backed out into the ditch to breathe some fresh air and to try and discover what was happening.

It was a beautiful summer evening, a fact which I had not had time to notice before. The strollers on the circuit above me were as many as ever. A message for me was being repeated again and again as successive groups passed by. I shook the sand out of my ears and listened.

'Charlie the ferret is inside the camp. Indefinite delay.'

I acknowledged and soon repetition of the message ceased. Jimmy's organization was working smoothly. Charlie the ferret was the cleverest and most dangerous of the German Abwehr staff. He could smell a tunnel from a hundred yards away and had a nasty criminal mind which worked on exactly the same wavelength as any escaper's. Charlie was a menace.

Back at the tunnel face, I started cutting sand again until I lost all count of time. When Tony hit the bottom of the ditch, I did not hear him arrive. It was only when he started pulling at my ankle that I knew he was there.

For a few minutes we sat in the ditch whispering. I gave him the digging tool.

'Give me a spell,' I said. 'I'll stay out here and spread this sand around. You'll find it's easy to push the sand back, because of the slope. I've just about reached the pine-roots, so you should be able to start levelling out soon.'

Tony disappeared into the hole and soon the sand started to come back really fast. I began to hope that the third man would not arrive. We really did not need him. He would delay our closing down by at least an hour and until we were sealed in we were very vulnerable to discovery.

A flying shadow suddenly obscured the sky and the third man arrived in a heap beside me. I looked him over again. He was a big man, much too big. He would need at least six and a half feet of tunnel to himself.

'You take over here,' I said. 'As the sand comes out spread it around evenly. You can't be seen on the bottom of the ditch, but kneeling up you're visible from the sentry towers. So watch it.'

I crawled into the tunnel. Tony did not want to be relieved so I set to work dragging the sand back to the ditch. After a long spell, I called Tony out. I wanted to talk to him. I told the third man to take over at the face.

'Just keep it straight and level,' I said, 'and dig fast. We won't be safe until we can all get inside and close the entrance.'

I gave him the little shovel.

'But I've never been in a tunnel before. I don't know anything about it.'

Tony and I looked at him in horrified silence. There was nothing to say. We had got ourselves a passenger. There is always a first time when one crawls into a tunnel. This man just did not want to crawl in.

'All right,' I answered. 'You get just inside the entrance and dig a pit in the floor of the tunnel about two feet deep and five long. That's just as good as tunnel space. Now get moving.'

He got to work, half in and half out of the tunnel. I stayed outside to whisper with Tony.

'We're going to have trouble,' said Tony. 'He's an obvious claustrophobia case. As soon as we seal in he's going to start screaming.'

'That's what I'm afraid of, but what can we do?'

'You and I will do all the digging at the face. We'll just push the sand back to him. Either he packs it behind him or he suffocates.'

'I suppose that's the only way,' I agreed. 'But I don't think I trust him to seal us in properly, nor to pack the sand really hard after we're closed in. Why don't we put him in the middle?'

'Then we'll both have to crawl over him when we want to change over,' objected Tony.

'I think we'll have to accept that. It can be done. You and I are both very thin.'

'Let's play it by ear. You and I will do the face digging and the sealing in. He'll just have to be moved around accordingly.'

'OK. Let's get to work. You realize we're a long way behind schedule.'

'We'll make it up,' said Tony confidently.

Our urgent worry was to get the entrance to the tunnel closed before darkness fell. The night patrols inside the camp used trained Alsatian dogs and we were terrified that they might sniff us out. So it was vital to get at least twenty and preferably twenty-five feet of tunnel clear before dark. After that point we would be moling and, in theory at least, our rate of progress should increase all the time, as the distance we had to move the sand got less and less.

By working frantically without rest, we made our footage. Tony and I alternated at the face and we left the third man near the entrance, pushing the sand out. While he could see daylight behind him and smell fresh air, he was happy enough.

'Time to seal,' I told Tony. 'I'll go back and do it.'

I called the third man forward and crawled over him.

'Shove the sand back to me as fast as you can,' I said to him. 'I'm going to close the entrance.'

'Wait a minute,' he called after me.

'What is it?'

'I'm going back. This isn't going to work.'

He was trembling uncontrollably. I knew exactly how he was feeling. Lots of prisoners before him and many after him had reacted in the same way to the confinement of a tunnel. Sometimes it was just a passing spell which could be dominated by will power. Sometimes it took control of the subject.

I did not know whether to be brutal or patient.

'You can't go back,' I said. 'You'll get shot if you try and anyway you'll ruin our chances. The only way you're going out is at the other end of the tunnel. Now just close your eyes and shove the sand back. Stop thinking.'

'I'm getting out,' he repeated with desperate obstinacy. But I had already closed the entrance and was packing sand tightly into the tunnel mouth.

'More sand,' I called.

There was a long pause and then he started to shove the sand back.

For about two hours he kept control of himself and we made progress, although it was painfully slow. When I was up at the face, Tony talked to him, calmed him and kept him working. But at one o'clock in the morning he started to break up.

'I can't breathe. There's no air.' He was gasping painfully.

In truth, there was very little air and what there was was foul. But we were not supposed to be spending the week-end at Brighton. We had two tiny air holes in the roof and it was more than enough to keep us alive.

A few minutes later he had broken down completely and was sobbing.

'Oh God. We're all going to be shot. I know it. We're all going to be shot.'

He soon relapsed into a sort of coma. He would not speak or move a muscle. But he was breathing and I was sure that there was nothing physically wrong with him.

Tony and I were in no mood to give up, so we enlarged the width of the tunnel at one point until we could move our unresisting passenger partly out of the way. Then we went back to work.

The sand came from the face fast enough, but it took a long time and a lot of energy to drag it back down the tunnel and pack it. Both of us were tiring fast.

At four o'clock I drove another air hole through the roof, close to the face. I was hoping to be able to get an indication of our position. I enlarged it gently until I had a pinhole view. I could clearly see the heavy coils of barbed wire which lay between the two fences. Tony had a look.

'Not outside the fence yet,' he lamented. 'That's really bad. We'll never make it to the ditch by the road. What shall we do?'

'Let's break right alongside the fence. But we've got to make it by five o'clock. After that it will be too light.'

We went back to work with renewed energy. After half an hour I uncovered a strand of barbed wire running across the roof of the tunnel. It was obviously part of the second fence.

'We're there, Tony. I'm going to start breaking now.'

'You can't, Tommy,' he shouted back. 'There's no more room for the sand unless we move our passenger along another few feet. I'm beginning to bury him.'

'God damn him. Why the hell did he decide to come with us? We've barely got twenty minutes before it's broad daylight.'

'Let's try,' said Tony.

We dug out another niche in the side of the tunnel and then dragged the third man into it. He was conscious but not making any sense. He was unwilling or unable to react to any of our proddings. By the time we had disposed of him so that he was out of the way, it was nearly five o'clock.

Frenziedly I attacked the face. Two more feet and we could surface. It took me ten minutes.

'Ready to go, Tony,' I reported.

'I'm afraid it's too late,' he answered. 'Push up an oblique air hole and try and get a view of the trees on the other side of the road. That will tell us how much light there is.'

It took me less than thirty seconds. I could see the sky above the wood. It was bright with dawn. There was no darkness left.

'Have a look for yourself, Tony.'

'I think it's too late,' he said. 'What do you think?'

'If it wasn't for our passenger here, I'd say let's go and take a chance on not being seen. But we can't just leave him here. We'll have to drag him out somehow. And then we're bound to be seen.'

'No, it looks as if we'll have to wait until tonight. If they can cover our absence on the two roll-calls, we can leave calmly and quietly as soon as it's dark. It's a better bet.'

Having taken our decision, we both fell asleep immediately. We were utterly exhausted.

It was about eleven o'clock in the morning when the dogs woke us. They were sniffing and scrabbling at the airholes. The Germans dug us out ten minutes later. Tony and I were marched straight to the cells at gunpoint. The third man was carried on a stretcher to the sickquarters.

Two

WHEN I had completed my sentence and was again back in the East Compound the greater part of July had gone by. This time my session in the cells had been boring and frustrating. But I had been able to pursue and torment Obergefreiter Schultz until I had a nearly exact idea of the documentation I needed for my next escape.

An insistent rumour was circulating that a big move was imminent. A few hundred prisoners were to be transferred to another prison camp in Poland. I was already tired of Sagan, so I volunteered to move. Stalag Luft III was a difficult and soulless camp. I had had more than enough of its hot arid sand. An old fashioned camp in Poland, I argued, might provide new opportunities. In any case, there was always the possibility of getting off the train.

Just as insurance, because these rumours so often proved to be false, I started planning an escape from the Vorlager.

The Vorlager had an area at least three times greater than that covered by the East Compound. It was strictly an administrative compound, housing the prison, the sickquarters, the parcel and book stores and the shower baths. There were no prisoners in the compound except for a handful of Russians and Russian prisoners did not attempt to escape. For one thing they had not the physical strength, their rations were too meagre. Secondly, they had no hope of covering the immense distances involved.

For these reasons I was convinced that the standard of vigilance in the Vorlager must be lower. If nobody was trying to escape, there was no reason for the guards to be on the alert. There were also a number of places around its perimeter where the chances of going through, under or over the wire looked particularly good.

When reduced to its basic essentials, the problem of getting from the East Compound to the Vorlager was simple. All I needed was a key to the gate. To me, any problem which involved keys was a welcome challenge.

During daylight the Vorlager gate was guarded by a sentry who had the key of the padlock which secured it. All traffic through the gate, pedestrian or vehicular, had to satisfy the sentry before the gate was opened. At night, however, there was no sentry. The German ferrets and dog handlers who patrolled inside the camp during the hours of darkness each had their own key to the padlock.

There was no formality about entering or leaving. Sometimes the guard in the nearest sentry tower, over a hundred yards away, would swivel his searchlight on to the gate, but a wave of the hand by the ferret or the dog handler always seemed to satisfy him.

My plan was to make my own key to the padlock, disguise myself as a ferret and walk out waving nonchalantly at the sentry in the tower.

It took me six weeks to make a key for the padlock on the Vorlager gate. The only problems I encountered were mechanical and their resolution demanded no more than time and patience.

The first time I had passed through the gate, coming into the camp from the prison, I had automatically noted the trade name on the padlock. I soon discovered that there were ten other padlocks of the same make inside the camp. Two of these were in the camp kitchen and the other eight attached to the letter boxes which were provided for each barrack. In all cases the keys were available. This gave me a rich supply of laboratory material with which to experiment. None of the ten keys were interchangeable which indicated a padlock of good quality.

After stripping down one of the padlocks and making accurate measurements and drawings of all ten keys, I was able, by a system of geometry and logic, to guess the probable shape of a master key which would fit the whole range of that particular make of padlock. I filed down one of the keys to this shape. After a considerable amount of trial, error and correction, I had a key which opened all the padlocks in the camp. The probability that it would also work on the gate was very high, but it had to be tested. Meanwhile, the move to Poland had been confirmed and its date was said to be imminent. It was obvious that I would soon have to decide whether to stay behind, changing places with one of the many who wanted to go but were not in the list, or abandon my Vorlager scheme.

It was a difficult decision. The Vorlager scheme had to work. If it failed and I was caught, it was a racing certainty that I would immediately be transferred to Colditz, the high-security prison fortress where all the incorrigible escapers ended up. Jack Best and his companions had been transferred there immediately after their recapture. The chances of escaping from Colditz were very nearly zero. It was one of those Spangenberg-like castles, designed with medieval expertise which, in the realm of escape security, was still decades ahead of modern technique. Furthermore, the competition at Colditz would be ruthless. Every one of the hundred-odd prisoners housed there was an individual fanatic, who had already made many attempts. The only thought in each of their minds was to escape and there were very many ingenious minds among them.

I would certainly have enjoyed their company but, for the moment, I could well do without it.

Two days later I proved that my master key worked on the gate. I had joined one of the regular shower parties which were escorted into the Vorlager. It was a matter of two seconds to fit my key into the padlock as we crowded through the gate. On the way back, I repeated the trial, again with success.

I now had the key to the door. All that remained was to prepare my ferret's overalls and make a good pair of wire-cutters.

The move to Poland was now expected to take place within the week. I still did not know which choice to make and, in my indecision, continued with my preparations. The ferret's overalls presented little difficulty. Roy Smallwood, who had discovered that he was a natural tailor, was modifying a pair of pyjamas for me. When these had been dyed black and decorated with a few pieces of tinfoil they would look exactly like the real thing, when viewed from fifty yards in a bad light. A pair of black flying boots would appear very similar to the high boots worn by the ferrets. The forage cap could be made of paper. The closest I intended to come to any German was a hundred yards from the sentry tower.

Manufacturing the wire-cutters was a complicated process. The sawing, filing, tempering and pinning together of two long pieces of iron could not be done in a hurry.

On 6 September, the Germans announced that the party for Poland would be leaving at dawn next morning. I had to decide immediately whether to stay behind, banking everything on the Vorlager escape or whether to discard the plan as too uncertain and wait to explore the new pastures of Schubin.

It was Peter van Rood who made up my mind for me. He was a tall, blond Dutchman who spoke German like a native and whose English was faultless. He came straight to the point.

'Tommy, the grapevine says you've got a key to the Vorlager gate. Is that right?'

'You can't believe half you hear, Peter.'

'This time I know it's true. If you're going to Schubin, will you give me the key?'

'I'm not at all sure I'm going to Schubin.'

We argued for over an hour. The conversation helped greatly to clear my mind and give me an objective view of the situation.

I told Peter of my great fear that, if I made another unsuccessful escape, I would immediately be transferred to Colditz.

'I just can't afford to try again until I'm fully prepared,' I said. 'I don't mean the ferret's overalls and the wire-cutters, those can be finished in a few days. What I'm worried about is good documents for train travel. As far as I'm concerned there isn't any other way of getting to the frontier.'

'You're absolutely right, it's the only way to travel and, you know, I don't believe it's all that difficult.'

'Not for you, maybe. You speak the language perfectly. You'll be taken for a German and probably not even be questioned.'

'Listen, Tommy, my problem is this. I want to go tonight. I've got good documents and I'm running very little risk in travelling by train. With luck I could be on the Swiss border tomorrow night. Of course, if you are not going to Schubin and are going to use the key yourself, I have to think again.'

'Peter, will you wait three or four days until I'm ready? Then we'll go together.'

There was an embarrassing silence.

'I'm sorry,' he said finally, 'but I can't wait. If I go tonight the Germans won't miss me in all the confusion there will be tomorrow, after the Schubin crowd leaves. It means I'll have an absolutely clear start.'

I could have insisted. Without my key he could not get out of the gate. I could have dictated any terms. Instead, I gave in. Peter van Rood had an outstanding chance of getting out of Germany. On the other hand, if he travelled in my company, he would be severely handicapped; with my dark glasses and burnt face, I was a conspicuous and suspicious figure, who would attract attention. I was beginning to realize that I was not a popular choice as a companion to escape with.

'All right, Peter. I'll do a deal with you. Make me a pencil copy of all your documents and I'll give you the key. Let's meet at eight o'clock, I've got to file myself another key.'

'What for? If you're going to Schubin you won't need it.'

'I probably will. That key will open all padlocks of a certain make. It's a common enough make in Germany and I expect it's used at Schubin, too.'

That night Peter walked up to the Vorlager gate, unlocked it, waved casually to the sentry in the tower and disappeared into the darkness. He was eventually picked up at Heidelberg, on a technicality, and spent the rest of the war at Colditz.

The train journey to Schubin took all day. The guards were grimly vigilant and hostile. We were forced to remain seated at all times and the guns came out if anybody got to his feet. Our boots were taken from us, which was a most effective way of preventing escape.

But it did not stop the Dodger. In broad daylight, in full view of half a dozen guards, he leapt from the fast moving train and disappeared into the woods amid a hail of bullets. He was recaptured, quite unharmed, a short time later, but his effort revived our flagging spirits and stopped the train for over an hour.

Major Dodge was a very unusual man. He was an army officer who, for reasons I never understood clearly, spent all his captivity among the air force and we were delighted to have him with us. The Dodger had served in the first world war and could give any of us twenty years and a beating. But his years seemed to mean nothing to him and he had as long a record of escapes as any prisoner I knew. The extraordinary quality of his courage, his complete indifference to danger, were legendary, even to us.

The lay-out of Oflag XXIIB at Schubin was a considerable shock. Even to our professional eyes it seemed to be an escapers' paradise. Never had any prison camp looked less escape-proof. There was cover right down to the trip wire; there were blind spots where the sentries could not see anything; there were fully grown trees; there were buildings close to the wire.

After the barren severity of Sagan, the apparent profusion of so many varied avenues of escape was overwhelming. Even hardened prisoners soon showed signs of neurosis under the strain of having to select, quickly before anybody else did, the most likely escape route from among so many attractive possibilities.

After a week in the new camp, the atmosphere was less feverish. A score of plans had been registered with the committee and furtive men were acting strangely in every corner of the camp.

I was busy in the middle of the asparagus garden, which was one of the many unusual features of Schubin. The previous inhabitants of the camp had been expert and industrious gardeners and there were extensive vegetable plots round the perimeter. In September the asparagus ferns grew tall and bushy and were covered with pretty red berries. My plan was to dig a short vertical shaft behind an asparagus bush and then to mole out. I intended to carry out the whole operation in broad daylight, right under the nose of the sentry.

For this escape I recruited Ian Cross and Robert Kee. The distance to dig was over sixty feet and there was going to be both the space and the work for three of us.

Ian was built like a small bull, compact and muscled. His strength and stamina were endless and he could excavate more footage in the hour than any man I knew. A naturally boisterous and extrovert individual, with the happiest of dispositions, he also had a hair-trigger temper. When Ian was provoked into losing his temper, those who knew him ducked for cover. He could explode with a violence which was primitive.

Robert, who was Ian's closest friend, could not have been more different. Studious, vague and entirely non-athletic, he had a brilliant mind. He was the most argumentative man in the camp, and his arguments were devastatingly logical. He treated escape as a form of recreation from his more serious occupations. He spoke excellent German and was rapidly mastering Russian.

This was the team which appeared one morning in the asparagus garden. Armed with crude, home-made gardening tools, we started hoeing the long rows of asparagus plants. We worked slowly and methodically, building the sandy soil up into high ridges. The sentry outside the fence took no interest at all and we found that we could work right up to the trip wire without arousing suspicion. Any similar activity at Sagan would have brought a dozen Germans to the scene.

On the first day I started a vertical shaft behind one of the ferns, about twenty feet from the trip wire. I was digging without concealment, relying on a warning from Robert or Ian, who were watching the sentry and raking away the sand as I threw it out. After a few days we had the shaft completed to its planned depth of four feet.

By now everyone inside the camp, as well as the sentry who did duty along the fence opposite the asparagus garden, were accustomed to seeing the three mad gardeners at work. We were very conscious of the dreamlike unreality of the scene, as we forever hoed the same row of asparagus plants. Sometimes it was difficult to remember that we were making a serious attempt to escape. The atmosphere was hilarious, we were the butt of every wit in the camp and were frequently so helpless with laughter that we could not work. But the tunnel progressed.

When we reached the stage where there was one man at the bottom of the shaft and another digging in the tunnel, which had started to bore out towards the wire, Robert and Ian stopped acting as though the scheme was just a big joke. Their scepticism vanished overnight and they were suddenly convinced that we were going to make it. We had fifteen feet of tunnel clear. After another fifteen feet we could close ourselves in and mole out in one night. But progress was slow while we were working openly in the asparagus bed.

I was digging in pitch darkness at the face, Ian was squatting in the shaft, pushing sand out to Robert whenever the sentry's back was turned. As I started to drag a heap of sand back to Ian, I felt what appeared to be a large piece of paper, screwed up among the sand. This was very much out of place and the suspicion entered my mind that the tunnel might be passing under an old rubbish dump. I decided to have a close look at this odd piece of paper, in the light of the shaft.

I had backed up about three feet when the roof of the tunnel fell in. An enormous weight hit me everywhere at once and I was completely unable to move my head, arms or body. My legs seemed to be free from the knees down. As I drew a first terrified breath, I inhaled so much sand that I nearly choked. I made a frantic effort to move my body but I was helplessly pinned under some tons of sand. I managed to twist my head sideways and get my face into a small pocket of air. For a few moments I stopped breathing pure sand.

I was kicking violently with both feet to attract Ian's attention. I felt him grab my legs and start hauling, but I remained firmly fixed. When he let go my legs, I prayed that he knew what he was going to do to get me out.

I had been trying hard to slow down my breathing in order to preserve the little oxygen there might be around my head. But I found, to my horror, that by no effort of will could I control my respiration. It had become quite automatic and its tempo was rapidly increasing. Soon I was panting like an exhausted dog and taking in more and more sand with each breath. I realized that I could survive for very few minutes and that they were going to be long, painful minutes.

My mind was clear and my thoughts were sad. Sad because of all the things I had not yet done, sad because it seemed so futile and meaningless that my life should end under a rubbish dump in an asparagus bed in Poland.

Then the digging started directly above me. Ian had organized a rescue squad. As the sounds got closer and closer, in frantic tempo, I held grimly on to my consciousness. I was now snorting sand in and out of my nostrils at an incredible rate. It was an entirely involuntary reflex action induced by breathing carbon dioxide.

A spade hit me in the middle of the back and a dozen hands grabbed my legs. I could hear the shouting.

'One, two, three, heave.'

On the fourth heave I came free and was suddenly hurtling through the air. I fell in a heap among the asparagus. My rescuers, a small army of them, were lying on their backs where they had fallen. I was still snorting.

I lay there gasping for some minutes, obviously alive and in no need of artificial respiration. The back of my hands were a dull blue colour. In fact, as Ian told me later, I was blue all over. The sentry outside the wire was standing rooted to the spot. He had watched the whole scene in open-mouthed amazement.

For the next twenty-four hours I had a splitting headache and for three days I coughed blood and sand. Otherwise I suffered no ill-effects and in a week was completely fit again.

Before the hard Polish winter set in, I made two other attempts. Both were failures and ended dangerously. I began to suspect, with good reason, that my judgement was deteriorating and that I was trying too hard. In a well planned escape there was no need to run the risk of being shot.

I was glad when the opportunity came to go to work on a nice, safe, long-term tunnel.

Three

THE original idea of the latrine tunnel was not mine. I had considered the site, which lay only a few yards south of the asparagus bed, where my disastrous mole attempt had begun and ended. But I was then still thinking in terms of an individual effort and not of a major engineering job with a big team of workers. I had not yet exhausted all the quicker prospects of a one or two-man escape.

I suppose it was on a day early in November that Eddie Asselin asked me to come round to his mess for a brew after the evening appell. I understood immediately that he wanted to talk business.

Seated with Eddie round the table were Tex Ash, Prince Palmer, Duke Marshall and a number of others. We were drinking hot cocoa and it was most welcome. The temperature outside was about ten degrees below freezing and inside perhaps two degrees above. We were all well wrapped in our greatcoats.

The plan for the latrine tunnel was presented to me in broad terms by one speaker after another. It was an efficient and impressive presentation, illustrated by pencil diagrams sketched on the spot and burned in the stove immediately they had been studied. Even in outline, for we had not yet got down to detail, the scheme seemed to smell of success. It was ingenious in its simplicity. All the major risks of detection had been very nearly eliminated.

The communal camp latrine, usually referred to as the abort, the German name for it, which had become part of our kriegie vernacular, was a long, low, one-storey building situated between fifty and sixty yards inside the western barbed wire fence. It was completely isolated, being at least a hundred yards from the nearest barrack block. In day time it was in constant use. At night, it was out of bounds. When working at maximum capacity, during the morning rush hour, it would accommodate some seventy sitting clients and another twenty standing.

The abort was of brick and basically simple in construction. Underneath its cement floor was an immense pit, between ten and twelve feet deep. This pit was lined with brick and sur-

mounted on all sides by the walls of the abort itself, with a simple
raftered roof covering the whole structure.

Inside the building, broad wooden benches lined three of the
four walls. They were roomy and comfortable. Made of soft pine,
they were not cold on the anatomy, even in winter. At three foot
intervals a generously sized hole had been cut, with smooth,
rounded edges. Between one hole and the next, there was a
wooden partition about three feet high. This gave each client
complete lateral privacy, but still enabled him to converse with
his neighbours. There was no frontal screen.

In addition to the three rows of open cubicles lining the outside walls, there was a double back-to-back row of thrones running
lengthwise down the middle of the building. These, too, had their
wooden partitions at the back and sides.

The cement floor did not extend underneath the benches. From
each hole the gravity drop was vertical into the slush below. The
seats were way above splash level. The whole atmosphere of the
abort was relaxed and club-like, even if it did not exactly smell of
old leather and cigar smoke.

It was a well planned, highly functional unit. During the popular morning session, one heard all the news, fact or fiction, BBC
or OKW,* real or wishful. It was here that all the lavatory rumours
started which flashed round the camp at the speed of sound. It
was here that one first heard that there was a trainload of Red
Cross parcels on the way, or that we were all about to be moved
to another camp. It was here that plots were plotted and griev-
ances grieved over.

When we first arrived at Schubin, the latrine did not have that
ambiance sympathique. The previous denizens of the camp had
been French and they had left the latrine in a truly filthy state.
There was ample evidence to show that they had been in the habit
of climbing on to the seats in their boots and performing their
functions in the squatting position. Their aim had, too often,
been bad. Some wit had summed up the situation in a short rhyme,
recorded on one of the partitions.

'It's no good standing on the seat,
The crabs round here can jump ten feet.'

* Oberkommando der Wehrmacht, the High Command of the German Army.

For three days we had scraped and scrubbed and disinfected. The labour was not organized, but there was never any lack of willing workers. Nothing is quite so sacred to an Englishman as his morning's performance. Nothing concerns him quite so much as being constipated. Unless we had cleaned up that abort, we would all have become chronically constipated.

The soft pinewood benches were now spotlessly clean and one could sit on them without qualms.

At the northern end of the building, for perhaps a fifth of its total length, were the urinals. Here there was no gleaming white, glazed pottery, just tarred cement walls on three sides and an open gutter. The contents of the gutter were piped through into the main pit.

This was the site of the planned tunnel, probably the most perfect tunnel ever to be driven out of a prison camp.

The urinal area also had a cement floor but, unlike the fauteuil section of the abort, there was no pit underneath it. The floor was laid on solid earth. The great pit ended where the floor of the urinal began. It was this admirable economy of design which had sparked the idea of our tunnel. It was this feature of the abort which ensured our eventual success.

Our intention was to excavate a large chamber under the urinal floor. From this chamber, a tunnel would be driven directly westwards, under the wire and to freedom.

It was to run deep below the surface and to be engineered in accordance with the latest tunnel techniques. This meant precision cutting at the face and wooden shoring for its whole length. Air was to be pumped to the workers at the face through an extending airline.

The chamber under the urinal was to be excavated to considerable dimensions before work started on the tunnel itself. There had to be room in the chamber for all our digging and dispersal gear, shoring frames, the airpump, and room for eight to ten people to work in comfort. But, above all, the chamber had to have space enough to accept spoil from the tunnel for a period of two or three days. This would enable us to work closed down, with no security risk. It would also enable us to complete the final yards of the tunnel without any risk of detection.

All these features had a vital bearing on the probability of the tunnel succeeding. The most dangerous clue to the existence of a tunnel was always the spoil, which was so difficult to hide. In our vernacular, we always referred to the spoil as dispersal and used the same word for the operation of disposing of the spoil.

In every prison camp our experience had been the same. The discovery of dispersal, whether it was the action of furtive men trying to spread sand in flower beds, or whether it was the discovery of the spoil itself, was nearly always the way in which the Germans detected a tunnel.

Once dispersal had been found and the Germans thus knew that there was a tunnel in being, they seldom failed to find it. Usually they could narrow down the probable location to one particular barrack block or building. After that it only needed a small army of Russian slave prisoners armed with spades to dig until the tunnel was revealed.

Our plan was to dump all our dispersal into the great pit, taking care to distribute it evenly over the whole area so that it did not show above the surface of the mixture.

But this was not all. There was still the ultimate refinement, the touch of genius, the factor which tilted the balance in our favour.

Access to our chamber under the urinal was not to be directly downwards through the cement floor. We were going to burrow in laterally instead of vertically, making our entry from the side of the great pit itself. It was this indirect approach which increased our chances of success by many hundreds of per cent.

The plan was to make a trap in the brick wall of the pit, below the level of the abort floor. Access to this trap was to be down through one of the seats in the back row of the stalls.

Eddie Asselin and Tex Ash were to be responsible for the construction of the tunnel. Both had had a long apprenticeship of tunnelling in other prison camps and could contribute a wealth of valuable experience which we completely lacked.

Prince Palmer, who was an expert carpenter, was to handle all the problems of shoring, trap construction, airpump and airline and lighting.

Duke Marshall was to be responsible for organization and supply, a vast field which covered most of the serious headaches.

I was to look after security and ensure that the Germans did not discover the tunnel or surprise us at work. It was a job which suited me. For months I had been studying the camp's Abwehr system, such as it was. I knew the movements of the sentries on duty to the last detail. I knew all the Germans who came inside the camp, where they went and when. In any case, I was still waging my private war and there was nothing I wanted more than the opportunity of once again outwitting the goons.

For some time we argued about who to recruit as our working force. The question was more complex than might appear. The camp was full of frustrated prisoners who would jump at any chance of being included in a tunnel scheme. Any well organized tunnel could enroll a hundred workers without difficulty. Indeed, twice that number could easily be recruited.

'This is your job, Duke,' said Eddie. 'What do you think?'

'No trouble at all,' answered the Duke. 'I can rake in as many as you need. Just give me the number.'

'No, wait a minute,' I intervened. 'There are a lot of advantages in keeping our numbers down to the minimum. For one thing, it's better security. And there are a lot of other reasons which I'm all ready to give you. First, let's see how many we really need.'

'As far as I'm concerned,' said Eddie, 'I just need a team to move the sand back from the face as fast as I dig it. But, in general, I agree that we should keep the numbers down. What about you, Prince?'

Prince Palmer was a Welshman and an inseparable friend of Duke Marshall. The Prince and the Duke—they were always accorded the definite article—were, like me, comparatively new prisoners. But they had adapted themselves to their new surroundings faster than most and already, at Schubin, they had emerged as important personalities. They had the reputation of being the best informed and the best provided. They could usually find the answer to any illicit request. If one wanted a hacksaw, a screwdriver or a radio valve, one asked Palmer and Marshall.

The Duke was a former London policeman and his insight into the criminal mind was a great asset to him as a prisoner. He also spoke fluent German. The Prince and the Duke were an invaluable pair and I was delighted to be working with them.

'Well,' said the Prince in answer to Eddie's question, 'I'm certainly taking on Charlie Swain to help me out. He's the best carpenter on the camp. What with the shoring, the trap, the air-pump and the lighting, I am going to be very busy. When I need more help I'll call on the Duke for it. I'll need a lookout system all the time I'm working. Tommy will have to provide that.'

'Any other ideas on recruiting?' Eddie asked the question of the assembled company.

There were a number of ideas and two or three people started talking at once. John, an old Warburg prisoner, was the most expressive.

'If this tunnel ever gets out,' he said, 'we could easily put a hundred through it. If it doesn't come off, well, it's just back to the old drawing board, as usual. But I can't see why we don't re-cruit a working force of, say, one hundred, so that we have labour to spare, don't have to exhaust ourselves and can easily cover all contingencies as they arise.'

There was a murmur of agreement. It was time I said my piece. The fact that I had already made one escape and had had a num-ber of spectacular failures, had given me something of a spurious reputation as an expert.

'Listen,' I said, 'I am convinced that this tunnel has a better than even chance of success. The tunnel itself is not important, ex-cept as a goon-infuriator. What matters is how many get away with a really good chance of getting back home. I'm not interested in sweating my guts out in a tunnel for three months unless, when I do get out, I get a clear start. I'd rather try another mole. One way or the other, it's over in two days.'

'Come to the point, Tommy,' said the Duke. 'We're with you so far.'

'OK Duke,' I answered, 'the point is this. Once we break the tunnel outside the wire, we have two choices. Either we keep it open as long as it lasts and the boys go on crawling through it until dawn, or until some poor bugger gets shot, or, which is the second choice, we just put out a limited number and then close the tunnel, still undiscovered.

'This is the way I want it. If the tunnel remains undiscovered until dawn, and the last man got away at midnight, everybody will have a real chance of being far away from this area before the alarm is raised. Do you realize that it's less than three hours by train to Danzig? Anybody who can get inside the docks before the heat is on stands a wonderful chance of making it to Sweden.'

'You can't do that.' The protest was heated. 'If the tunnel is open to the outside, everybody in the camp should be allowed to have a crack at it, as long as the luck lasts. Hell, we might get a hundred out, even more. What a triumph!'

'This is the whole point of my argument,' I replied. 'The more we get out, the bigger our triumph in a certain sense. But we are not trying to break the record for the greatest number of prisoners ever to escape from a tunnel. We are trying to give those of us who dig the tunnel the best possible chance to get back to England. That's our real aim. The conclusion is that the less we are, the better our chances.'

For a long time we argued back and forth but, in the end, the mini-theory won the day, much to my relief. We would, it was agreed, keep our numbers as low as possible and only take on essential workers. It was to be a private tunnel for the benefit of those who had made it and nobody else.

'What about the escape committee?' asked the Prince. 'They could help us a lot with stooging and security.'

'No.' I vetoed the idea. 'If I am to be responsible for that side of it, we'll do it all with our own team. It's the only way to avoid slip-ups. The escape committee can pressgang unwilling stooges who haven't got their heart in it, because they won't have a place on the tunnel. This means they are liable to let us down at a crucial moment. Let's do it all ourselves. It's more work, but it's safer. We can only really rely on enthusiasts, the ones we pick now, the ones who have a direct, personal interest in the success of the tunnel.'

'How many do we need, then?' asked the Duke.

We all made our calculations and finally reduced the figure to an absolute minimum of 25. We accepted the fact that we would all have to work long hours, but felt that it was the only way we could retain our independence and not run the danger of a critical slip-up on the part of the central organization.

After this point had been finally settled, it was not so much a question of selection as of discarding, so many were the possible candidates. What we wanted were confirmed escapers who, in one way or another, had already shown their determination to get out, even if they had never been successful.

Ian Cross was the first to be proposed and unanimously approved. Ian was a fanatic. He was always trying something impossible and ending up in the cooler. Never have I met a man as single-minded about escape than Ian. He had worked with me and Robert Kee on the asparagus bed job and had, in fact, literally saved my life on that occasion. He was small and bulky, with incredible endurance. If told to dig twenty feet of tunnel, Ian would dig those twenty feet, even if it took him three days without relief. He never gave up.

Ian Cross was murdered by the SS at Gorlitz in March 1944, after escaping from the big North Compound tunnel at Sagan.

Other nominees followed rapidly and each was clinically examined, dissected, approved or discarded. We had a lot of talent to choose from. We ended up with a team of twenty-five prisoners who could be relied upon to put their last ounce of energy into the work, without ever complaining or slackening their efforts.

The Duke took a note of the names.

We started to get down to detail.

'Stooging,' said the Duke, 'that's your headache, Tommy. How will you work it?'

By stooging, Marshall meant the system of look-outs.

'I'll work out the coverage needed for each phase of the operation, digging, dispersing or odd jobs, and let you know how many bods I need. OK? Time on dienst will have to be worked out when we know the overall requirement. I think the boys we've picked won't argue if we keep them working long hours.'

'Right,' said Marshall. 'I've got a lot of other problems. First, is there anything else on security?'

'Yes, one very important point. We've been talking about the Abort Dienst. We've got to cut that out completely. It only needs one stupid goon to report that he has heard the words and the Abwehr will start tearing the abort apart. We have to use another name.'

'So what do we call it?'

'Anything. Eddie's Exit. The Duke's Hole. The Shithouse Job —SHJ for short. It doesn't matter as long as we forget the Abort Dienst.'

We went on to discuss labour problems. With only twenty-five men, we were going to be fully extended as soon as we got under way.

The Duke had a query.

'As I understand it, I organize the labour force. Each one of you tells me his requirements and I provide. Now what about ourselves? Those of us with particular sectors of responsibility sitting round this table represent at least twenty per cent of the whole force. Do I organize you lot too?'

'Me for certain,' I responded, 'any time you want me. I'll have a number two and as long as we are not both put on dienst together, we're available. As for Eddie and Tex, I think they are excluded. They'll be underground all the time. I should think that the Prince is going to be busy twenty-four hours a day, too. As for you, Duke, I don't think you are going to get any sleep until we break out.'

'Tommy's right,' said Eddie. 'Let's leave it that way to start with. We are all going to have to sweat it out and if anybody can't stand the pace, he gets dropped at once. If this job really gets going, the whole camp will be begging to join us.'

The Prince had a technical point.

'What about lighting?' he demanded. 'Do you want electricity, or will fat lamps be good enough.'

Tex was all for electricity. Eddie said no, reminding us of the unfortunate prisoner in another camp who had been electrocuted by faulty wiring in a damp tunnel.

'What do you think, Tommy?' the Prince asked.

'No electricity.' I was firmly negative. 'The lead off the mains in the Abort will be too dangerous. I know we can disguise it, but if the goons should find it, it will bring them straight to the tunnel. It's not worth it. Fat lamps have always been good enough before and, if we've got an airpump, there's no trouble about the oxygen they burn. I say no electricity.'

This was agreed.

'What about bed slats for the shoring?' asked Eddie. 'We are going to need stacks and stacks of them.'

'No sweat,' answered the Duke. 'Just leave it to me and don't ask any questions.'

When the Duke spoke like that nobody doubted that he had a

certain, but probably illicit, source of supply. And one never questioned the Duke's sources.

'It might run as high as a couple of thousand,' persisted Eddie.

'I told you not to worry. I'll fix it.'

'Jesus, I'm glad you're with us, Duke,' said Eddie. And we all felt the same way.

Four

THE first job was for the carpenters. The end lavatory seat in the back row, the one nearest to the urinal, was chosen for our tunnel entrance. The whole section of bench between the partition and the wall had to be adjusted so that it could be raised sideways to rest against the bricks. It was a delicate piece of work.

It took two days to complete the job and it was a dangerous period for us, when we necessarily had to take big risks, protected only by an elaborate system of look-outs. The carpenters worked on the spot and tried, as far as possible, to make their modifications in stages, so that the lavatory seat could be replaced within a few minutes in the event of any warning of approaching Germans.

When it was finished the trap was a masterpiece. To operate it one released a hidden catch and the wooden partition could be swivelled a few inches to one side, revealing a hairline saw cut across the full breadth of the bench.

The lavatory seat could now be raised sideways, rotating smoothly on concealed hinges. When in the fully open position, it rested against the side wall, revealing an entrance nearly three feet square which led directly into the great pit. Below the hole in the lavatory seat, on its underside, a hand-rail had been securely attached. This was to help us perform the gymnastics necessary to get into the chamber under the urinal, once we had breached the pit wall. It took less than five seconds to open or close the trap and return everything to normal. If any German came into the abort, one of us would whip down his trousers and sit on the replaced seat. The rest would disappear.

Our next task was to breach the brick wall of the pit itself so as to get in underneath the floor of the urinal.

As I was small and light, I was a natural choice for this job. I had to lower myself head first into the pit, while two strong men held my legs. Then, with a hammer and cold chisel, I went to work on the bricks, in semi-darkness and surrounded by an aroma which I can only describe as strongly elemental. A few feet below me was a swamp of nauseous fertilizer, our British contribution to the Polish agricultural economy, for none of this produce was wasted. About once a month a Polish contractor arrived driving a horse drawn cart on which was mounted a great metal tank. With a hand pump, he did his best to empty the pit. His load ended its journey on the fertile fields of Poland.

Fifteen minutes was my absolute maximum duration for working upside down. After that there was so much blood in my head that I could not see to hit the chisel. The tools were so precious that, if, as a result of hitting one's thumb a nasty clout, one dropped either the hammer or the chisel, there was only one rule and remedy, which was to go down on a rope into that noxious sump and recover the tools. In spite of crushed fingers and mangled thumbs, nobody ever dropped anything.

At this early stage we were still very vulnerable to discovery. The only protection we had was the lavatory seat trap and our system of look-outs. A thorough search of the latrine would have revealed the hole in the brick wall of the pit. But there was no reason for the German Abwehr to be suspicious of the latrine as long as we were careful. In a casual check, we felt certain no German would go so far as to stick his head down through the end hole in the back bench and shine a torch over the side wall of the pit.

Nevertheless, we were nervous and our system of look-outs covered every possible line of approach to the abort. We could expect at least three minutes warning of any possible danger. This gave us plenty of time to replace the lavatory seat and clean up.

Cutting through the wall did not take long because the work had to be precise only within certain overall limits. Eventually we needed an exactly rectangular opening, so that a close fitting trap could be installed. The finishing work on the hole, the exact trimming of the edges, would be done, we had decided, from inside the hole, from the chamber we intended to dig behind it.

For the time being, the wall bashers just had to work inside the limits of a faintly drawn chalk circle, whose outline was brushed off every evening when we closed down.

After three days, we were digging sand from behind the wall. After five days there was room enough to put a man inside, under the urinal. After that point we started to make rapid progress.

We worked in short shifts all through the day, stopping only for the appell parades. We were most careful not to dump any sand or dislodged bricks into the pit immediately below the hole in the wall. The bricks we saved for constructing the trap. The sand we spread evenly over the whole surface area of the fermenting solution in the pit below. It sank without trace.

Digging sand, even if it is really hard packed and virgin as it was under the urinal, is not difficult, provided there is plenty of space and tired workers can be frequently substituted by fresh ones. Our digging teams worked frenziedly. Eddie Asselin was the first through the hole in the wall and soon he had enlarged it enough for Tex Ash to join him. From that moment the sand to disperse started coming out by the bucketful. Container after container was handed through the hole, to be grabbed by a worker leaning down through the lavatory trap and immediately passed on to the dispersing team. The sand was then poured down through any of the available seventy holes, taking care never to spill any on the floor and to spread the spoil evenly.

Soon we were able to put a third man through the hole and the rate of dispersal again increased. By now every one of us on the twenty-five-man team was working in shifts from morning until dark. The team inside the hole was changed at two hour intervals.

My first spell in the hole under the urinal came late. I had been too preoccupied with security problems to make myself available sooner. We were still working in highly vulnerable conditions. With three men underneath the urinal, three minutes warning was barely sufficient time to get them all out.

The way into the small chamber behind the wall was complicated, but not very difficult. All one had to do was to get a good grip on the hand rail, lower oneself into the pit and jackknife one's legs up and into the hole. The first one in fought his own way through, using hands and elbows. Those who followed had the help of the diggers already inside the hole.

When I first saw it, the chamber inside the hole in the wall was already big enough to house four people, two digging, one filling and one handing the containers up to the surface. The roof of the chamber was the underside of the cement floor of the urinal, with an area of about four foot square. Immediately through the pit wall, the level dropped, giving space enough for movement in the crouched position. In two corners margarine lamps were burning, giving a soft yellow light. Two men were digging furiously, using small coal shovels, another was filling the sand into aluminium jugs and the fourth handing the jugs out through the hole. The man I was relieving disappeared backwards through the hole in the wall, reaching upwards for a grip on the hand rail.

Inside the chamber the air was breathable, but stank of the pit. Eddie told me that one forgot the smell very quickly.

'Nice going,' I congratulated him. 'How big are you going to make this?'

'Real big,' he answered. 'Lengthwise, we'll take it right to the end of the piss house. Wide, about ten feet. That will give us all the space we need. And plenty of room for dispersal when we break.'

'When can we get the carpenters in here?' I asked, thinking of the trap which still had to be fitted.

'There's room for them now, if we cut this team down to two. Let's wait until the day after tomorrow. Then there'll be room for all of us and the rate of digging won't drop. We'll give them a quiet corner to themselves.'

I worked my shift, sometimes digging, sometimes filling. All four of us were going flat out. It was only a two hour shift and there was no point in not exhausting oneself. We moved tons of sand.

As Eddie had predicted, we put the carpenters in two days later. They had everything prepared. We passed in to them all their tools and materials, cement and water, saws, nails, hammers, chisels, bricks and bits of iron. They stayed down all day, surfacing only for appells. It took them two days to complete the trap and we waited another two for the cement to get hard. Fitting the trap into the hole in the pit wall and getting the pivots and coun-

terbalances to work perfectly took another three days. Dispersal of
spoil was slowed down because the carpenters were busy working
on the opening itself.

When finally the wall trap was completed and worked perfectly,
we moved into a new rhythm. The look-out system was reduced
and streamlined, thus releasing more labour for digging or dispersal. We practised our close down procedure until it was faultless. If we left the digging team below, we could complete a
crash close down in twenty seconds. If we wanted to get the
digging team above ground, we needed just less than three minutes to get four men out. As most alarms were short term, we
adopted the policy of leaving the diggers down whenever the
stooges called an alarm, closing both the wall and the lavatory
traps behind them.

By Christmas the dispersal chamber under the urinal was enormous, its dimensions being roughly fifteen feet long by ten wide
by six feet high. This gave us space to work in comfort and room
to store all our equipment where it was safe from searches. A
start on the tunnel had already been made. Its entrance, well
shored and protected against wear and tear, was at the floor level
of the chamber, at least six feet below ground level. Beyond the
dark square hole which lead into the tunnel, about ten feet had
been dug.

We were on our way. We were also in a hurry. Rumours of a
move back to Sagan were beginning to circulate. Furthermore,
Dickie Edge had started a rival tunnel from a barrack block a
hundred yards north of the latrine. We had to break our tunnel
first.

As the tunnel started to grow in length, and to grow fast, the
work load on the carpenters increased. The established and well-
proven method of shoring a tunnel was to construct square frames
from our wooden bed slats. These slats were placed at about two
foot intervals all along the length of the tunnel, whose dimensions became exactly two feet by two feet in cross section.

Although it may not seem credible to the uninitiated these
dimensions permitted comparative ease of movement and only
engendered a small degree of claustrophobia. It was even possible
for one man to crawl over and past another, if the need arose.

The roof of the tunnel was supported by fitting other bed slats longitudinally, whose ends rested on the shoring frames. This system prevented falls in the tunnel and protected the diggers if a fall should occur.

The shoring frames were carefully carpented so that they could be assembled in the restricted space of the tunnel itself. All joints were dovetail fits and the greater the pressure on them, the solider was the frame. For each two feet of tunnel, nine bed slats were needed. Four went to the making of the frame and another five were needed for supporting the roof between each frame. As the tunnel was going to be close to 300 feet long, we were going to need some 1,400 bed slats for shoring alone.

The straw-filled mattresses on our two tier bunks were supported by bed slats, simple pieces of wood about two feet three inches long by six inches wide, which fitted inside the frame of the bed. The full ration for each bed was eight slats, on which one could sleep comfortably even though there was room for twelve. But when one was reduced to only four or five slats, the discomfort was acute and there was a real danger of falling through the bottom of one's bed.

That winter in Poland was the coldest I have ever experienced. Instead of undressing to go to bed at night, one dressed. Double and triple layers of underwear, all one's sweaters, two or three pairs of socks, covered by all the blankets and greatcoats one possessed. Everything combustible had gone into our stoves, including many of our bed slats. We were all reduced to the ultimate minimum necessary to defeat gravity.

The provision of bed slats for tunnel shoring was therefore a major problem. This was the Duke's headache and, as was to be expected, he solved it in a manner all his own.

He could have gone to the escape committee, which had the authority to impose a levy on the whole camp of, say, one slat per person. This would not have satisfied half our needs and would, in any case, have caused a mutiny. No prisoner could be expected to sleep on less than five bed slats and most were already down to that number. A levy would have made us the most unpopular people on the camp and that would not have helped us.

Duke Marshall did not go to the committee. Instead he went to the German quartermaster's stores. His visit took place at a time when neither the quartermaster himself nor any of his staff were present. We entered the storeroom through its main door. The Germans at Schubin were still naïve enough to believe that locked doors gave them security.

It was a treasure house of valuable material. There were two rooms stacked to the ceiling with two tier wooden bunks and literally thousands of bed slats. There were also many other items which made our mouths water.

But we were on dangerous territory. We were breaking both German and British rules by robbing the quartermaster. If the Germans discovered a theft, they would immediately report it to the Senior British Officer who would be forced to appeal to the thief to return the stolen goods, to avoid whatever communal sanctions the Germans threatened. This had happened more than once when some poor technician doing an urgent repair job inside the camp had lost half of his precious tools. So our decision to rob the quartermaster's stores had to remain a very close secret.

The Duke and I decided that it would not be difficult to disguise the fact that anything had been stolen. It was mainly a matter of working with care and ensuring that, at a casual glance, the piles of bed slats appeared to be untouched. This would be compara- tively simple. Greatly in our favour, too, was the fact that these stores were not in constant use. The German quartermaster rarely visited them and they were situated in the basement of a great ramshackle building, the White House, which was locked, barred, shuttered and out of bounds to us prisoners. Only those of us who had a penchant for lockpicking had ever explored it.

We also decided that the most secure place to keep our bed slats was the quartermaster's stores. Until there was room to house them in the chamber under the urinal, we would only steal enough to keep up with the carpenters' requirements. And not a word to a soul.

The spacious dispersal chamber enabled us to work to a maxi- mum production schedule in complete security. Even if malodorous, the air in the chamber was good and the optimum sized team of workers could be put down for hours at a time. The spoil from the tunnel could remain in the chamber until it was the right moment to initiate the dispersal operation.

As the tunnel grew rapidly in length, the number of workers needed below ground increased. Even the carpenters found that they could do their work faster in the dispersal chamber, where they were never interrupted by alarms from their look-outs. Our working force was beginning to be extended to the limits of physical endurance. It was becoming difficult to maintain a fully secure network of look-outs throughout the day.

In the circumstances it was logical and practical to change our method of working. The operations of digging and dispersal were separated. The underground team worked with the wall trap closed and concentrated all its efforts on getting the sand back from the face into the chamber. There the spoil was accumulated in a convenient position to pass it out through the lavatory trap when the operation of dispersal started. The chamber was big enough to accommodate spoil from several days digging, if necessary.

We calculated that in less than an hour of concentrated dispersal operation, we could dispose of about a hundred aluminium jugs of spoil. This represented a full day's work by the digging teams. During this short period, it was well worth our while to use the maximum force for dispersal operations, even at the expense of the underground teams. If we only dispersed once a day and for less than an hour a day, the disruption to the progress of digging the tunnel would be little. Once the dispersal session was over, the underground teams could work with the wall trap closed and in complete security. The system of look-outs could be reduced to a minimum, even two men were enough. This released more labour for more productive tasks. During dispersal, however, when both the wall and lavatory traps were open, we had to protect our vulnerability with an extensive screen of look-outs, which was costly in manpower.

It was easy to conclude that the best time for our dispersal operation would be between half past eight and half past nine in the morning, when the whole camp had just breakfasted and, the British constitution being what it is, the abort was at its busiest. During this period the traffic to and from the latrine was so intense that no German observer, however astute, could have noticed that a dozen or more men had gone into the lavatory, who did not emerge again for over an hour.

The first morning we put our new plans into practice, we ran into trouble. Everybody had had a pep talk and we were all eager to prove the new system. Eddie and Tex were down at the tunnel face, with just two helpers, to haul the sand back. Inside the chamber was a dispersing team of four, one filling the jugs, one holding the jugs, one handing the jugs through the trap and one general relief for whoever tired first. Inside the abort was a two man lifting team, who stretched down through the lavatory trap to take the full jugs as they came through the wall. These jugs were really heavy. Waiting to receive the jugs as they came out of the pit was a team of four dispersers. Spread around the camp, in direct visual contact, were five lookouts. The carpenters and their helpers were busy. This accounted for all of our working force.

When the first jug of sand surfaced, a disperser grabbed it and rushed down the corridor between the lines of thrones, to dump it at the far end. He was in a hurry to complete his job and bring back the empty jug, which would immediately be passed down into the chamber. He had been told to use only the holes at the southern end of the abort building.

As this was the rush hour, all the cubicles were occupied. When the eager disperser arrived at his destination, he found the hole blocked by a large body firmly seated over it.

'Quick. Move your great ass. I want to dump this sand.'

It was not, of course, the most tactful of approaches. The response was coarse and immediate.

'You can stuff that sand and the jug too. Now bugger off and leave me in peace.'

The second disperser with his jug of sand had no better luck. Nor the third, nor the fourth.

We had made the great error of not remembering that there are some moments sacrosanct to an Englishman, when he may not be disturbed for any reason. We had certainly picked one of those delicate moments.

Eventually we got our spoil dumped into the pit, but it took us far longer than we had planned.

The next morning we changed our system. By cutting down ruthlessly on all other activities, we increased our dispersal team to seven workers. Of these, four occupied lavatory seats through which the sand would be poured, changing their station whenever the departure of a client permitted it. The other three ran back and forth with jugs of sand. The sitting dispersers provided relief

for any member of the lifting or carrying team whenever necessary. And, of course, they obligingly removed their posteriors from
the seats whenever a jug of sand arrived. In this way we were able
to push through a rapid dispersal operation every morning. Gradually, too, our activities came to be a familiar feature of the morning session and more and more of the customers would cooperate
to the extent of getting off their asses for the brief moment necessary.

Five

By mid-February, the tunnel had passed underneath the wire and
was well over 150 feet in length. It was time to establish exactly
what point it had reached in relation to the ground above.

The system we used to locate our true position was primitive.
A thin iron rod was driven vertically up through the roof of the
tunnel, at its far end, while a number of experts stood by above
ground to get a bearing on its position.

Eddie was up at the face with the iron rod and both traps were
open so that messages could be relayed back and forth. It was a
tense moment for all of us.

'Can you see it yet?'

The message came to us from Eddie.

'No. Nothing in sight.'

The answer was passed down to the chamber and along the
tunnel.

A dozen pairs of eyes were searching the rough grass outside the
wire.

'Eddie says it must be sticking out at least a foot above the
ground. Get a bloody move on before the goons see it too.'

We all stared intently. There was nothing protruding above
the ground. Eddie's messages became more furious and impatient. Of course, we were all looking where we thought the tunnel
ought to be.

Suddenly there was a shout.

'I've got it. Hold still while we get bearings.'

We all followed the direction indicated. We could not believe our eyes, the disappointment was so great. The end of the iron rod was clearly visible, but only a very short distance outside the wire and nearly thirty feet south of what should have been our line.

Our navigation experts quickly took their bearings and the order was passed to Eddie to bring the rod down. Ten minutes later a very angry Asselin emerged from the pit.

'What the —— hell were you clots doing?' was his greeting.

The situation was explained to him and it was a very chastened Eddie who sat down with us to conduct a postmortem. Keeping the tunnel straight had been his responsibility.

It was fairly obvious what had happened. Instead of taking a line which was at right angles to the wire, we had gone off some fifteen degrees to the left. It was a common enough error, as many tunnellers after us were to discover. The fault lay not so much in the protractor and string method of lining up a tunnel, as in the fact that it was almost impossible, below ground, to establish a reliable baseline on which to orientate one's protractor. Inside our dispersal chamber there were no absolute indications of azimuth. Our tunnel navigators had to work with primitive instruments and had probably been misled by the alignment of the walls through which and under which we had dug.

Our depression soon evaporated. Two positive facts had emerged from the morning's operation. We knew exactly where we were and we were outside the wire. There was not very far to go.

All digging operations were closed down for the day to give our navigators time to work out the best solution to the problem and a new course for the tunnel. We picked, as our exact point of exit, a noticeable depression in the terrain which lay some fifteen yards beyond the sentry's beat and which would give each of us some cover as we emerged from the tunnel. The navigators' problem was thus reduced to simple terms. They had to produce an accurate course to steer and establish the exact distance between two known points outside the wire. Although the terms of the problem may have been simple enough, their resolution, without accurate instruments, was a big headache. A team of navigators worked all day, well protected by a network of stooges. That evening they produced their answer, neatly drawn on a large scale plan. This time, they guaranteed accuracy to within a foot.

When digging re-started the following morning, I was on the tunnel shift. Immediately after morning appell, all the underground crew made their way individually to the abort. With the ease born of long practice, I hung suspended over the pit, holding onto the handrail. Then I jack-knifed neatly through the wall trap and into the chamber, which was already a hive of activity.

The fat lamps, placed in little niches cut from the sand wall, illuminated the scene with a soft, smoky light. One man was already at work on the airpump, clearing the stale air from the tunnel. This was an infernal machine, made of a canvas kit bag some three feet long and a foot in diameter. To operate the pump one sat at one end of it and, with a rowing-like motion, compressed and expanded the kit bag throughout its whole length. This concertina-like motion, which was carefully restricted by a wooden frame and wire loops, drove fresh air up to the face through a line of tins buried in the floor of the tunnel. Working the airpump was the hardest job of all. After twenty minutes one got a severe pain in the guts, but it did develop one's stomach muscles.

The aluminium bowl which, hauled on a rope, brought the sand back from the face, had already been filled with lighted fat lamps. It would be drawn up the tunnel as soon as the diggers were ready, to provide light for their work.

In one corner a carpenter was busy cutting and assembling shoring frames. The team which hauled sand back from the face and stacked it for subsequent dispersal was ready. In all there were eight of us in the chamber.

That morning there was to be no dispersal through the trap to the abort above, so there was no dispersing team in the chamber.

I changed rapidly into my digging overalls, which consisted of woollen combinations provided by the Red Cross. They were stiff with sand from long use. Eddie disappeared into the tunnel and I followed him at a few yards interval. I was followed, in turn, by the man who was stationed at the midway point, lying inside a small cavity in the tunnel wall, and whose job was to help with the hauling back of the spoil.

It takes a long time to crawl along 150 feet of tunnel, using one's elbows and toes. I was out of breath when the journey was over. Very gently, so as not to upset the lamps, I hauled up the aluminium washing bowl. Eddie and I both cut little holes in the hard sand of tunnel wall and disposed the lamps to our satisfaction. Eddie immediately set to work, cutting sand from the face. Soon I was fully occupied filling sand into the bowl. When it was full I gave the signal to haul away.

That morning the work was not hard. Eddie was concerned with getting the new direction of the tunnel exactly right and spent more time taking measurements than digging. When the signal came from the chamber that we were to be relieved, I was hardly tired. Usually, I crept backwards out of the tunnel in an exhausted state.

Back in the comfortable spaciousness of the dispersal chamber, I watched the relief team disappear into the tunnel entrance. I was feeling cold and the penetrating damp of the sand was beginning to chill the marrow of my bones. The man on the airpump was labouring, nearly exhausted. I decided to take over from him and restore my circulation with some hard physical exercise.

For ten minutes I pumped air, leaning alternately fully forward to my toes and then right back again to past the vertical, rhythmically, without a pause. Soon I was warmer and the chill of the damp sand was defeated. But again I had that sharp pain in the guts. It was more acute than usual and getting worse. I stopped pumping and handed over to the man I had relieved.

Once above ground, I had a cold shower and retreated to my bunk. I was feeling a little sick. The pain in my stomach persisted through the afternoon, so I decided to walk over to the sick bay and see what the doctor could do for me.

The doctor was a British Army major. His sick bay had half a dozen beds in it. He was a kind and dedicated man, too frequently faced with the agonizing problem of having to cure seriously ill patients without the medicines and drugs he desperately needed.

I lay on a bed half-stripped, while my temperature and pulse were taken and the doctor prodded my stomach. I was fully expecting him to diagnose a pulled muscle and prescribe a few days rest.

But no. It was appendicitis.

It was a grave mistake to get appendicitis at Oflag XXIIB in Poland. The doctor had neither operating theatre, anaesthetics nor instruments. The Germans would only transfer a prisoner to a proper hospital when the case became desperate, which was after the appendix had burst and peritonitis had set in. The doctor told me this quite bluntly. There was no point in not being frank.

'So what happens now?' I asked.

'You go to bed and stay there. With complete rest, starvation or something close to it, liquids only, and some sedatives, if I have any left, we might calm it down. It's your only chance. I can't offer anything else.'

For the next two weeks, I lay on my back in the little sick bay. Usually, I kept my right knee bent, which eased the pain. I ate no solid food at all but lived on sticky brews of Horlicks, Ovaltine and cocoa. Gradually the pain subsided. The tunnel went ahead without me.

Irregularly, I got progress reports about the tunnel and began to worry whether I would be cured by the time it was finished. It was going to be a very close thing, the tunnel was in its final stages. Fortunately, all my preparations were made. I just needed to be fit.

On 4 March I was still in bed, but feeling much better. The pain had completely gone and, for a few days, I had been enjoying a slightly more substantial diet. In the morning, the Duke came to see me. He gave me all the news.

The tunnel was to be broken the following night. It had already reached the point at which we intended to make our exits and its exact location had again been checked by the iron rod method. Eddie needed another day to complete his preparations for breaking out.

The escape committee had intervened and nominated another eight prisoners, who had not worked on the tunnel but who were to be given a place on it in reward for services rendered to the community. This last item of news made me furious. If the escape committee wanted to nominate extra bodies to our tunnel, why not do it in good time, when we could make them do some work.

The Duke was no happier about this development than I was.

'Well, Tommy, are you coming?'

'Of course I'm coming. When's the draw for places?'

'At noon tomorrow, in our block.'

'I'll be there.'

'You're going with Robert, aren't you?'

'Yes.'

'Well, your names will go into the hat together, so that you follow one another out of the exit.'

'That's fine. Suits me.'

'How's it going, Tommy? Are you fit? Are you really in shape?'

'I think so Duke. I'll check with the doctor now. But don't you give my place away, because I'm going to be there.'

I went in search of the doctor. In his tiny office, we discussed the situation.

'You're not supposed to be out of bed.'

'Doctor, it's something of an emergency. Anyway, I'm feeling fine on my feet.'

'What's the great emergency.'

'A tunnel. We're breaking out tomorrow night and, as one of the founder members, I'm leaving with the rest.'

'You're not well enough. Admittedly, we've cured your appendicitis and you should be damned thankful, but after fourteen days in bed, you'll still be convalescent for quite a time. You're in no condition to go escaping, believe me.'

I believed him. I knew well that I was not in the best of condition to escape. But, at the same time, I was in no mood to let that tunnel break without me. I told the doctor so.

Wise in the ways of prisoners, the doctor did not argue. He just warned me that I was taking a big risk. In other circumstances, he indicated, he might have taken more effective measures to prevent me from going.

We shook hands and I thanked him warmly for the care he had taken of me. After collecting my meagre belongings, I walked up the hill to my barrack block. When I arrived, I was panting and exhausted. It looked bad for my prospects.

It was good to be home again in our tiny mess, its dimensions delineated by five sets of two-tier bunks and, in the middle, the unvarnished wooden table with its two hard benches.

Greetings were warm and welcoming, but brief. Everybody was intensely busy and there was a tangible tension. I recognized the atmosphere immediately; it reminded me of the briefing room before a big operation, part fear, part excitement, with the inevitable reaction on stomach and temper.

'I thought we'd see you just about now, Tommy. Had a good rest?'

'Better than a week at Brighton,' I answered. 'But I'm damned hungry. I suppose you ate all my rations? Just in case they went bad?'

There was no immediate answer. Before the silence got too embarrassing, the mess cook intervened.

'Well you know how it is,' he said apologetically. 'We did eat them, as a matter of fact. But we saved your chocolate and Robert has drawn your escape rations. Are you really hungry?'

'As a Russian prisoner. I've been living on Horlicks for two weeks.'

'Well, as this is a special occasion, how would you like two slices of Spam and some bread and marg?'

This was a really generous offer.

'Just dish it up.'

'Where's Robert?' I asked between mouthfuls.

'At his Russian class, I should think.'

This was typical of Robert Kee, who was going to be my companion on this escape. He remained entirely unaffected by the high fever which had gripped the rest of the tunnellers. After all, the escape was not planned until the following night, why should he disturb his planned schedule for the day? Robert's attitude was calm, placid and, in many ways, enviable.

I had wanted Tony Barber to come with me. His approach to escape was the same as mine and he was both determined and resourceful. But Tony had one and only one plan after getting out, which was to make for Denmark, where he had close relatives. I did not like this route. To my mind, occupied Denmark, even the island of Bornholm, was a dangerous place. I wanted to go west to France or south-west to Switzerland. I was quite convinced that the Germans would put an intense watch on all the Baltic ports as soon as our tunnel was discovered and that they were, therefore, to be avoided.

In spite of long days of argument, Tony and I had failed to find any solution agreeable to both of us.

After my train jump on the journey from Spangenberg, I had reached an entirely final decision. Never again would I escape alone. The lonely human, I had found, cannot dominate his elemental fears. Although he can, consciously and with an effort of will, control those fears, he cannot prevent the subconscious effect they have on his actions. During those cold days spent in ditches or thin woods, my morale had been so low as to be almost non-existent. I knew, with absolute certainty, that the comforting presence of one companion would have been the most effective antidote to this fear complex. In company one suppresses one's reactions to fear. Alone it is nearly impossible to do so.

With Tony eliminated as a companion, I had to look closely at the rest of our team. So many, too many, were suffering from wire psychosis. They had a compelling impulse to get outside the fence. At that point, however, their thinking stopped. From then on it was a matter of luck and providence. They had no plans.

Every tunnel depended on prisoners with this attitude. They were the hardest workers, the most fanatic, the indefatigable. But once outside the wire they were lost.

I knew where I was going, exactly and down to the most minute detail. From Schubin I was walking to Bromberg, the nearest railway station. From Bromberg I would travel by train in a westerly direction, always in short stages, to Cologne. From Cologne I would take the early morning Workman's train to Aachen. From Aachen I would walk down the road towards Eupen, which lay in Belgium. I had a detailed map of the frontier crossing into Belgium, drawn for me by a Belgian officer whom I trusted completely as a local expert.

The journey from Belgium, through France and into Spain was still an unknown quantity, but, at least, some of the population would be friendly. An escapee from Poland would not be looked for on the German—Belgian border.

Of our team, I calculated that there were hardly a dozen who had an exact aim and plan for getting out of Germany. The remainder, once outside the wire, would have achieved their major objective and would then wander, hopefully but unprepared, across the Polish countryside.

Robert's entirely independent spirit, his very personal sense of values, his complete immunity from conventional or traditional concepts, put him in a class apart, one-off, rare and singular.

If you asked Robert to work on a crazy mole scheme, he agreed without hesitation. If you asked him to come and cut through the wire, he was enthusiastic. But he was not a dedicated escapist. He never exercised his mind to produce original ideas for getting out of the camp. He never thought of where to aim for after getting out or the best way of getting there. I had the impression that he did not truly believe in escape; that he had assessed the probability of success as nil and did not therefore want to waste his time thinking about it. He had better things to do.

This quite infuriating attitude of Robert's that escape was just a little game one sometimes played for amusement, did not disguise the fact that he had all the qualities and talents which a successful escaper needed. Nothing took him by surprise and he was never at a loss for an answer. In English he could outargue and and talk down anybody. With his fluent German, I had no doubt at all that he would be able to dominate any conversation, even with a suspicious German policeman. These were exactly the qualities I needed in my companion.

Robert was perfectly content to leave all the preparation and planning to me. I had found him civilian clothes, prepared his documents and worked out our route, without any objection or contribution from him. The arrangement suited me well. Once we were outside and in close contact with the dangerous reality of wartime Germany, Robert was going to be invaluable.

Six

EVENTUALLY I tracked Robert down in his Russian class. The instructor was a Polish officer who had escaped to England in 1940, joined the RAF and was now, in 1942, again in Poland as a prisoner-of-war. Like the many Poles and Czechs among us, his was an uncomfortable situation. Inside the camp he was safe enough. But should he escape and be re-captured, there would probably be a firing squad waiting for him.

'Excuse the interruption, Zilly,' I apologized. 'May I talk to Robert?'

I felt rather like a visiting uncle asking the head's permission to take his nephew to tea. Robert, as he came towards the door, looked like a guilty schoolboy.

We started walking slowly around the circuit. Slowly, because I insisted. Robert usually moved at a gallop.

For once, I talked and Robert listened. It was quite essential to get him organized for the escape. As I expected, he had made no preparations. He was one of those lucky individuals who did not have to struggle to escape. Opportunities just came to him and he accepted them with a casualness which was disconcerting.

I had hidden all our clothes, documents and other paraphernalia behind the rafters in the roof of the White House. They were safe there, but it was a difficult climb to reach the rafters and I just did not have the strength for it. I gave Robert detailed instructions and returned to my bunk.

That day I ate all the food I could beg as well as a good part of my escape rations. This was a heinous crime for the inviolable rule was that they could be consumed only outside the wire. But I had, somehow, to build a store of energy for the exertions of the following night. I walked round the circuit a few times to exercise my leg muscles.

Later that evening we held a dress rehearsal. Not only Robert and I, but most of the others in the block who were going out with us.

I was wearing a naval officer's uniform, with the gold braid removed and black instead of brass buttons. It looked like a businessman's double-breasted suit. It was well worn, with shiny patches and suited my status as a low grade foreign technician. My shoes were black, strong and comfortable. I wore a faded blue shirt and a sober tie. Over this I wore a bottle green, half length overcoat. These half length overcoats were then the fashion in Germany. It was warm and badly cut. The colour was not the one I would have chosen to go with my dark business suit, but in wartime Germany nobody cared. I had also obtained myself a fine black Homburg, Anthony Eden style. But I looked so ridiculous wearing it that I decided to go bare headed.

Robert was dressed in a converted airman's uniform which looked like a smart and serviceable blue-grey suit. The cut, perhaps, was a little avant-garde, a forerunner of the Carnaby Street style, but it looked respectably civilian. He also had a short length overcoat of dark blue. It had been made from blankets and dyed. The dye tended to run in the rain. His shirt and tie were impeccable. His boots were horrible.

'Robert,' I protested, 'I told you weeks ago to get some new boots. You can't go out in those.'

'Oh, these are fine. They're comfortable and I'm used to them. We're not travelling first class, you know!'

'But will they hold out? They looked just about finished to me.'

'Oh, don't fuss,' said Robert. 'They're in perfect shape. Just need a touch of polish.'

Robert, too, was going bare headed. He hated hats.

Each of us had a small attaché case which I had obtained from a friendly Pole. Into these we had packed our food for the journey, consisting of rock hard cakes of Lubbock's mixture, a small water bottle and a few items of clothing such as spare socks.

David Lubbock had found his way into a prison camp via the Fleet Air Arm. It was the hard way to do it as it involved surviving the most suicidal of all operations, that of flying an old and obsolete aircraft against well armed enemy warships in order to drop a torpedo from close range and at sea level. Most of those who tried it were shot down and few who were shot down survived. Those who did joined us in Germany.

Before becoming a temporary naval officer, David Lubbock had been a dietitian and certainly had many other qualifications. However, calories and food values were his speciality. He had therefore taken upon himself the task of concocting a recipe for the ideal food for an escaper. The requirements were simple. It had to be easily transportable, very long lasting, highly concentrated and provide the maximum calorific nourishment. Lubbock's mixture was thus invented and became the standard, official hard-ration for escaping prisoners.

As far as I remember, it consisted of a fused mixture of oatmeal, chocolate, sugar, glucose, raisins, milk powder, Horlicks tablets and any other high-energy goodies David could lay his hands on.

It was produced in moulds some eight by four by two inches and was hard as a rock. A half-inch slice sawed from this block contained enough calories to keep one going for a day.

David had quickly achieved official status as the escape committee's expert on the subject and, whenever it was possible, the high energy foods he required were diverted to him from Red Cross parcels. As our tunnel had arrived at its planned destination, all the escapers had been provided with their ration of Lubbock's mixture.

Robert and I paraded ourselves for critical examination and were naturally the butt of a variety of ribald remarks. The kindest comment was that we looked like a couple of out of work road sweepers. But the more serious and experienced of our audience approved. We looked the part we were playing.

My new identity for the escape was that of an Italian technician employed by Krupps, the great armament complex. My name was Tommaso Calabresi and I had been invalided out of the Italian army. My burns dated from the North African campaign where I had been one of the crew of a tank set on fire by British artillery.

Robert was to be a Frenchman, also employed by Krupps and who worked with me. Our job was to supervise the installation of new plant at various Krupps subsidiary factories all over Germany and Poland and to instruct the local workers how to operate the new machines. The whole project was thickly covered by a veil of secrecy and was top priority.

Our documents were designed to back up this story. Each of us had a German identity card, complete with our photographs and personal details. These identity cards were a big risk and their value an unknown quantity. I had designed them myself without having any original to copy from. Although they were a product of my imagination, they did give all the normal details required and had, across the corner of the photograph, the essential police stamp.

In those early days the highly efficient forging organization, which eventually became known as Dean & Dawson, did not exist. Forging documents was in its infancy and largely a matter of individual effort.

I had made our identity cards from stiff, pale blue cardboard, which had originally been a box containing some expensive note paper. The colour was unorthodox, but looked reassuringly official, long patient work with a pen and Indian ink had produced all the essential printed headings—name, nationality, date of birth, etc.—Against each of these headings our personal details were recorded in typescript.

Reproducing typescript was beyond my skill. There were no

typewriters in the camp and typescript could only be imitated by using a very thin camel hair paint brush and black paint. The precision demanded of the forger in this case called for the experienced hand of a practised painter.

There were a few amateur painters among us who had the necessary skill. Often they were not themselves active escapers, having an entirely different temperament. But they could nearly always be persuaded to help.

If the identity cards I had manufactured for Robert and myself were of doubtful value—they were palpable forgeries if viewed in a good light—the Krupp letter was a masterpiece. The heading was embossed in rich black print of impressive dimensions. It was all Indian ink and careful brushwork and the embossing had been achieved by delicately pressing out each single letter in the title with an exactly formed wooden block, cut with a penknife. The final result was imposing.

The address, telephone number and cable address were genuine, obtained from newspaper advertisements. The text of the letter, in brush-forged typescript, required all and sundry to support and assist the bearers, who were named, in their work, vital to the German war effort. It also explained the rather vague itinerary which Robert and I might be following, using the broad phrase 'at our factories or associates within the territory of the Third Reich.'

The letter terminated with a formal 'Heil Hitler' and was apparently signed by the equivalent of the Director General.

The German text had been drafted by Steve who had been educated more in German schools than in English. He was completely bilingual. The typescript was a little irregular, an inevitable feature when each letter is painted by brush. But the overall effect was of solid respectability and great authority. It was the only document I might have risked showing in broad daylight. In fact, I intended, as far as possible, to travel only by night in blacked-out trains. In the dim light of a railway carriage or by the faint glow of a policeman's torch, the forgeries would not be detectable.

We had a number of other documents which we believed were necessary. These were, in appearance, roneo-ed typewritten forms and were not difficult to reproduce if one had a delicate touch with the paint brush. One was 'Urlaubsenlaubnis' and the second a 'Reisebescheinigung.' We had a whole sheaf of these, stamped and signed by the Breslau police. All we had to do was fill in the blanks and date them to coincide with each various stage of our journey.

The draw for the order of leaving the tunnel took place next morning. The eight escape committee nominees were also there, looking, as well they might, a little sheepish and uncomfortable. The reception they got from our team was hardly welcoming and they had to suffer a great deal of partly malicious banter.

'I've dug your tunnel for you, sir. Just let me know when you want to leave and I'll be there to carry your bag.'

'Mike, you'd better go last, you're so damned fat you'll get stuck. Why didn't you tell us you wanted to escape, we could have worked off all that surplus fat for you.'

'I'm surprised to see you here, Al. Whatever happened to your pet theory that tunnelling is a waste of time?'

And so it went on in this vein. But the resentment which we had originally felt had mostly evaporated.

Among the nominees was Jimmy Buckley, head of the escape committee, all of whose days and many of whose nights were entirely devoted to organizing and controlling escape activities. Jimmy deserved a place on our tunnel, just because he was so entirely occupied in helping others to escape that he had no time to make plans for himself.

Pricky Day was another in the same category. His headaches as Senior British Officer were unending. Daily and relentlessly he fought the Germans, with the few weapons he could use. Escape was the most telling weapon he had. Coming out through the tunnel with us was both a gesture of defiance and a declaration of war.

Steve, the German expert, was another. Without him, none of the documents we were using would have been even slightly plausible. All of us who were travelling 'legitimate' with forged documents were delighted to have him with us.

And so it was with the others. They were all worthy characters who had contributed something of importance to our prisoner community. The only ones we still resented were those who were not so fully occupied that they could not have joined us earlier and got their lilywhite hands dirty.

The draw for places was made out of a hat. I drew number 13 and Robert automatically was number 14. The unlucky number did not worry me. I just would have preferred an earlier one, like 5 or 6. Eddie and Tex, who were to break the tunnel, were numbers 1 and 2. The Prince and the Duke were numbers 3 and 4. They, as was their right, had not gone into the hat. The last man out, and I felt sorry for his loneliness, was number 33. After him, the tunnel would not be used.

The Duke stepped forward to give us our final instructions.

'Right,' he commenced, 'we'll start going down half an hour after evening appell. These are your times to be at the abort.

Nos. 5 to 9 inclusive at 17.30
Nos. 10 to 14 at 17.40
Nos. 15 to 19 at 18.30
Nos. 20 to 24 at 18.20
Nos. 25 to 29 at 18.30
Nos. 30 to 33 at 18.40.

'You'll note that there is a big gap between numbers 14 and 15. That's because there isn't room for all of us inside the chamber and we've got to be sure that the early batches are already inside the tunnel before we let anyone else into the chamber.

'Now have you all registered your times? OK. Let's synchronize watches. You've got to be punctual. If anybody does not turn up at the right time, he's had it. And don't come early. The batch in front of you has to be safe inside the chamber before you appear on the scene.

'Don't approach the abort without checking the lookouts. If you can't see any stooges, the coast is clear. If you can see either Jake or Freddie here, hanging around the latrine, it's a danger signal. Beat it and try again five minutes later. Exactly five minutes. And repeat every five minutes. If there is a hold-up like this, it's up to the batch which is delayed to inform the next batch. So make your contacts.

'Any questions so far?'

He paused.

'Next, dress. You will all be dressed in your escape clothes and will wear a greatcoat over them to go to the abort. If you're going out in the greatcoat, that's fine. If you're leaving it behind, bring somebody with you to the abort to take it from you. Whoever comes with you for this purpose has to go to the abort without a greatcoat. Is that clear?

'If you're wearing combinations over your suits to protect you in the tunnel, these are to be carried and put on after you are inside the chamber. As you've already been told, these combinations have to be dyed black. Otherwise they'll be too conspicuous when you get out.

'Now luggage. If you're taking shoulder packs or attaché cases or any other luggage, you'll deliver them to the abort between 13.30 and 16.00 this afternoon. Remember the tunnel is only two foot square. Cabin trunks will not be accepted, nor bicycles. Nor, for that matter, will any unsafe parcel which might break. You've got some 300 feet of tunnel to go through and it's a very wearing process. We can't afford to risk any sort of obstruction from a broken pack. How you get your luggage to the abort is your own affair. But be clever and check with the stooges. Normally there are no goons inside the camp at this time. Make your own arrangements to space out your arrivals.

'All packs and cases will be stacked for you inside the dispersal chamber. Put your exit number on them and you'll find them all in order, ready to be picked up.

'How you get luggage through the tunnel is important. It is essential not to lose it, because it may block the tunnel.

'If you have an attaché case or briefcase which will slide easily over the sand, I suggest you wrap it up well in a vest or underpants and push it ahead of you. For a shoulder pack, the best idea would be to tie it to one of your feet, but tie it very securely, and drag it after you.

'Any questions?'

'What about my guitar, Duke? The sand will ruin it.' This was a voice from the back row.

'Any other questions?' The Duke was in a serious mood.

'Now those of you who haven't been down into the chamber or the tunnel will stay behind and get a briefing on how you go through the traps. It's easy enough, but we can't afford to have anybody drop into the fertilizer tonight.

'Another point. No smoking and dead silence in the chamber and the tunnel. The only people who may talk are Eddie at the face and whoever's on duty in the chamber, just to pass messages. Is that understood?

'When you get into the chamber, you move immediately away from the trap and wait until you're told what to do. Eddie and Tex will be opening the tunnel. The Prince and I will be backing them up. You'll move up the tunnel when you're told and you'll be lying there head-to-toe until we break. I guess that there will be about 23 of us inside the tunnel and the rest in the chamber. It may take two or three hours to break out, so breathe easy.

'Those in the chamber will work the airpump in shifts. As soon as the tunnel is open at the far end, you stop working the airpump and get into the tunnel in the right order. There'll be plenty of air once we've opened up.

'I think that's everything.

'Eddie, do you want to add something?'

Eddie took the floor.

'There's just one thing and it's important. It's not going to be easy to crawl along the tunnel fully dressed and with packs and attaché cases, especially for the bigger ones.'

His glance took in Michael Kane who was comfortably portly and Fessler who was a giant of a man.

'You fight your way along with your toes, knees and elbows. What you must not do is grab at the shoring frames to pull yourself along. If you collapse a shoring frame, you might easily drop the tunnel roof on top of yourself. Don't touch the shoring.

'The best of luck to all of you. See you in Sheppards.'

A Second Attempt

For the last time I lowered myself through the lavatory seat and jack-knifed into the dispersal chamber. The flickering orange flames of half a dozen fat lamps illuminated a scene from Dante's inferno. Enormously bulky figures, covered from head to foot in black dyed underwear, pulled on over all their clothes, were jostling one another for the little space available. Grotesque shadows danced on the sand walls. It was difficult to identify individuals, because most had black hoods pulled down over their heads.

But the commanding figure of Eddie Asselin was unmistakable. He was a tall man and no one else had those wide, square, hockey-player's shoulders. Standing near the tunnel mouth in his black overall, he was a satanic figure conferring in whispers with his lieutenants. There was no smell of brimstone, but the overwhelming taint of the great pit was appropriate.

I crawled over to him.

'Good luck, Eddie. I hope you make it home. I'll buy you dinner at Prunier's in a week's time.'

'That'll be the day.' Eddie smiled briefly. He was tense and nervous.

'Well, so long, Tommy. I'm off. See that I get plenty of air, I've still got a lot of work to do.'

He disappeared into the tunnel.

With a rapidity which surprised me, the chamber emptied as, one after another, the escapers crawled away. Robert and I stayed behind to work the airpump.

I looked at my watch. The next batch would be coming into the chamber in five minutes. Then we could go. The Duke's timing, I reflected, had been remarkably accurate.

When we had been relieved at the airpump, we collected our attaché cases and started the long crawl down the tunnel. It was pitch black and I did not see the boots of the man ahead of me until I bumped into them. He kicked gently, indicating he did not want to be crowded. I kicked to warn Robert that it was time to stop crawling. The air was foul. The airpump was supplying the face, but little oxygen found its way back to our position, mid-way along the tunnel.

My shoulders were touching the tunnel walls on each side. If I raised my head, it hit the roof. I felt the first shivers of claustrophobia.

Since my experience in the asparagus bed, I had been just plain afraid of tunnels. But this tunnel, which was the safest and most solidly constructed I had ever been down, had never frightened me unduly. I had always been able to suppress and dissimulate my fears.

I tried not to think of the tons of sand above me, supported only by flimsy pieces of wood. But the closed-in feeling was growing. The absolute darkness, the physical impossibility of making any but the slightest movement and, worst of all, the knowledge that any retreat was completely blocked by the long line of men lying behind me, all these sensations were beginning to strain my self-control to its limits. As I would have to lie where I was for another two or three hours, I knew that I had to get a firm hold on myself or I was in for a very bad time.

Fortunately for me, the spell of claustrophobia passed quickly. The familiar touch of the wooden shoring frames and of the damp sand on which I was laying again became ordinary and reassuring sensations. My exaggerated fears dissolved and, after a while, I was able to doze with my head resting on my forearms.

It was a long, long wait. At ten o'clock we were all still lying in the same position and I was beginning to worry about what was happening up at the face. Until then a complete silence had been observed but now discipline was beginning to break. From behind me whispered messages were being passed from man to man.

'What the hell's gone wrong?'

'When are we going to break?'

'For Christ's sake, hurry it up or the last ones won't be out before daylight.'

Only one message came back from the face and it was rudely unhelpful.

'——well shut up and keep pumping.'

After that there was complete silence for half an hour. I could imagine the difficulties confronting Eddie.

Breaking open a tunnel is a precise art which calls for a special technique. Eddie had brought the tunnel to within an estimated three feet of the surface. To have come any closer would have been dangerous. A heavy footed goon or a farmer's horse and cart might have collapsed it.

The task of opening the tunnel involved digging vertically upwards for three feet and disposing of the sand. As it was not possible to pass the sand back along the tunnel, Eddie had prepared a dip pit in the floor of the tunnel, right at the face, which was designed to accommodate all the spoil.

In a tunnel with a cross section of two feet by two, one foot of linear progress in an hour was an excellent average. Eddie would therefore need at least three hours to dig to the surface.

Digging vertically upwards was more difficult and uncomfortable than digging horizontally, so the figure of three hours should be increased. In addition, the vertical exit shaft had to be fitted with some robust wooden shoring, or it would have collapsed under the wear and tear of thirty-three bodies scrambling their way out.

It was also possible that Eddie's estimate of the depth of the tunnel had been low and that there was, in fact, more than three feet to excavate. This would require more time and would also give rise to new difficulties if the amount of spoil produced should exceed the capacity of the pit.

I imagined that Eddie was facing all or any of these difficulties. But I was not very concerned. As long as we were out before midnight, my plans would still work out.

It was while I was thinking of Eddie's problems that a sudden gush of warm stale air passed over me coming from the chamber. It could only mean one thing, the tunnel was open.

A few minutes later, I lost contact with the boots in front of me. We were moving. Already Eddie must be outside.

As I crawled forward, I smelled the fresh air. It was now coming back from the face in a strong current. I filled my lungs, breathing deeply. There was no need to pass any message back to the chamber. Everybody could now smell the cold air of freedom.

Progress forward was in a series of short jerks. As one man left the tunnel, the whole line crawled forward. Then there was a pause while the next escaper negotiated the vertical shaft leading to the night sky and got his bearings before slipping away. Each time the long horizontal queue stopped I counted, knowing that another was away and my turn was coming closer.

It was taking them a long time to get away, nearly three minutes per man. That meant about forty minutes before it would be my turn and another hour before the last man was clear. I hoped the luck would hold. Subconsciously, I was waiting for the sound of a rifle shot.

I worked my way forward in short bursts of crawling until, according to my count, there were only two ahead of me. Then the boots in front of me moved away from my touch and it was my turn, next. I followed the boots into the darkness. Three minutes, I thought, and I will be away too.

There was intense but uncannily silent commotion in front of me. The boots were working frantically, kicking sand into my face. Then the body in front relaxed and lay still.

'I'm stuck.' It was a desperate whisper. 'I can't move at all.'

I inched forward and took a boot in each hand.

'Try now. I'll give you purchase. Kick as hard as you like.'

I braced myself as best I could and the boots strained against my hands in the darkness. I was pushing forward with all the strength I had. There was a violent kick and the boots moved away from my hold. After that all was silence. I wriggled my way forward.

The tunnel had suddenly narrowed. My bottom was touching the roof and my shoes were scrabbling for leverage. But I could not move forward. Without being able to raise my bottom, I could get no purchase for my toes. I too was stuck, right at the exit.

'Keep calm,' I told myself. 'Keep real cool.'

I relaxed and Robert, who was behind me, pushed his attaché case hard up against my feet.

Struggling violently, I managed to turn over so that I was lying on my back. Now, with my knees slightly raised, I could get some purchase for my heels. I shoved forward with all the force I had, moved and kept moving. My head came up against a solid wall of sand and above me I could see a bright patch of sky framed in the exact square of the exit shaft.

I twisted myself into a sitting position and, after many contortions, was crouching in the tunnel shaft with my head just level with the ground. My attaché case was within reach at the bottom of the shaft.

Outside the blaze of light was blinding. The perimeter lights round the barbed wire fence bathed the terrain in a harsh, unforgiving brilliance. It was like being in the middle of a fair ground.

I could see a sentry patrolling the wire. His rifle was slung over his shoulder and he had his back to me. Twenty yards away was a ditch. I slipped out of the tunnel and made for the ditch, flatter to the ground than any snake has ever been.

Once safely in the ditch, I paused. I wanted to breathe the clean air of Poland and to savour to the full the rare pleasure of looking at my prison camp from the outside. Again I was free to run like a fox. But this time I knew where I was going and believed that I could keep ahead of the hounds. In any case, it was going to be a good run.

My eyes had re-adjusted, after the pitch dark of the tunnel, and now the country around me did not seem to be so brilliantly lit. The camp itself still looked like Piccadilly Circus, but the fields in front of me, which stretched for quarter of a mile to a line of dark woods, were mostly in shadow. No sentry would see a crawling figure.

There was a rustle and a thump as Robert dropped into the ditch beside me. We did not dare even to whisper. The sentry's beat was less than twenty yards away.

I set off for the woods in the best deer-stalker style, with my head and bottom well down, using my elbows and toes for propulsion. It was the first time I had tried this method of locomotion across plough and I hope never to have to do it again. Not only is progress frustratingly slow when one is in the first flush of excitement after a successful escape, but it is also remarkably exhausting as well as being a very muddy process.

I persevered for a hundred yards and then raised my bottom and started crawling on hands and knees. Before I had covered another fifty yards in this fashion, I was overtaken by Robert who was moving across the plough like a demented turtle, propelled by all four thrashing limbs.

At the edge of the wood, Robert was waiting for me.

'Come on,' he said impatiently. 'We've a long way to go yet.' This set the tone for the rest of the night's march. Me tired and lagging, Robert eager and energetic. I knew then that I was going to have trouble holding him back to my slower pace.

But Robert's impatience was mostly nervousness and I talked him into a five minutes rest. I badly needed it to get my breath back after the exertions of getting stuck in the tunnel and the crawl across the plough. While we rested, I stripped off my protecting underwear and threw it into the wood. In the morning the Germans would find thirty-three pairs of excellent British woollen combinations among the trees.

We had picked a moonless night for the escape and the sky was overcast. I got out my tiny collar-stud compass and selected a course. We wanted to be in Bromberg by dawn and had a little more than twenty miles to cover. Our plan was to march northeast by compass until we hit the railway line and then to walk along the tracks, which would lead us directly to Bromberg. We set out into the darkness.

Walking on a compass course at midnight across a completely dark and unknown terrain is something which only happens to escaped prisoners. I suppose that with practice one could develop a technique, but we fell into ditches, walked into fences, tripped over logs and startled a number of animals out of their wits. Frequently we frightened ourselves.

Quite early in our progress, Robert fell into a pond. He emerged cursing and wet from the chest downwards. Thereafter, he started walking faster than ever and I lagged further behind. But I had the compass and he had to wait for me whenever he got too far ahead. I felt sorry for him. The night was freezing cold.

We were on a course which passed a little to the north of the prison compound. Its bright lights remained visible for hours and were a constant spur. When we had left those lights behind, we felt we would be safe.

We hit the railway about two hours after we had started marching. We were in a sorry state, bruised, scratched and exhausted. Robert was nearly freezing to death after his ducking in the pond. But our first target had been achieved. That cheered us.

For a while the going along the side of the railway track was good and we marched briskly, averaging at least four miles an hour. Then the path gave out and we were forced to walk on the sleepers in the middle of the track.

The distance between the sleepers did not correspond to a normal stride and the result was that we had to constrain ourselves to a short, mincing toe-to-toe pace, which was both tiring and slow. Every now and again the distance between sleepers varied and one of us would miss his footing and fall. It was painful progress.

Long before dawn, I was exhausted. In spite of five-minute rest periods in each hour, I was lagging farther and farther behind Robert. He was alternating between fury at having to wait for me and kindness in offering to carry my case.

And so it went on, endlessly, until we came to the bridge where the railway crossed a canal.

This was a hazard I had foreseen and it was marked on my map with a red circle. Our information, inside the camp, had been that all such bridges were guarded. We approached the bridge with great caution and lay down to listen. There was no sound of steel-shod boots.

After a few minutes blind vigil, we decided to risk crossing the bridge, rather than swimming the canal. Robert volunteered to go first. He took his boots off and went cautiously forward in stockinged feet. There was no alarm and I followed him at a discreet interval.

The bridge was unguarded.

Two

Long before dawn it was obvious that we had no hope of being in Bromberg in time to catch the six o'clock train to Schneidmuhl, which had been our original plan. We eased the killing pace we had kept up all night and took a long rest. When we had washed and shaved in a stagnant pond and brushed the mud from our boots and clothes, we walked openly into Bromberg down the main road. It was half-past seven and broad daylight. The town was bustling with life.

This was our first public appearance and we were painfully self-conscious. It seemed as if everyone must recognize us immediately as escaped prisoners. Our confidence was not increased when the

sole of Robert's boot became unhinged and started to make a loud
flapping noise with every step he took. I was furiously angry with
him. I had told him to get new boots.

Robert tied his sole back in place with a piece of bootlace and
we went on. The streets were getting more crowded and we were
getting more nervous.

'Don't forget the drill,' said Robert.

The drill we had planned, if we met anybody on the street,
was to appear to be conversing animatedly in German. Robert,
the expert, had coached me in what to say.

We turned the corner and immediately saw a group of Germans
coming towards us on the same sidewalk. There was no way of
avoiding them. As they came within range, I was supposed to
say in a firm confident voice 'Meiner Meinung nach . . .' and
then fade as the Germans got out of earshot. It was a very collo-
quial phrase which meant 'In my opinion . . .' . I could pro-
nounce it with a very passable accent.

I drew a deep breath and opened my mouth but only managed
to produce a squeak. I had stage fright. The Germans walked by
without glancing at us.

It was Robert's turn to be furious and he gave me hell for the
next hundred yards.

'Don't worry, Robert,' I apologized. 'I'll get it right next time.'

The opportunity came only too soon. As another group of Germans approached, I got ready. When they were three yards away
I went into my act.

'Meiner Meinung nach . . .'

This time the phrase came out in a booming shout which
echoed up the street. All the Germans immediately looked at me
with great interest and stopped walking. They were curious to
hear just what opinion I wanted to proclaim so loudly. Unfortunately, my phrase was not meant to be completed and I had no
opinion to offer. I could only glare at them indignantly and hurry
past.

'You bloody fool, Robert,' I swore. 'Why the hell didn't you
say something?'

'You didn't have to shout at the top of your voice, did you? Anyway, if I'd said anything it would have made matters worse.'

We were now arguing heatedly in English, oblivious to where

we were. Suddenly conscious of the stupidity of our behaviour, we pulled ourselves together and hurried on. Tacitly, we agreed to abandon that particular gambit.

The station hall was crowded and it was heartening to see that there were others almost as badly dressed as ourselves. In that crowd we would not be conspicuous. But it also looked just the sort of place which might be swarming with plain clothes police. It was a dangerous place to hang around.

'I'll go and get the tickets,' I whispered to Robert. 'Then we'll go and hide in the lavatory.'

My getting the tickets, when Robert was more qualified, was partly bravado. But I also wanted to prove to myself that I was capable of uttering the simple German phrases necessary.

There was a long queue at the ticket window and, to my relief, nobody in front of me was asked for any documents. When my turn came, I spoke clearly and distinctly and two tickets were pushed towards me. I paid the amount asked and returned in triumph to Robert.

We found the public lavatory and, for the expenditure of ten pfennigs each, were able to lock ourselves into two adjacent cubicles. We intended to stay for an hour until our train was due at quarter past nine.

Lavatory seats in Polish railway stations have a strictly functional design. They are not built for comfort and I found it impossible to take a nap, which I would dearly have loved to do. Instead I opened my attaché case on my knees and started to eat some of my escape rations. I was very hungry.

Suddenly the door of my cubicle rattled briefly and was flung wide open. I stared aghast at a fat, dirty woman who stood there with a bucket and mop. She gave me a contemptuous look and slammed the door shut again. I was more embarrassed that I had my trousers up than I would have been if they had been down. It seemed to be a highly suspicious way of occupying a public lavatory.

To my horror, I heard exactly the same process being repeated with Robert. As quickly as we could we abandoned our cubicles and slunk away shame-faced. We passed through the ticket barrier without encountering any problem and sat down on a bench to await our train.

It was a tense period of waiting. In all probability our tunnel would be discovered soon after the morning roll call at nine o'clock. The first logical step for the Germans to take would be to put an immediate watch on Bromberg station. I prayed that the train would not be late.

I was watching a very smart young man as he walked up and down the platform. He was wearing a neat blue-grey raincoat, carrying an attaché case and had a folded newspaper tucked under his arm. He looked like a superior bank clerk. There was something vaguely familiar about him, but I did not recognize him until he passed close to us.

It was Tony Barber.

Tony recognized me at the same time and very deliberately looked the other way. But I could not resist getting up to greet him. His look of panic when he saw me coming should have discouraged me, but I was enjoying the moment too much. I gave him a nicely casual Nazi salute and greeted him.

'Heil Hitler,' I said.

He was forced to respond in the same way and to return my salute.

I then shook hands with him and told him how delighted I was to see him.

'Go to hell,' said Tony. He was shaking with anger.

'And stay away from me. You look like a tramp.'

With great self-control, he shook hands again and bowed himself away. When the train came in he made a point of boarding it a considerable distance from us.

The journey to Schneidemuhl was long and uneventful. I had a corner seat and slept most of the way. When I was not sleeping, I kept my eyes shut. I wanted to avoid any risk of being drawn into conversation.

When we got off the train at Schneidemuhl, I sent Robert to buy two tickets to Kustrin, our next planned stop. I checked the departures board and found that there was a train leaving in two hours time. It was now noon and the last thing we wished to do was to loiter around the station. We set off down the road at a brisk walk, trying to look as if we knew where we were going.

Tony Barber soon overtook us and we walked together until we were clear of the town. Tony had completely recovered his good temper. There was nobody about and we talked freely and happily, relating our experiences of the night before. We were all in high spirits. Soon Tony left us to return to the station. He was taking a different route, aiming at the Baltic coast. He had some rather mysterious plan for getting to the island of Bornholm. We wished him luck, sorry to see him go.

We timed our return to the station just fifteen minutes before our train was due. We presented our tickets and went straight through to the platform. I had a theory that we would be safer there than in the waiting room or the hall.

Robert and I were strolling slowly from one end of the platform to the other, conversing quietly in English when there was nobody near us. Our meeting with Tony had done us all good. Even Robert, who was never an optimist, was now beginning to think that we might be successful.

As we made a turn at the end of the long platform I saw we were about to be intercepted by two Germans. They were conspicuously well dressed, with excellent warm overcoats, Homburgs and the inevitable black briefcases. They might have been taken for two prosperous business men, but I had no doubt at all that they were policemen. We were greeted politely and asked for our documents.

I suppose we both remained outwardly calm as we started fumbling for our papers. But inside me I was feeling sick with disappointment. In broad daylight our papers would immediately be seen to be crude forgeries. And then there was our carefully prepared story. As I went over it in my mind, it seemed so far fetched, so lacking in credibility that I thought that Robert might as well start telling Grimm's fairy tales to these two professionals.

But I should not have doubted Robert. He was now proving that my original judgement of his particular qualities had been entirely correct. With a self-assurance and precision which was impressive, he had started to talk. Within seconds he was dominating the conversation, while the two Germans listened with growing respect and attention.

Hearing Robert re-tell our much rehearsed story, it suddenly sounded genuine, normal and convincing. The way in which he hinted that our work for Krupps was both highly secret and of vital importance to the war effort was a masterpiece of apparent under-

statement and suggestion. I was amazed to see that both policemen were following every word with intense interest.

While talking, Robert was shuffling our miserable documents
in his hands, as worried as I was about letting the policemen look
closely at them. Then he boldly played our ace, the Krupp letter.
This was an excellent forgery, but I did not think it would survive
close examination in good light by a professional. Like all our
documents it was only meant to be produced in the dim light of
a war time train.

When he handed over the Krupp letter, Robert did not pause
for a moment. He kept talking. The two policemen read the letter
together, still impelled to listen to what Robert was saying. I suddenly realized that they were reading the text of the letter and
not examining it as a document.

The letter was politely handed back. It had been accepted as
genuine.

Robert now flashed our identity cards in front of the Germans
but they waved them aside.

'Where are you going now?' asked one of the policemen. There
was a genuine interest and curiosity in his voice which was not at
all menacing.

'We have the most urgent job to do at Kustrin. I expect we'll
be working all night. There has been the most serious hold up in
production. We need that material for the Russian front. Production must be started again by tomorrow.'

As he said this, Robert was declaiming. I wanted to clap.

The senior policeman extracted a card from his pocketbook and
wrote a name on the back of it. He gave it to Robert.

'If you need any help at all,' he said most earnestly, 'telephone
the Gestapo headquarters and ask for this man. Don't hesitate.
My name is on the card. Just tell him that I sent you.'

The two policemen raised their hats, bowed stiffly and walked
away.

My admiration for Robert knew no bounds. I wanted to buy
him a brandy in the station restaurant. He deserved it and I
needed it. But our train was coming in.

It was already dark when we arrived at Kustrin. We had slept
fitfully during the journey and had no adventures. Our next stop
was to be Berlin and this excited us greatly. But we were tired. It

was now more than twenty-four hours since we had disappeared
through the lavatory seat and we had had very little rest during
that period.

At Kustrin station we went through our now established routine.
Robert bought tickets for Berlin while I studied the departure
board. The news was bad. There was no train to Berlin before
two o'clock in the morning.

Again we walked away from the station, holding a southerly
heading and aiming for the open country where we might find
somewhere safe to sleep. The night was cold and the shelter of a
barn full of warm hay would have been welcome. But such comforts are not easy to find in the dark and we had to be content
with a copse of trees and sparse undergrowth. It was far too
cold to sleep, so we ate, smoked and suffered. We were both relieved when the time came to make our way back to the station.

The walk back through the town was dangerous. It was nearly
one o'clock in the morning and all honest people were long ago
in bed. Anybody we might meet was bound to be a policeman or
a drunk, encounters we preferred to avoid. Twice we heard footsteps in the distance and made detours, but we reached the station without incident. There were hundreds of people travelling
to Berlin that night and the waiting rooms were crowded.

We failed to get seats on the train and stood in the corridor
just outside the lavatory. This enabled us to take turns in locking
ourselves inside the smelly lavatory cell, where we tried to sleep.
Two sharp raps on the door from the one outside was the signal
for the other to emerge and let some impatient German relieve
himself.

When the police came we were not even concerned. The light
in the corridor was so dim that all documents, forged or genuine,
looked alike. We presented ours and received them back without
comment. I was highly elated. It proved my theory that, as long
as daytime journeys were avoided, train travel presented few dangers for the escaping prisoners.

The great Schlesischer Bahnhof in Berlin was an enormous
cavern, dark and smoky. Even at that early hour, just before dawn,
it was thronged with hurrying people. Soldiers were everywhere
and military police stood guard at every platform. The biggest
danger we ran was that of being arrested as suspected deserters.

We intended to spend the whole day in Berlin and the thought excited us. We both wanted to see the city but we were so tired that the prospect of having to remain on our feet all day appalled us. At that moment twelve hours in bed was our idea of heaven.

The Schlesischer Bahnhof was an unhealthy place for us, being the principal station for eastern Germany, Poland and the Russian front. We took the S-Bahn to Charlottenburg and found our station of departure which had the attractive name of Bahnhof-am-Zoo. From there we would leave for Stendhal immediately it was dark.

The first thing we did at the Bahnhof-am-Zoo was to buy our tickets. By now this procedure was practically a religion with us. I believed that it was always essential to have our tickets for the next stage of the journey in our pockets. It justified our presence at the station and gave plausibility to our story if we were questioned.

Greatly daring, we went into the crowded station restaurant. While we were waiting for a place, we listened carefully to what others were ordering. It seemed that one could obtain unlimited amounts of beer and that there was also one dish on the menu which did not call for the presentation of food coupons. This was called the Stammtisch and was a large bowl of thick vegetable soup. We eventually found seats at a table sloppily wet with beer, in the company of half a dozen Germans. Their proximity made us uncomfortable but did not spoil our appetite.

We wolfed down our bowl of soup and had three glasses of beer each. We lingered for nearly two hours over our beer, enjoying the warm, stale atmosphere.

All the morning we walked round Berlin, occasionally taking a short rest on a park bench. At noon we returned to the station restaurant for more beer and another bowl of soup. Then, wearily, we set out again. We did not dare remain stationary in any one place. We only felt safe when we were walking.

It was the longest afternoon of my life. Not only did we have to keep walking, but we also had to appear to be walking with a purpose. Our train to Stendhal did not leave until seven in the evening and we thought it prudent not to return to the station before six o'clock. There was no escape from our fate. We just had to keep moving. I was in such a state of exhaustion when we returned to the Bahnhof-am-Zoo that I could not remember a single feature of the city we had been promenading all day.

The train to Stendhal was a local one, stopping at nearly every station on the way. The crowd on the platform was so dense that we had to fight our way aboard and stand in the corridor for the whole journey. We gathered that the nightly exodus from Berlin, to avoid the bombing, accounted for the popularity of this train. Twice in an hour the train stopped and all the lights went out. There was an air raid in progress. Once we heard the out-of-phase rumbling of formations of heavy bombers overhead.

The train was very late at Stendhal, where we disembarked. It was now near midnight and I was walking like an automaton, in a daze of weariness. My spell in hospital had weakened me more than I expected. I can only assume that we found a place to hide and sleep somewhere out in the country because my memory is a blank until our arrival at Hanover the following night.

On Hanover station we met Steve, who greeted us warmly. As he had been largely responsible for drafting the miraculous Krupp letter, he was most interested to hear of our adventures. He looked like a thoroughly respectable business man and, as he was completely bi-lingual in German, he was full of confidence. Although he was a little ashamed of being seen in the company of two tramps, he insisted on buying us beer and another Stammtisch. We spent a happy hour in his company and then left the station. He stayed behind in the warmth of the second-class waiting room, discounting the possibility of a police check. I believe he was arrested there.

There was an express train, a D-Zug, leaving for Cologne soon after midnight, which was due to arrive at five o'clock in the morning. Robert and I had argued for a long time before deciding to take it. By doing so we would be breaking our 200 kilometre rule. So far, all our journeys had been less than that distance, but Cologne lay nearly 300 kilometres away. It also meant travelling second class and our appearance proclaimed us to be third-class citizens. Steve told us that he had had no trouble travelling second class, but he looked the part.

What finally convinced me to take the express was the fact that it arrived in Cologne before daylight. There was no other way of completing the journey in darkness. Arriving at five o'clock, we

could catch the half past six workmen's train to Aachen which, I
had been told, was never checked by the police. From Aachen,
we would take a tram ride towards Eupen and the Belgian frontier.
It was a very tidy programme which avoided the danger of having
to stay long in Cologne and meant that we could be over the
frontier the same evening.

Again Robert and I walked endlessly round another city, looking at everything and seeing nothing. Automatically we were walking briskly and with a purpose. Never did we hesitate or loiter.
We returned to the station in time to spend half an hour in the
public lavatory, where we washed, shaved, changed our shirts and
cleaned our shoes. We were now second-class citizens.

The comfort of our upholstered second-class seats was celestial
bliss. Our tired muscles began to relax and we could have been
in a deep sleep within minutes. But both of us could not sleep at
the same time. This was practically the last stage of our journey
inside Germany and we had no intention of being careless.

'You sleep first, Tommy,' suggested Robert. 'I'll wake you in
a couple of hours' time.'

Robert was being very generous and I did not have the strength
to argue. I was asleep before the train left the station.

I awoke a long time later when Robert shook me. He was talking calmly and confidently to a policeman. Half asleep, I showed
my identity card and the policeman went away. He had inspected
our documents in the faint glow of a tired torch.

'You'd better get some sleep now, Robert. I'll wake you before
we get to Cologne.'

I was feeling very much refreshed.

The train passed through Hamm at about three o'clock in the
morning and not long afterwards came to a complete halt. We
remained motionless for two hours and all the time I was getting
more impatient and nervous. But we were in the Ruhr area and
heavy air raids on the German industrial complexes there were a
nightly occurrence. I should have taken it into my calculations.
As it was, every minute we lost brought us much nearer to all
the dangers of arriving in Cologne in daylight.

When eventually the train rumbled over the long Rhine bridge,
the sun was already above the horizon. I thought back to the
last time I had crossed that river, thirteen months before, when

Bill Joyce and I were on our way into captivity. I hoped fervently that I would never have to cross the Rhine again.

The city of Cologne lay immediately the other side of the river and the train was now slowing perceptibly. This was the moment the police chose to come back. Suddenly, there was a policeman in the compartment.

Confidently, Robert started to tell our story, but was abruptly cut short.

'Your identity cards.'

We had no alternative but to hand them over. The German studied them, glanced briefly at our faces and then put them in his pocket. All the other passengers in the compartment were treated in the same manner and, except for a suspicious looking individual in the corner seat, all had their documents returned to them.

It looked very bad for us.

Robert made another effort.

'May we have our documents, please. We have very little time to make our connection and our work is most important.'

He spoke haughtily, in the tone of a man very sure of himself. He was waving the Krupp letter under the policeman's nose.

'Später,' said the policeman with chilling indifference. He left the compartment.

After a few seconds, I moved into the corridor followed by Robert. The train was now running slowly into the station.

'Out on the wrong side and run for it,' I whispered.

Robert nodded agreement and we made our way towards the end of the carriage. Another policeman was guarding the doors.

'Back to your seats,' he ordered.

Impotent and worried, we sat on our second-class seats. We disembarked with the other passengers and immediately the police segregated us. With a motley crowd of half a dozen individuals who had also been picked out on the train, we were escorted to the police office on the station.

There we stuck obstinately to our story, still hoping to talk our way out of trouble. Robert put on a superlative act, insisting on being allowed to telephone to Krupps. But there was something wrong with the atmosphere. The policemen were not taking us seriously. They seemed to be highly amused.

'Search them,' ordered the sergeant.

And that was the end.

We might have produced a plausible story to account for the sticky cakes of concentrated food which were our escape rations, but there was no way of explaining our Players cigarettes or the collection of maps.

The sergeant behind the desk was laughing hugely at our discomfiture. It was obvious that he had guessed who we were.

'So you are the escaped air force officers from Schubin,' he announced with great satisfaction. 'We know all about you. You've caused a lot of trouble. Every policeman in the country has been looking for you. We did not expect you to come so far.'

There was no hostility, no bullying. The atmosphere was excited and triumphant. They had captured two well-advertised criminals and would get the credit for it. We were the only miserable people in the room.

After that all was anti-climax. We knew we were beaten and suddenly our exhaustion enveloped us like a wet blanket. The endless jokes at our expense did not provoke any reaction. It was a relief to be locked in the cells.

The next day we were taken to the Gestapo headquarters at Wuppertal. The paternoster lift in the building fascinated us. It was an endless chain of wooden cubicles which never stopped. There were no doors. As the cubicle came by the aperture on each floor, one jumped in or jumped out, one at a time.

Robert and I had the same thought. If we could step out on the wrong floor, we could run for it and create a remarkable pandemonium right inside the Gestapo headquarters, even if our chances of escaping were probably nil.

But our guards quickly disillusioned us. We were to step out on the sixth floor. On the seventh floor a policeman was waiting to shoot us if we were still in the lift. There were also guards on all the other floors.

The ceremony with which we were ushered into the office on the sixth floor was typically fascist.

The senior of our guards knocked firmly on the door.

'Herein.'

He threw open the door and immediately went into a stiff Nazi salute, clicking his heels neatly as he did so.

In a sustained shout he made some sort of report which I failed to follow. Then he turned about and screamed orders at our two escorts.

We were marched in.

The man behind the desk must have been in his early fifties. He had a pale, ascetic face, with sleek hair, slightly greying, and an aquiline nose. His mouth was thin and his ears rather prominent. He was smoking a cigarette in a long ebony holder.

He dismissed all the guards and we were alone. He did not ask us to sit down. Behind him on the wall were portraits of Hitler and Himmler. On his enormous polished desk was a small silver standard with the Nazi flag. The carpet under our feet had a deep expensive pile. He was obviously a very senior man in the organization.

'I have some questions to ask you.' His English was nearly faultless. 'Let me warn you that I expect completely truthful answers. Your situation is very serious. The penalty for espionage is death.'

He stubbed out his cigarette as he said this, looking sideways at us to see the effect of his words.

I caught Robert's eye. We did not need to speak. We knew exactly how to handle this man. If this was the Gestapo, the so much feared secret police, it was going to be a pleasure for us to cut this pompous, self-important individual down to size.

Throughout Germany and the occupied countries, the mere name of the Gestapo induced terror. The Gestapo was used to dealing with frightened people and fear was one of their prime weapons. But Robert and I, secure in our belief that the Geneva Convention protected us from all but a formal punishment of 21 days in the cells, found the man in front of us melodramatic and slightly ridiculous. Deliberately and with a very nicely balanced coordination, we started to bait him. I was so pleased he spoke English, it permitted me to get into the act instead of leaving it all to Robert.

'How did you get out of the prison camp?'

Robert took this one.

'The gate was open and we just strolled through by mistake.'

'The gate is always guarded.'

It was my turn.

'We didn't see any guards.'

'There are always guards.'

It was Robert's turn.

'Perhaps they were drunk. You know how German soldiers are.'

After a few minutes we had the Gestapo chief turning his head automatically from one to the other of us for each successive question.

Suddenly he realized what was happening and made an effort to regain control.

'That's enough,' he said sharply. 'I want the truth. Answer my questions correctly or you will be punished.'

Robert and I nodded encouragingly.

'How did you travel?'

'We had a taxi waiting outside the gate.'

'Which taxi?'

He said it sharply, as if he had believed us. Then he saw his mistake and took a long, slow breath.

'How did you travel?' he repeated. He was addressing me.

'It's his turn to answer,' I said, pointing to Robert.

He made a great effort to control himself and turned to Robert. 'Well?' he said.

'I didn't hear the question,' said Robert. 'Would you repeat it?'

Robert walked forward and sat on the edge of the desk. I thought the man was going to have apoplexy.

'How did you travel,' he said with slow deliberate emphasis, spacing each word.

'Why ask such a stupid question?' I answered. 'You know we were arrested on the train.'

I joined Robert on the desk.

With a violent sweep of his hand, he drove us away.

'Stand up when you answer my questions.'

We retreated to our previous positions.

'Where did you get your money?'

'We paid by cheque,' said Robert.

'Where did you get your food?'

'We brought our own,' I answered. 'German food is so revolting.'

We kept this up for nearly an hour before he lost his temper completely.

He screamed at us for perhaps half a minute and then, suddenly, was completely calm. But his face was white and his hands were trembling.

'You arrogant British.' He was talking quietly. 'You think you are going to win the war.'

Robert and I nodded enthusiastically.

'We are going to destroy you. I don't think you realize how impertinent you have been. I don't think you know that I have the power to put you in jail for the rest of your lives. Perhaps you don't realize,' his voice dropped to a whisper, 'that I could shoot both of you where you stand and never answer for it. Do you think that the Geneva Convention means anything to us?'

For the first time, I was scared. There was a menace in that whispering voice which I recognized as real. That man had immense power and could have carried out his threat with complete impunity.

Suddenly he rang all the bells on his desk. Half a dozen thugs rushed through the door and we were thrown bodily into the passage.

'English pigs,' he screamed and the door slammed.

Later that evening we left Wuppertal with an escort of four Gestapo men. The journey back to Schubin took two days by a long roundabout route, which avoided Berlin. Our Gestapo guards were determined to enjoy themselves, this was a holiday for them. They drank beer every hour of the night and day, sang songs in chorus and played cards.

Robert and I were very careful not to make any suspicious move. We had got the very clear message that any one of these men would shoot us happily and efficiently if given the slightest excuse. We abandoned all thoughts of escape. Instead we accepted their beer and shared our cigarettes with them. It was better than a bullet in the back.

We were the last arrivals in the cells at Schubin. All the others, except for Jimmy Buckley and Thomson, had already been recaptured. We did not know it at the time, but Jimmy Buckley and his companion were dead.

We finished our sentence just in time to pack our belongings and join the move back to Sagan.

Walk Out

BACK in the sandpit of Sagan, all of us who had escaped from the Schubin tunnel found we had achieved, almost overnight, a new status. Now we were all recognized as experts. Even the old Warburg hands, who knew everything and had a painful superiority complex, were grudgingly willing to let us play with the big boys.

It was flattering to be asked for one's advice on the widest variety of problems—which route to take, what documents to carry, how to disguise a tunnel trap or whether some harebrained scheme had a slender chance. Invitations to join new tunnel projects were so numerous that we could pick and choose. We had come a long way since our wet-eared apprentice days at Spangenberg a year before. We had been accepted by the establishment.

This was very gratifying but, as the more determined and rebellious of us realized, it had its dangers. Recognition by the establishment we had earned, absorption we feared. A restricting blanket of orthodoxy would not help us to get out of Stalag Luft III, which had been designed as an escape-proof camp, and very nearly was that. Convention and conservatism would rapidly blunt the sharp edge of individual invention.

I decided to play the establishment rules while keeping my own council. Between April and July 1943 I spent all my time digging tunnels for recreation and exercise. As soon as the ferrets discovered one tunnel, I joined a new one. It was a long hot summer and I preferred to spend my time in the cool dampness underground. Meanwhile I was thinking during my waking hours and dreaming while I slept of an original way out of the camp.

I had a half-formed idea which I discussed with nobody, so complicated and devious was it, involving so many stages, so many intrigues, such delicate manoeuvring, that it could only be done in the strictest, loneliest secrecy. But I was convinced that no conventional plan would get me out of Stalag III. Tunnelling, I was certain, was a waste of time. The Abwehr were discovering tunnels at the rate of two a week and few of them had a life of more than ten days.

The essence of my idea was that the escape should be from the Vorlager and not from the East Compound itself. The Vorlager lay immediately outside the main gate of our East Compound and, technically considered, it was just as impregnable as our rectangle of sand. The machine guns on the towers and the guards rifles were just as lethal. But it did not contain any RAF prisoners and that made a big difference. There was nobody inside the Vorlager who wanted to escape. There was no convincing reason for the defences to be always alert.

There were prisoners living inside the Vorlager—the Russians. There were perhaps forty of them, a tragic jetsam from the East front. Their problem was survival from one day to the next. The food the Germans gave them was enough to sustain life at a steadily diminishing level. In truth, they were being very slowly starved. Whether or not they plotted or planned escape, I did not know. The important fact, from the narrowly selfish aspect of my own plans, was that the Germans did not credit them with the energy to escape and were contemptuous of them.

These men were being deliberately destroyed by a long drawn out and carefully phased programme of cruelty. Each one of them, almost without exception, had once gloried in his great physical strength, which had been his chief pride and the mainspring of his personality as a soldier of the Red Army. Now they were doomed men, destined to die painfully of malnutrition unless the war ended before their strength failed them. For their escape was a physical impossibility. I did not then know whether their morale had been affected.

To our comfortable British consciences, they were a nasty embarrassment. It was easier to pretend they were not there, much as one crosses the street to avoid passing a begger. Their offence was that they did not fit into the rightful scheme of things, but provoked uncomfortable thoughts. Towards us the Germans behaved themselves with a disciplined formality and correctness. They liked us to think they were gentlemen and we were often stupid enough to think this way. The starving Russians, moving their emaciated bodies with painful slowness, did not fit the pattern and it was easier to ignore their existence than to re-adjust our ideas to grim reality.

In those days we were innocent and ignorant, sheltered and protected by our barbed wire fences. We had never heard of Belsen, Buchenwald or Dachau and knew nothing of the desperate plight of the Jews and the other declared enemies of Hitler's Third Reich.

I still remember one single horrifying sight of reality, glimpsed in the summer of 1943 through the back window of a small closed truck in which I was being taken from the camp to the dentist in Sagan. At a level crossing, I saw ten or a dozen figures, herded in a group and surrounded by SS guards. They were not human figures, just angular skeletal forms clad in pyjamas with yellow and grey vertical stripes. There was no substance to them and no personality. They could hardly walk.

The vision was gone in two seconds, as the truck pulled away and turned the corner. I was left with a strong sensation of evil and an unexpectedly powerful fear of something unknown. Instinct prevented me from asking questions of my German guards.

I failed completely to explain the vision to myself, although it persisted in my dreams. But even my nightmares could not reveal to me the Germans' ruthless organization for exterminating the Jews. Later, of course, it became clear enough that the group of relics I had seen at the level crossing were from a local concentration camp, probably on their way to their last ride in a cattle truck.

The Russian prisoners who lived next door to us were not in this category. They had more to eat than the Jews and their bodies would stay alive longer. If the life expectancy of a Jew in a concentration camp was six months, leaving the gas chambers out of the equation, that of a Russian prisoner was two years.

The German Vorlager was far bigger than the East Compound but contained only a few wooden barrack blocks. One housed the parcel store where Marcus Marsh was in control. A second was our sick quarters and the third the book store. In one half of the book store, which was partitioned off, the Russians lived.

The only other geographical feature of any interest was the rubbish dump. Here all the empty cans from our compound were deposited and the pile had reached impressive proportions. These cans had come to us in food parcels and had contained corned beef, Canadian spam, sardines, jam and everything else with which the Red Cross supplied us.

At all hours of the day, there was always a Russian prisoner sitting on the dump, carefully scraping out the remnants of each can with his index finger. What he found he licked from his finger. This privilege was obviously strictly controlled by the Russians for there was never more than one Russian at the dump at any one time. Certainly, the miserable butolic scrapings left in the tins would not have provided a mouthful for more than one Russian a day.

My hope was to plan an escape from the Vorlager itself. This meant getting myself appointed to one of the only two German-sponsored sinecures open to us. One was the officer in charge of the parcel store, who was Marcus Marsh. He spent his whole day in the Vorlager and had a most responsible job. The other appointment was that of book censor. Thousands of books were sent to us by friends and relatives and they all had to be censored by the Germans before being released. The German system was that a British officer and two German interpreters should read all these books before they were issued. It was a fair practical system even though it was, naturally, the Germans who made the final decision.

The British censor who was appointed to this three-man board could always argue and dispute a decision even if his protests were usually ignored. He could also use his own initiative and ban a book immediately without waiting for German protests.

If, for instance, the title of the book was 'The Secret Vices of Adolf Schickelgruber,' he could firmly ban it without further ado. It certainly would not obtain the German imprimatur.

This was the job I wanted. Unfortunately, my credentials and curriculum vitae were unfavourable. As a two-time escaper I was considered dangerous by the Germans and normally no privileged occupation such as that of the book censor would have come my way. The Germans in this case accepted a short list of nominees from the British and chose the one who they considered most suitable. I thought that I could browbeat the British authorities into putting me on the list, if I could assure them that the Germans would accept me. The key to the problem was therefore the Germans.

It took me many months but I worked on the problem with carefully deliberate tactics. The two German interpreters who formed the majority on the censorship board came into the East Compound nearly every day. I cultivated them assiduously discovering their favourite topics of conversation and softening them with generous gifts of cigarettes and chocolate.

One was a stiff-necked clot and stupid to boot. Cigarettes and flattery were enough for him. The second was highly intelligent and genuinely anti-Nazi. He was already convinced, in 1943, that Germany was going to lose the war and wanted desperately to have something in his favour on the records which he was certain we British maintained on our captors. Nikki was a nice honest kid, quite open in his views and absolutely terrified of being sent to the East front.

I worked on these two until we were all bosom friends and I had their promise to support my nomination as the next book censor. The job was becoming vacant. As they explained, their support carried no weight at all but was, at the same time, probably decisive. The German Kommandant received a list of names from the SBO of half a dozen nominees. The Kommandant, being far too busy to take a personal interest, would pass the list to these two interpreters asking them to select a name, which he would then approve.

When I was entirely sure of German support, I went to talk to Authority. The first reaction was of immense amusement, the funniest joke of the week.

'Don't be ridiculous. They'll never pick you. You've got too long a record.'

'If you'll slip my name on the bottom of the list, I'll bet you a Red Cross parcel that I get the nomination. Just don't draw attention to me. I don't need any help. The Germans will pick me.'

'Are you really serious, Tommy?'

'I'm dead serious. I've been working on this for months and I can assure you that the appointment is mine, if my name is on the list. It's a racing certainty.

'I've got a lot of plans for the Vorlager, not only my own escape. The censorship job is a key post and you need a good man there—not some literary type who is just going to read books all day. I can also work closely with Marcus. It gives us access to all sorts of people who never come into the camp and we can use them to our advantage.'

'But we were thinking that the Beaver would be ideal for the job. Right up his street.'

The reference was to one of the long-haired types who was extremely well read, highly opinionated and voluble on any subject. But he was impossibly impractical and a non-escaper. The establishment was being conservatively naïve, as usual.

'Excellent choice,' I answered, 'I can think of nobody better qualified to censor books. Leave his name on the list. Just add mine in small print. I'll do the rest.'

My name went on the list and in August I was appointed, without further argument.

This was only the first stage of my complicated plan. I was not then at all sure how my eventual exit from the Vorlager would be achieved, but I favoured a walk-out through the main gate. I felt that a walk-out at Stalag Luft III would be a triumph and I suspected that the defences would be vulnerable at that point. The main gate to the Vorlager was reputed to be impregnable, with the strictest system of identity checks and passes. But as it had no contact with our compound it would not, I calculated, be expecting an attempt by any prisoner. Surprise, as Clausewitz probably said, was half the battle.

Two

On my first morning in the Vorlager, I strolled over to the parcel store to call on Marcus.

'Here's trouble,' he said smiling, as I walked into his comfortable office. 'Sit down, Tommy, coffee's just coming up.'

He offered me a cigarette.

'I won a nice bet on you,' he continued. 'Bill Skinner laid me five to two against you getting the job. A racing certainty wasn't it, Tommy? But I would like to know how you did it.'

'It cost me a lot of chocolates and cigarettes,' I answered with a grin. 'It wasn't very difficult, I bribed the judges—those two interpreters who work in the book store.'

'Are they thoroughly tame?' Marcus was immediately interested.

'One is, the little fair one. The other I would not trust an inch.

In fact, if he wasn't so stupid he'd be dangerous. But I can handle him.'

'Oh, I am sure you can, Tommy. Now what are you plotting? You're certainly not here because you like reading books. Of course, what you do in the book store is none of my business, that's your own private empire. But if there's going to be any funny stuff which might involve me, I'd better know about it. My set-up here is too valuable to risk any balls-up. I imagine you know what I mean.'

'I know exactly what you mean, Marcus, and I've no intention of upsetting the apple cart. In fact, the reason I'm here is to tell you my plans, so that you know what's going on. And I promise I won't involve you.'

Over a mug of Nescafé and Klim milk, brewed by one of Marcus's well trained slaves, I told him of my still vague idea of walking out through the main gate.

'All I want, at the moment, is information about the main gate —what the checks are, what passes are used, who comes in and where do they go. Until I have studied the problem thoroughly, I can't plan anything.'

I was looking out of the window as I spoke. Marcus's office overlooked the main gate which was less than a hundred yards away. There couldn't have been a better observation post.

Marcus, too, looked out of the window.

'All right, Tommy, you can use my office whenever you like. But make the visits fairly short and try not to look too damned furtive. If Charlie Piltz ever sees you in here, he's going to be suspicious immediately. He knows there's bound to be something shifty going on wherever you appear on the scene.'

Marcus's caution was more than justified. His job as parcels officer had two aspects, the one official, the second clandestine, and both were extremely important.

He had thousands of Red Cross food parcels in his store and thousands of prisoners to feed. It was the central store supplying not only our East Compound where our strength was less than 1,000, but also the Middle Compound which housed some 2,000 NCO aircrew and the newly-opened North Compound which had a total capacity of between 5,000 and 6,000 although, at the time, it was only just beginning to be occupied.

Marcus was the undisputed parcel king. It was he who decided how much we ate. The optimum and luxury level of parcel distribution was one per prisoner per week, a standard we seldom enjoyed. Thus, if there were 5,000 of us prisoners and there were 5,000 parcels in store, it meant one week's supply. In such a situation Marcus would only issue one parcel a week for every four prisoners, so creating a three-week reserve on very limited rations.

If there were 10,000 parcels in the store for 5,000 prisoners, he would only issue one parcel for two prisoners per week. If his stock got higher still, we got an individual parcel each per week.

Nobody argued with Marcus's decisions. The Germans did not care, the British did not dare.

The parcel store was entirely staffed by Germans, probably a dozen of them. But the boss was Marcus and he ruled them with that strict discipline which only the Germans love. Whenever he shouted, they jumped to it. It was a pleasure to watch.

This was the official side of Marcus's work. The cloak-and-dagger aspect of his activities was also vital. Nearly all the essential contraband which reached us inside the camp came via the parcel store. This contraband arrived in parcels which were not sponsored by the Red Cross, but by commercial or semi-charitable organizations which specialized in supplying, packing and despatching all sorts of extras and comforts which relatives of prisoners-of-war wanted to send to us unfortunates. These might arrive from Gamages or Harrods or the Ex-Convicts Friendly Association. Most of them were innocent parcels and might contain anything from camel hair sleeping bags to chess sets, packs of playing cards to poker chips. Every now and again, however, there was a loaded parcel. Back in England some official guardian angel was taking care of our most illicit needs.

Not in all cases, but in many, Marcus knew from the label on the parcel whether or not it might be loaded. If there was this possibility, the parcel had to be made to disappear from the store before the Germans opened and searched it. It was at this sort of manoeuvre which he excelled.

In those days I was awaiting a consignment of documents for myself which were to cover me on my next escape. I did not know how they would reach me, but I was very confident that they would. The channel I had established had been proved and was working well. When one day I got a parcel from a particular organization, which was well known to deal sometimes in contraband, I was happy as a sandboy. Marcus smuggled it into the East Compound for me and I opened it with intense expectation.

It contained an expensive set of chessmen and a beautiful marquetry chess board. With not the slightest qualm or hesitation, I took a hammer and chisel and split the chess board through every possible plane, until it was reduced to matchwood. There was nothing hidden inside it. I then dissected every chess piece larger than a pawn—again nothing. All that was left of my parcel were sixteen pawns and a pile of tinder. This was the fate of many similar parcels, although sometimes we found treasure in the form of money, maps or documents.

In addition, Marcus's well trained goons brought in a lot of forbidden items which could only be obtained locally. These might range from railway timetables to radio valves, all of which were paid for in chocolate or cigarettes. There was also a great deal of potentially valuable information to be obtained from the parcel store goons. It was miscellaneous and often unimportant. Nevertheless it was carefully sifted and classified. Any information which appeared to have an intelligence value found its way quickly back to England.

This was the set-up which I neither dared nor wished to disturb. But Marcus was a man in a million. He was not in any way disturbed by my activities in the Vorlager and was fully prepared to help me in any way he could.

From the very first day I performed my official duties with meritorious dedication. Every morning at nine o'clock one of the two German interpreters would escort me through the gate into the Vorlager. I would remain there until lunch time and return again in the afternoon. All day I read books and conscientiously marked all passages which were blatantly anti-German or took the mickey out of Adolf. I was doing my job.

Nikki, the junior interpreter, proved to be a friend and I got to feel that I could trust him. The senior interpreter, the stiff-necked one, had many other duties and appeared only occasionally, making a point of being present when we issued our weekly list of approved and banned books. He signed the form.

Nikki, too, was a busy man and often left me alone in the book store. This gave me all the opportunity I needed to snoop around and study the lay-out.

One of the earliest contacts I made was with the Russian prisoners. They were not, at the time, part of my plan, they were only on my conscience. With the cooperation of Marcus in the parcel store, I arranged to have a consignment of forty Red Cross parcels delivered to the book store disguised as sacks of books. Nikki agreed to be absent at the right time. The food parcels were quickly hoisted into the loft of the book store which communicated directly with the loft under which the Russians were housed. I was thus able to present the Russians with a parcel per man, a quantity of food which exceeded their wildest dreams and was the equivalent of, at least, a month of German rations.

The meeting I arranged with the senior Russian was frigid and disillusioning. He was closed and suspicious. I had the strong impression that he both disliked and distrusted me.

After a very stylized and sterile conversation had run out of steam, without showing any sign of a break through, I threw all my trumps on the table.

'There are forty Red Cross parcels in the loft. Collect them tonight or the Germans will find them and I'll be in trouble. Meet me here tomorrow.'

I was sorry for the man. He hated me for my generosity. He wanted not to believe me. He was too proud and bitter to be able to accept pity.

He fell back on formality.

'The Red Army is most grateful for your generous cooperation.'

'Tomorrow at three o'clock,' I answered.

Next morning, as soon as I had been able to get rid of Nikki, I climbed up through the trap door in my office, into the loft. All the parcels were gone. I was extremely relieved. If the Russians had been obstinately proud and refused to take them, there would have been endless trouble and I would have immediately lost my job.

After lunch I returned early to the book store and sent Nikki away on an errand to the East Compound. At exactly three o'clock I heard furtive movements in the loft and then a gentle tapping on the trap door.

'Come on in,' I called. 'There is nobody here.'

One after the other, three Russians dropped to the floor. There was my chum of the day before, looking sheepish, and two others who were grinning all over their faces. I was warmly embraced by the two grinning Russians and hesitantly by the third. We all talked in bastard German.

That there was now a new rapport between us was obvious. The alliance was on again. One of the Russians produced a bottle of colourless liquor and handed it to me, carefully wiping the spout with his thumb. I took the bottle.

'To the glorious Red Army,' I said, as I raised it. I took a very cautious swig, well knowing how dangerous these home made brews were. My caution was justified, both my tongue and palate took fire. I handed the bottle back.

'To the incomparable Royal Air Force.'

They drank one after the other, each repeating the phrase. It was my turn again.

'To Stalin,' I declaimed.

This time I took a bigger swallow. This stuff was not so bad.

'To Churchill.'

I got three responses in rapid succession and the level in the bottle was way down below the half way mark.

My turn again and I could not think of another toast. As I grabbed the bottle, inspiration came to me.

'The Victory of Stalingrad,' I said.

The bottle finished and the ice thoroughly melted, we got down to more confidential exchanges. They told me their story of the previous night. They had not believed that there were parcels in the loft but had sent a man up to have a look, just to be polite. When he had come back with a couple of parcels and reported that there was a great stack of them up there, they had decided, by a completely unanimous vote, to organize immediately the biggest celebration dinner of all time. And they had eaten the lot—the whole damn lot.

This was nearly unbelievable. I had seen men, for a bet, try to eat the contents of a Red Cross parcel in a sitting, and all, except perhaps for Robin Beauclair, had failed. It was a superhuman achievement.

But one had to believe these Russians, they were so hungry.

They told me that three of their men were very sick that morning. They had terrible stomach pains.

We all roared with laughter, although nothing funny had been said.

Three

AFTER about ten days of direct observation and some discreet questioning, I had put together a detailed and comprehensive picture of how exit through the main gate was controlled. This knowledge brought me no nearer a solution to my problem. The security system in force was tightly efficient. There seemed to be no loophole through which I might squeeze.

The gate itself was wide and high, strongly constructed of a framework of rough pine. The open spaces within the framework were closely latticed by barbed wire. The gate was always kept locked and the key was held by a sentry who stood outside the gate and had a clear view of anybody approaching the gate from the inside of the Vorlager.

From inside there was only one avenue of approach to the gate which led past a sort of ticket window in a small wooden hut placed directly in front of the gate and some twenty yards from it. A system of wooden railings channelled one's approach and permitted only one person at a time to present himself at the ticket window.

On duty behind the window was one of the German administrative staff, usually an NCO and frequently one of the many interpreters. He could be expected to be an intelligent and responsible man who also certainly knew by sight all the Germans who had any business inside the Vorlager.

No one could leave the Vorlager without positively proving his identity at the ticket window. The duty watchman had to satisfy himself, first, that the individual leaving had already been recorded in the log book as having entered the Vorlager and secondly that his pass, with photograph, corresponded in all respects to the details recorded in the log. If the duty NCO was satisfied, he ordered the sentry to unlock the gate.

It was beginning to look as if there was no way out through the main gate. I had been hoping that it might be possible to walk out disguised as one of the ferrets, who always wore overalls which were easy to fake, or as a sentry going off duty, which was more difficult, but we did now have some goonskins and dummy rifles. I had even dreamed that I could disguise myself as a German officer. I had a perfect German officer's uniform, made by the best London tailors, and I was longing to get it out of mothballs.

But it was now obvious that with the security system in force it would be necessary to impersonate a particular German individual. Not only would I have to have a pass which was an exact copy of that of the man I was impersonating, but I would also have to look like him. This was clearly impossible.

The only other way was to disguise myself as a Russian prisoner. The Russians were frequently taken out through the gate in small, well guarded working parties. The control of their identities was perfunctory. All Russian prisoners were faceless and anonymous. Their names were not recorded by the duty NCO. He logged ten Russian prisoners out and as long as ten Russian prisoners came back again nobody worried. These parties were always guarded and the responsibility was with the guards who accompanied them.

I could change identity with a Russian prisoner and go out with a working party. It would probably be easy enough to escape from the party. But the consequences of such an action could be very unpleasant. If I was re-captured it would be impossible to persuade my captors that I was a Russian prisoner. When I escaped I intended to be well dressed, with a solid French identity and a lot of excellent documents. Without a word of Russian, I could not hope to maintain the pretence of being a Russian prisoner. Once my real identity was discovered, the Russian who had taken my place would immediately be discovered and the consequences for him would be very painful, perhaps fatal. Even if my escape was completely successful and I got back to England, it was very doubtful that the Russian could successfully take on my identity in a prisoner camp without being detected sooner or later. In that case, too, it would be the Russian who paid the bill possibly with his life. It was not a plan I could contemplate, the stakes were too high and it would not be my own neck which I was risking.

Eventually it was the Russian prisoners who gave me the key to the gate—figuratively speaking. Since the first parcel delivery, I had maintained contact with them and there were four or five of them who used to drop in regularly through the trap door for a chat. We got to know one another well and could talk quite intimately. But we never became real friends. They always maintained a certain reserve, a certain distance. I felt that if it were not for the fact that we, too, were fighting the Germans and hurting them badly with our bombing, there would have been no rapport at all between us.

Delivery of food parcels to Russians was continuing through the loft in the book store and for this they were genuinely grateful. But we never again made the mistake of delivering forty parcels in one consignment. We were trying to educate them to be more restrained, to ration the food they received from us.

My most regular visitor was a tank commander named Igor, who had been captured at Smolensk. He spoke good German and a few words of French. I was closer to him than to any of the others.

I told him of my plans to escape, not in secret, but in the presence of any other Russian who was visiting me, and kept him up to date on the progress I was making. There was absolutely no danger in this. No Russian prisoner ever exchanged a word with the Germans. They hated them with a sullen, smouldering venom which was unextinguishable. Rare cases had occurred of a Russian prisoner becoming too friendly with the Germans and, for personal gain, which always means food, betraying his comrades. The fate of these unfortunates was horrible. They were inevitably executed by their own companions and their bodies made to disappear. One morning Ivan the traitor was there, the next morning he had vanished without trace.

One day Igor came to see me with two Russians I had not met before. He introduced me. The two Russians were part of a group of six who worked in the German stables, outside the main gate. Every morning two or more of these six Russians left the Vorlager by the main gate about half an hour before dawn. Their duty was to clean out the stables where the Germans had over forty horses. Most of them were cart horses, but a few of the German officers, in the old tradition, kept riding horses in the stable.

Igor's proposal was simple and generous. If I wanted to go out through the gate, all I had to do was to disguise myself as a Russian prisoner and walk through the gate half an hour before dawn.

This was something that my patient observation of the gate had not revealed. I had never been in the Vorlager before dawn. I began to be very interested.

It was a little difficult to get the basic facts with three voluble Russians all talking together in ridiculously bad German. I fixed four rich brews of Horlicks and Klim and calmed everybody down. Slowly and methodically, I pieced the story together.

The quite remarkable fact which emerged from our conversation was that the Russians who left the Vorlager every morning to go and clean the stables were not accompanied by any German guard. They had been issued with passes and were permitted to go out of the main gate unescorted.

It looked as though this might be the loophole I was looking for.

The procedure followed by the Russians to get out of the main gate was straight forward. They usually went out in pairs and always about half an hour before first light. At the ticket window inside the main gate they presented their passes. These were retained by the NCO on duty who gave them, in exchange, a blue armband which they buckled on to their left arm, above the elbow. The blue armband was the authority for the sentry to open the gate to them. It also enabled them to get back into the camp again after they had finished work, when they went through the same procedure in reverse, exchanging their blue armbands for their passes.

I was given one of the Russian passes to study. It was a piece of thick, stiff paper, pinkish in colour, with a photograph of the holder and all his personal details. It had the usual Stalag Luft III rubber stamp on it and was typewritten throughout. There was a great deal of typescript including an authority for the bearer to proceed from the Vorlager to the stables in the German compound.

It would not be very difficult to forge, but it would be a long, tedious job.

I looked at the Russian who owned the pass and then at the photograph. The photograph might have been of anybody. It showed a sullen looking man with a fur cap pulled well down over his forehead and his ears. For identification purposes it was

valueless. I would not have recognized the original from his picture. This was encouraging, because providing photographs for
passes was not at all easy. However, I was fairly confident that it
was a problem to which a solution could be found.

'Can I keep this pass for a day?' I asked.

'Two days, three days if you like,' was the owner's careless answer. 'The others will work, I will stay in bed.'

'I'll make a copy. I won't use your name, of course.'

'I trust you, comrade.'

He shook my hand and embraced me. They were emotional
types these Russians. They seemed to think I was already back
in England. I foresaw a host of difficulties before this idea became an exact plan of action.

'How do you see this walk out, Igor?' I asked. 'How would you
do it?'

Igor had been dying to tell me just this and he got so excited
that he forgot his German and lapsed into Russian. Eventually, he
became intelligible and I listened with close attention.

'You go out ten minutes before the real ones—our comrades
here. I'll tell you the exact time the day before. When you get
to the guichet, you look through the window and the interpreter
is asleep. You understand?'

I did not understand, but I nodded. I did not want to interrupt
his flow.

'You are dressed like us—like a Russian soldier—yes?'

I nodded again. That would be no trouble.

'The sentry outside the gate is watching you. You hold your pass
in your hand, you put it in through the window and when you
pull your hand out you have the blue armband. You nod to the
interpreter inside the window who is still sleep and you walk out.
It is simple. You understand?'

By now I was lost. There was some slight of hand I had not followed which made it all seem too easy.

I looked at my watch. It was time for the Russians to go. Nikki,
the interpreter, would be back within five or ten minutes.

'Can we discuss this tomorrow, at the same time?' I asked Igor.

'But of course.'

'Good, I'll be waiting for you. I think it's time to go.'

Within thirty seconds the three Russians had disappeared and the trap door in the roof was closed. I wiped their boot prints off my desk.

That evening I made an exact drawing of the layout of the Russian pass, which recorded its dimensions, the exact spacing of the typescript, the position and size of the photograph and all other relevant details. I also copied the text and, with a razor blade, cut a strip from one side of it, barely one sixteenth of an inch wide. This would give me a colour control when I needed to make a replica.

The next day Igor came to see me alone and this made it far easier to get the information I wanted. Over and over again, during the night, I had gone over what he told me. I hardly dared to believe what he appeared to be saying. Now I was going to get the facts.

The facts were amazingly simple. There was one German interpreter who was regularly on duty behind the ticket window in the small hours of the morning and who always went to sleep in his chair. When he was on duty, the Russian stable cleaners had to wake him up before they could exchange their passes for blue armbands. If, when I went out, I did not wake him up, but produced my own blue armband, nobody would ever know that I had gone out of the gate.

'Which interpreter is this?' I asked.

'We call him hedgehog because he always sleeps.'

Igor described him in detail. I knew the man. He was tall and pale with a prominent Adam's apple and copious spots on his face. He had receding black hair and wore glasses. He normally worked in the Middle Compound but I had met him more than once in the parcel store. I did not know the hedgehog's name, but I could easily find out.

Four

My plans had now crystallized and I could see the whole operation clearly in each of its separate phases. It looked to me like the surest and safest escape I had yet contemplated. But there was a great deal of complicated work to do, as well as considerable intrigue, before I could be ready. It was then nearly the end of August. I calculated that, if I met no unforeseen problems, my preparations would be completed by the end of October.

Inside the East Compound everybody was digging tunnels. I had no faith in any of them. It was too difficult to dispose of the spoil without being discovered. The German Abwehr, particularly Charlie Piltz and his gang of ferrets, found every new tunnel long before it got to the wire. There was only one original scheme, the now famous Wooden Horse, which I had been watching with close interest.

This was a two-man tunnel being dug by Eric Williams and Mike Codner. Starting in the open, underneath a vaulting horse, it had progressed some forty feet towards the wire by the end of August. It was the narrowest, meanest underground passage, dark and airless, running just under the pine-root level. Eric's intention was to turn it into a mole when he had gone far enough.

Eric and Mike Codner came to see me.

'How about a circuit?' they asked.

To be invited to walk round the circuit meant that serious business had to be discussed. I was immediately interested. We made several circuits.

'How's the dienst going?' I asked. Dienst, which in German means duty, was one of the many words we had incorporated into our daily vernacular. When we used it, it meant a tunnel or any other escape activity.

'We've done about forty feet,' said Mike, 'and it's going well. The trouble is it takes so long to get the sand back from the face. At our present rate we won't be out before Christmas.'

'That's the point, Tommy,' said Eric. 'We're overworked. We need another man underground. We wondered whether you would like to join us.'

This I had not expected and it took me entirely by surprise. Eric was very frank. He said they needed a small man, with experience of tunnelling, particularly moling and that I fitted the bill perfectly.

I was equally frank with them. I told them of my Vorlager plans which, I calculated, would get me out before they were ready.

'The real problem is this,' I said; 'my next attempt has got to succeed. If I get caught on another mole, they'll ship me to

Colditz. They've already promised that. And I don't want to go to Colditz.'

'Don't you think our scheme has a chance?'

'I think it's got a very good chance. I can tell you that it's the only one inside the East Compound which has. But I think mine is more certain. Let's hope they both work.'

'So you won't join us?'

'I would if I could keep my own scheme going. But for mine I have to spend most of the day in the book store in the Vorlager. Will there be enough time left for me to pull my weight on your show? You tell me.'

'No, Tommy. There obviously won't. I'm sorry.'

'So am I, Eric. But any time you want me to help out, I can always take a day off from the book store.'

We left it at that and a few days later I heard that Oliver Philpot had joined the Wooden Horse team as the third man.

The longest and most tedious job I had to do was to reproduce the Russian passes. Tim Walenn, our master forger, had prepared the blanks, exactly matching the sample of paper I had given him. I intended to complete the typescript myself.

There was a typewriter in the parcel store, used by one of the German clerks, who guarded it jealously. But Marcus was able to get rid of the clerk for short periods at a time and then I would immediately start work. These opportunities occurred irregularly and often I would achieve no more than five minutes productive work, typing only a few words.

It was a nerve-wracking procedure. I could not afford to make a single mistake and would pause for long seconds between each letter to make absolutely sure I was going to hit the right key. By the end of September the passes were still unfinished.

It was at this stage that I started to consider the feasibility of bringing Nikki, the interpreter, into the act. For a long time he had been bringing in all kinds of contraband when asked and also reporting a lot of miscellaneous information, some of which had intelligence value. It was from him that I heard the first rumours of a new secret weapon being produced at Peenemünde on the island of Rügen. But he was careful never to accept a bribe and to stress that what he did was done of his own free will because he was anti-Nazi. All he wanted for his services was eventual recognition, when the war ended, that he had cooperated. He had no doubt that Germany would be defeated. I was sure that he could be trusted.

But there were also very good reasons why I should keep this German interpreter entirely ignorant of my plans. In the first place he was the one who was going to be blamed for my escape. After it was discovered, he was going to be in real trouble. Never before had I worried about what happened to the Germans whose mistakes or carelessness had allowed me to escape. It just did not enter into the equation. Whether they got shot or sent to the East Front was not my affair. There was no place for such sentimentality in an escaper's attitude. I did not see why the fact that Nikki appeared to be a 'good' German on our side should make any difference. If he was for the high jump, it was his own fault. He had got himself into this situation with his eyes wide open. He knew my escape record.

Of course, if I did make use of him, everything would be much easier. He could borrow the typewriter from the parcel store; he could get hold of one of the essential blue armbands for the short time necessary for me to make a pattern and take a colour sample; he could provide me with the roster of the interpreters on duty behind the ticket window; he could help in a hundred ways, and greatly accelerate the process. If he was clever, he could also plan an alibi for himself.

It was this final consideration which decided me to talk to Nikki. The risk was that when he realized that my escape via the book store was going to be blamed on him and that he faced the probability of an immediate posting to the East Front, he would baulk. If he decided to save his own neck, my plans would be ruined.

On the other hand, if he was genuine in his anti-Nazi attitude, he could give me all the assistance I needed and, knowing my plans, could take his own precautions to keep himself in the clear. I was glad I was not in his shoes.

Nikki was not a brave man and had never pretended to be. When I told him what I was planning and what I expected him to do, he was terrified. But he was clever and after thinking over my proposition, he decided to help. In truth, he had little choice.

If he had refused, he would have lost all his credits with the British and could have been in very serious trouble with the Germans. We would not have had any mercy on him.

After that everything became much easier. Nikki, who did his turn on duty behind the ticket window with the other interpreters, purloined a blue armband for the bare ten minutes I needed. He borrowed the typewriter from the clerk in the parcel store for afternoons at a time and brought it to the book store where I could work in undisturbed peace. He discovered when the hedgehog, the sleeping interpreter, was on duty and he planned his own alibi.

By the end of October, Robert and I were ready to go. I had hesitated a long time before deciding to ask Robert to come with me. It was so difficult to get him to make any preparations and he just did not think in terms of escape. But once outside the wire, there was not a better man. I doubted if anybody else could handle a German policeman in the masterful way in which he did.

Fortunately it was much easier to get Robert equipped this time. The escape organization at Sagan now included expert teams of forgers and tailors. Robert's papers were prepared for him and he was provided with very adequate civilian clothes. Our cover story was much the same as before but, instead of Krupps, our new employers were a big chemical firm in Leipzig. The forgers had produced a most impressive sheet of headed notepaper and I had done the typing in the book store. I also typed a similar letter for Oliver Philpot.

On 29 October Oliver got clear away through the vaulting horse tunnel with Eric and Mike. Robert and I were still waiting for the hedgehog to be detailed for duty between midnight and eight o'clock in the morning. Then it would be our turn. But we were having bad luck with the hedgehog. He had been on leave, he had been sick and he had had a whole series of spells on the duty roster at the wrong time. We just had to be patient.

It was while we were waiting that the parcel arrived. It was a flat wooden box and its contents were stated to be a dozen gramophone records. But it had a distinctive label on it which told Marcus that it was loaded. He smuggled it out of the parcel store. When he had opened it, he came to see me.

'Tommy,' he said, 'I've got a parcel in my room which is full of loot. It's mostly documents and your photograph seems to be on most of them.'

'Thanks, Marcus.' I was excited. 'I've been expecting it for months. I'll come straight over and collect it.'

'No, you can't do that. I have to hand it over to the boss.'

'Well, thanks for the tip, anyway. I expect he'll let me know.'

Half an hour later the Senior British Officer sent for me. I found him with all his staff standing round the parcel which was open on the table.

'Ah, Calnan,' he said, 'I'm very glad you came along.'

He did not sound at all glad.

'Not at all, sir.' I was being very polite. The atmosphere seemed a little hostile. I was not very popular with the establishment at the time. They considered me to be too independent and something of a rebel. They were right. Only in extremes did I ever tell them what I was doing.

'We've just opened this parcel and there seems to be a lot of stuff in it for you.'

He said it accusingly, as though I had committed some crime. The assembled company all looked at me with disapproval.

I glanced round the ring of faces. We all knew one another very well but although my personal relationship with most of them was reasonably good, our official relationship was terrible.

I suddenly understood the situation. The Senior British Officer was a group captain and was a brand new prisoner. He had only arrived a few days before. He hardly knew me and he knew little or nothing about escape documents. His staff had obviously told him that I was going too far in organizing my own un-official supply of documents. Their pride was hurt. Everything should go through the proper channels. So I was being put on the carpet.

The group captain was still talking.

'There are identity cards and passes with your photograph on them.'

He paused and looked at me severely.

'How do you explain this?'

'I sent for the stuff, sir. It's what I need for my next escape.'

'And when do you expect to escape, may I ask?'

He was obviously disbelieving.

He knew nothing of my plans and the others very little.

'Next week, sir,' I answered as casually as possible.

He looked around for confirmation. Nobody could confirm my statement but nobody dared contradict it.

'Now just explain how you sent for this material.'

I had never told anybody of the code I used in my letters home. But now there was no point in keeping it a secret.

'I use a code, sir.'

'But you're not allowed to use a private code.'

Now he was being petulant and I was beginning to get angry. There were no regulations which prohibited me from using my own code. I was quite prepared to start an ungodly row but I did not see what purpose it would serve. To calm everybody down I told the whole story in detail. How I had prepared a simple code long before I was shot down. How I had used it first to obtain a naval uniform, which provided me with my business suit and then a complete Luftwaffe officer's uniform when I was working on a gate walk-out plan at Schubin. And finally how, after the tunnel escape at Schubin, I had made a complete list of all the documents a foreign worker in Germany should have and sent it back with a request to be provided with all of them.

'My wife decodes my letters and passes on the message to Air Ministry,' I explained. 'They obviously end up in the right place, because I get results.

'I don't think you fully realize just what treasure you've got in that box,' I continued.

I picked up a handful of documents and started to go through them.

'Here is a complete set of documents for me, and half a dozen photographs, but there are another twenty sets which anybody can use. Look at this, French identity card for Jean Blanc, that's me. Address in Avignon. German identity card issued to foreign worker Jean Blanc. Employed in Leipzig. Travel passes for Jean Blanc. Issued by the Leipzig police, still blank. And this, this is the real masterpiece.'

I held up a pink form.

'This is a frontier pass which has to be carried by a foreign workman going back on leave to his own country. With this pass you can ride over the frontier in the train. There's a whole sheaf of them here.'

I rummaged in the box again.

'Look at these rubber stamps. With these we can put a police stamp on all the travel passes and validate them. And look closely at the documents themselves. Nobody carrying them must think of them as forgeries. They're originals, even if they are printed in London.

'All this is exactly what I asked for and it's what we badly need if we are going to get anybody home. The only thing that worries me is that they might be too good. Anybody who gets picked up with these on him is not going to be able to pretend he made them himself and he may find himself accused of being a spy.

'Frankly, sir,' I went on, 'I don't feel the slightest bit like apologizing for organizing this. But I'd like to collect my documents.'

The group captain was examining the contents of the box with great interest. As he looked up I could see that he was trying hard to control his temper. But his anger was not for me.

He turned to his staff.

'See that Calnan gets just what he needs,' he said curtly. 'He obviously organized this and I think he deserves credit for it, not blame.'

The door slammed behind him.

I was now alone with my friends. We smiled nastily at each other. Methodically I put aside my set of papers and collected a second set for Robert. I selected one or two maps and counted out a generous amount of money.

'See you in the Old Bailey,' I said and walked out of the room.

Five

NIKKI brought me the news that the hedgehog was on the roster at the time we wanted him on 20 November. That gave me three days to make my final preparations. The forgers could now fill in the travel passes and put on the date stamp and the police stamp. Photographs could be applied to the passes and duly stamped. Everything else was ready.

On 19 November I came up from the book store with a hand cart on which were loaded five sacks of books. Nikki escorted me back into the compound. These were books which had passed the censor and were for distribution. Half an hour later I pushed the cart out of the gate again and back to the book store. This time there were four sacks of books which had to be sent to prisoners in the new North compound. In the fifth sack was Robert.

As I was escorted by an interpreter he knew, the sentry did not check the sacks. We released Robert in the safety of my office in the book store and he disappeared through the trapdoor into the loft. He was wearing his best civilian clothes.

Again I went back into the East compound with the cart loaded with sacks of books. When it came out again, I was inside one of the sacks while another prisoner was helping Nikki to push the cart. I joined Robert in the loft.

Nikki's complicity was now at an end. He went on leave that very evening, calculating that absence was the better part of discretion.

We spent a very cold night in the loft of the book store and slept little. At four o'clock in the morning, we started to prepare ourselves. We were due out of the gate at exactly five thirty. I had arranged with Igor for the two Russian stable cleaners to be late that morning.

Our first layer of clothing was that of two respectable, well-qualified Frenchmen, employed by a chemical firm in Leipzig. We stowed all our money and papers in convenient pockets. We were each carrying a briefcase containing the few essentials we required and a small supply of food for emergencies. This time there were no Players cigarettes or Air Ministry maps. As our briefcases could not be carried openly through the gate, we had to tie them securely round our stomachs with string. Working in pitch darkness, this was no easy task. We rolled up our hats and put them in our pockets. That completed our French costume.

Now we had to convert ourselves into Russian stable cleaners. This meant donning a filthy fur hat, as worn by all Russian prisoners and a shapeless garment which had once been a Red Army greatcoat. Igor, of course, had supplied these items. I had had unexpected trouble in getting exactly what I wanted. When I first told him that I needed two Russian greatcoats and two hats, he had been delighted to help.

'Just leave it to me,' he said and I knew I could rely on him.

Two days later he brought in two magnificent greatcoats, at least by prison camp standards, and two fur hats which were works of art. Somebody had spent many hours cleaning, restitching and ironing these garments. They had been somebody's Sunday best. I suspected that one set had been Igor's own.

Igor was very hurt when I refused them and it took a long time to get him to accept the fact that I wanted the sort of torn, tattered and stinking garment which the Russians wore when cleaning the stables. The same was true for the hats.

At first Igor said that he would be ashamed to give me such garments, but soon his practical mind saw the logic of my argument and the two greatcoats which Robert and I put on over the top of our other costumes were worthy of the filthiest stable cleaners.

At exactly twenty-five minutes past five we slipped out of a window on the darkest side of the book store. Although it was only five feet from the ground, the window was very difficult to negotiate without bursting the bodice of string which was holding our briefcases in place.

Three minutes later we were shuffling along the well beaten path which led to the hut guarding the gate. Arc-lights illuminated the scene as if it were day. We could see the sentry outside the gate was watching us. We were imitating the walk used by all Russian prisoners, hands in pockets, eyes staring at the ground ahead and feet dragging through the dust in slow time. In my right pocket I could feel the pink pass. In my left, I clutched the blue armband.

As I approached the ticket window, I drew the pink pass from my pocket and held it so that the sentry could see it. I was very tense. This was the crucial moment. I stopped opposite the ticket window and looked in.

The interpreter was sitting in a chair on the far side of the room. His arms were resting on the table in front of him and his head was on his arms. He was fast asleep.

I did not dare look at the sentry, a bare twenty feet away, the other side of the gate. But in case he was watching closely, I went through the mime we had planned.

I waved my pink pass in front of the ticket window and then put my arm in through the window. I nodded a couple of times as though answering questions. With my left hand, which was hidden from the sentry by my body, I put the blue armband just inside the ticket window. Then I palmed the pink pass and picked up the blue armband with my right hand. I shook it out so that the sentry could see it. I nodded again at the sleeping interpreter and made a vague gesture of saluting.

I stepped a few feet away and stood still while I strapped the blue armband in place. I was covering Robert from the sentry while he repeated the same act. The sentry followed the whole process.

We walked towards the gate, making no sound as we shuffled through the dust. The sentry watched us come. He made us wait for a few taut seconds, wondering whether we should speak, and then he opened the gate.

We shambled through and turned off in the direction of the stables, not saying a word.

The broad path we were following curved away to the right and after a hundred yards we were out of sight of the sentry. Abandoning the path we looked for cover in the woods. It was time to change our identities.

There were only some low bushes to hide us and we struggled to get out of our Russian clothes half sitting, half lying on the ground. We cut our briefcases free with a penknife and unrolled our civilian hats. A quick wipe over our dusty shoes and we were ready to go. Sagan station was less than half a mile away and our train left at five minutes past six. I looked at my watch, it was exactly a quarter to six.

Sagan station was a dangerous place. A large number of the German camp staff used it and the possibility of being recognized was very real. Both Robert and I were fairly well known.

Robert bought the tickets and we immediately retired to the lavatory. In front of the mirrors over the washbasins, we checked the appearance of Jean Blanc and André Boucher. It was very encouraging. We looked like strangers. There was nothing to suggest that we were escaped prisoners.

The train was on time and we found seats in a crowded third-class compartment. I had vetoed the idea of travelling second class. It was better, I argued, to be well dressed in third class than to be not quite well enough dressed in second class. I was also determined that after the first day, when daylight travel was unavoidable, we would revert to night travel. Even though our papers might be faultless, darkness was always a friend.

Our plan was to change trains at Kottbus, some eighty kilometres from Sagan and go on to Leipzig. At Leipzig we had a choice. Either we would use our frontier passes and rely on the full authority of our documentation to buy ourselves a through ticket to Paris, or we would travel by night in shorter stages and cross the frontier on foot.

We would decide this in Leipzig. In any case, we intended to leave Leipzig that same evening travelling westwards.

The first police check occurred when we were about one hour out of Sagan. We had expected and dreaded it. But our story was carefully detailed and very simple. We were returning to the factory in Leipzig after doing a job at Sagan. We knew the name of the factory at Sagan where we were supposed to have been working. Our travel papers supported this story.

The policemen were busy and unsuspicious. They nodded uninterestedly while Robert told our story and glanced casually at our documents. I was beginning to relax again, feeling that this rehearsal had been good for us. It would give us much more confidence. We might even take the gamble of buying through tickets to Paris.

'Let me see your identity card again.'

The policeman was addressing Robert. He handed it over.

The policeman studied it very attentively.

'Now yours please.'

He studied them together, holding them side by side. Then he showed them to his mate.

'Is anything wrong?' asked Robert.

'There's something a little unusual,' he answered. It was not the tone of voice which threatened immediate arrest. If anything the policeman sounded puzzled. This gave Robert the courage to keep talking.

'There can't be anything wrong,' he insisted. 'As you see they were issued to us by the Leipzig police only a few months ago.'

'There's nothing wrong with this one.'

He handed mine back to me.

'But look at this.'

He held Robert's identity card open in front of us.

'The police stamp should be put across the corner of the photograph. Here it doesn't even touch the photograph.'

'I suppose they made a mistake,' said Robert weakly. He was very shaken.

'They must have done,' answered the policeman, 'but, as I said before, it's most unusual.'

He handed the card back to Robert.

'We'll let it go this time but if you want to avoid a lot of trouble in future, go round to the police station as soon as you're back in Leipzig and get it corrected.'

'Thank you very much,' we answered in chorus. 'We'll do it immediately we arrive.'

Robert and I were very worried. The forging department who had been responsible for the preparation of the documents had made a quite incredible mistake. All they had had to do was to paste Robert's photograph inside the little rectangle indicated and then apply the Leipzig police stamp across the corner of the photograph. They had applied the stamp, but it did not touch the photograph.

My identity card had arrived with the photograph and stamp already applied and London had not made the same mistake. It was only the obvious genuinity of the documents which had persuaded the policeman to let us go.

'How the hell could they have made such a stupid mistake?' asked Robert. 'They've always been so good. I just don't understand it. What are we going to do now?'

We were talking in the corridor but we could not continue. There were too many people about.

We got off the train at Kottbus and bought ourselves some beer. We had less than an hour to wait before our connection to Leipzig was due.

'We've got to find somewhere we can talk,' whispered Robert.

'Let's go onto the platform,' I answered.

Right at the end of the platform we found a vacant bench.

'You'd better go on alone, Tommy. They'll pick me up at the next check.'

'Don't be damned silly, Robert. You know perfectly well that

I couldn't survive a check unless you're with me. Why do you think I keep dragging you all round the German countryside?'

'With your papers, you wouldn't have to open your mouth. Anyway, you speak a lot more German now than you did six months ago. The best thing is to separate.'

'Forget it, Robert. We're in this together and we'll get out together.'

'So what do we do now?'

'First we've got to get out of Kottbus. It's nine o'clock and, if they didn't cover our absence on appell, the warnings will be going out within half an hour. Kottbus is too damn close to Sagan to be healthy. I suggest we take our train to Leipzig and risk it. You can always tell the cops that the error on your identity card has already been pointed out to you and that you're reporting to the Leipzig police as soon as you get back. You've got away with it once. You can do it again. The fact that my papers are in order all helps. Let's risk it.'

'And after Leipzig?'

'We'll decide when we get there.'

We boarded the train for Leipzig. There was no corridor in the third class and being enclosed in our uncomfortable compartment gave us a false sense of security. We were alone and could talk freely. We had only one topic of conversation: what to do to avoid trouble with Robert's identity card.

The train was stopping frequently at stations along the route. This made Robert nervous.

'We should have taken a fast train,' he said.

'I don't think so. The police are much less likely to check a local train like this.'

I had hardly finished speaking when a policeman climbed into the compartment.

'Guten Morgen meine Herren.'

At least he was polite.

'Your papers, please.'

I presented mine first. It was a new tactic we had worked out. The policeman asked a few questions which I answered easily. He was not suspicious.

'And yours?' He turned to Robert.

Robert spread out his papers in a wide fan in two hands.

'They're exactly the same as his,' he answered. 'We work for the same firm.'

For a moment I thought the trick had worked. But no. He picked out Robert's German identity card and looked at it. Then he looked at mine again.

'This is very strange,' he said.

Robert started his explanations. The policeman listened with interest.

'We had better clear this up at the station. You can't travel with a document like this.'

For half an hour, until the train ran into Finsterwalde, Robert argued and pleaded. But the policeman remained firm.

'We'll clear it up at the station,' he repeated.

As the train came to a halt, I played my last card.

'Don't worry,' I said to Robert in German, 'as soon as I get to the factory I'll speak to the manager. He'll clear you immediately. Goodbye for the moment.'

I shook hands with him.

The policeman looked at me.

'You're coming too,' he said flatly.

'But why? My papers are in order.'

'Don't argue.'

We knew it was the end but a small thread of hope impelled us to stick to our story when we got to the police station. Our briefcases and documents were taken from us and we were locked up.

Half an hour later we were again standing in front of the station chief. He did not waste any time.

'I've talked to the factory you claim to work at,' he waved at the telephone, 'and they've never heard of you.

'So who are you?'

The comedy was over. We told him who we were.

'I thought so,' he said. His voice lacked the usual satisfaction to which we were accustomed. Instead it was grave and serious. I was beginning to feel a little uneasy.

'Bring me that file on escaped prisoners-of-war,' he shouted. He studied the file for a few minutes.

'Yes, here we are,' he said. 'Both of you. You escaped from Schubin on 6 March and were arrested in Köln on 11 March. I don't know if you realize that your last escape caused a Gross-fahndung, a nationwide alarm. Thousands of soldiers and police were searching for you and your companions. Every hotel, every barn and every train in the country was searched. Do you recognize your pictures?'

It was the typical 'wanted man' police poster. We easily recognized our own photographs among half a dozen others.

'Now you have some very difficult questions to answer and I advise you to answer them most carefully. Your position is very serious. Much more serious than you think.'

He was speaking very earnestly and I had the strongest impression that he was not threatening us but warning us. My uneasiness increased.

'Where did you get these documents?'

It was the question I was most afraid of.

'I am not permitted to answer that question. The Geneva Convention only requires me to give you my name, rank and number.'

He nodded slowly.

'I expected that answer. Well, I'll tell you where you got these documents. As a policeman I have a lot of experience of these matters. In the first place they were not produced inside your prison camp. I have seen many of your prison forgeries but they are always quite evident forgeries. These documents were printed on modern presses. One of these forms,' he held up the pink frontier pass, 'has the name of a Leipzig printer in the corner here. But that company has no contract for printing these forms. I can deduce with absolute certainty that these documents were printed in England.

'What have you to say?'

We remained silent.

'Now take these travel passes. They're all signed by the chief of police in Leipzig, whom I've known for twenty years. I know his signature as well as my own. He could not have signed these, yet I would be willing to swear that this is his signature. How do you explain that?'

The silence was absolute. I loosened my collar.

'You understand what I'm saying? These are the sort of documents used by spies, not by escaped prisoners-of-war. Spies are treated very differently to prisoners-of-war. If you were not now in the hands of the Kriminalpolizei, I would give nothing for your chances of ever seeing your homes again.'

Now I was convinced that the grey haired policeman in front of us was giving us a very serious warning, not with the intention of frightening us but for some humanitarian motive I could not analyse. He had told us clearly that we had not yet been put in the hands of the Gestapo, which we had not realized. The implication was that, if we were good and careful, we might not fall into their hands. The Gestapo were Himmler's men and very dangerous.

'What will happen to us now?' asked Robert.

'A decision will be taken about you. Meanwhile you will be locked up. If it can be shown that you have not committed any civil crimes against the state, it is even possible that you will be returned to Sagan.'

The End of the Journey

Four days later we were back at Sagan. After spending twenty-one days in the cells there, we rejoined our friends in the East Compound just before Christmas.

I had two urgent tasks. First I saw the senior British officer and the assembled escape committee and told them that I thought there were new dangers, possibly very serious ones, for prisoners who were recaptured with the London documents in their possession. A charge of espionage would be very difficult to avoid.

'So what do you suggest?'

'Continue to use the ones we forge ourselves. They are good enough, especially if one travels by night, and they are so obviously hand-made when inspected under a magnifying glass. Save the others for special people on special occasions. Certainly, don't let anyone use them unless he knows the risks very clearly.'

'Anything else?'

'There's something I can't put my finger on, but it's bad news. I think the Geneva Convention is wearing very thin. I don't believe we can rely on it for protection as we always have done in the past. I also get the impression that the Gestapo is making a powerful bid to take over responsibility for all prisoners-of-war.

'I got this feeling after talking to both the police and the military. If that happens we will have to be very, very careful. The Gestapo don't obey any rules but their own.'

I then went round to see the forgers and told them of the mistake they had made on Robert's documents.

'Oh, but we always do it that way.'

'Well, it's time for a change. The police don't like your methods.'

The East Compound was changing in many ways. During the long summer there had been a steady outflow of old prisoners on the North Compound. Some just wanted a change of scenery, others were attracted by the very secret rumour that the biggest tunnel of all time was being dug there and that experienced workers would be welcome. Ian Cross and Charles Hall had gone, so had Tim Walenn and a host of others. The East Compound was filling up with new faces as freshly shot down prisoners arrived with increasing regularity. The war in the air was working up towards its zenith and the casualties were high.

I had started a new tunnel which was based on quite the most feverish idea that my tired brain had yet conceived. The tunnel started twelve feet above floor level, in the side of a chimney. My theory was that the Germans would not look for a tunnel entrance twelve feet above the ground. But the chimney was narrow and the work of enlarging its interior, until it could provide passage for a man, was laboriously long. Eventually the tunnel would go vertically down through the foundations of the chimney and then strike off towards the wire. It was a long term project.

On 25 March 1944, the north compound broke its big tunnel. This was thirty feet underground and 350 feet long. Seventy-six prisoners escaped. Ian Cross, Charles Hall and Tim Walenn were among them. The north compound organizers were disappointed. They had planned on getting 200 men away. But it was still the biggest coup we had ever made.

Our excitement and jubilation were short lived. Less than three weeks after the escape, the Germans made a formal pronouncement that forty-one of the escaped prisoners had been shot 'while resisting arrest or attempting further escape after arrest.'

It was not believable. We could not take it in. Even when the list of those executed was published and the total had increased to a round figure of fifty, many clung to the desperate hope that it was all a bluff to frighten us into being good boys.

Yet the fear that it was true pervaded all of us and the sorrow of reading the names of so many true friends was hurting each one of us. Ian Cross was on the list and I could not imagine him dead. He had more vitality than any five men. Charles Hall was there, the kind, conscientious, ever-helpful pilot officer. Tim Walenn was there, the man who had forged a thousand passes for others and never had time to plan an escape for himself.

Of the many non-British RAF officers who escaped, nearly all were shot including my old friends Marcinkus and Mondshein and the irrepressible Norwegians, Espelid and Fugelsang. Only three got safely back to England, Bob Van der Stok, a Belgian, and Rockland and Muller, two Norwegians.

When fifty urns containing the ashes of the dead men, who had all been cremated, were delivered to us, we could no longer escape the truth. We were in the hands of murderers.

The order for the shooting had come from Hitler and Himmler had carried it out. Himmler's second in command, Kaltenbrunner, had immediately issued what has since become known as the 'Sagan order.' The essential part of this order is quoted textually:

'The Fuehrer has ordered that more than half the escaped officers are to be shot. Therefore I order that the Kriminalpolizei are to hand over for interrogation to the Gestapo more than half of the recaptured officers. After the interrogation the officers are to be taken in the direction of their original camp and shot en route. The shootings will be explained by the fact that the recaptured prisoners were shot whilst trying to escape, or because they offered resistance, so that nothing can be proved later. The Gestapo will report the shootings to the Kriminalpolizei giving this reason.'

We buried the fifty at Sagan with such pathetic military honours as we could give them. I saw nobody crying at the funeral although many must have felt like it. But there was such a feeling of consuming hatred for the German race that it was like electricity. It sparked from man to man and, for those of us who lived through those events, I think it still endures.

The murder of the fifty put a stop to all further escapes, which were rigorously forbidden by our own senior officers. We were winning the war and the end was too near to risk any more lives. The atmosphere of the camp changed from one of comparatively cheerful activity to a sullen, morose boredom. Now we were truly prisoners. We had nothing to do but to wait for the final German defeat.

There was now only one way to get home and that was by being repatriated on medical grounds. It was a very long-odds chance, but it was still worth a try. A Swiss-German Repatriation Commission, sponsored by the Red Cross, visited the camp once a year to interview the hopeful applicants. If the Commission approved a particular case, he might possibly get repatriated if the Germans ever got around to it. In the spring of 1944 nobody had yet been shipped home.

Although there was only a handful of prisoners who genuinely qualified for repatriation because of the state of their health, there was always a great crowd of candidates. Most of them were tough, able-bodied individuals who had never had a day's illness in their lives. Their faces were more familiar in the dim glow of a margarine lamp in any of the tunnels in progress. It was accepted that any prisoner, however fit, was entitled to try and fool the Commission. This was considered to be a somewhat underhand, but quite legitimate form of escape. It was also generally thought to be a forlorn hope.

I had already been before the Commission on three previous occasions and had been turned down each time. Now the Commission was due again in the month of May and it was very strongly rumoured that an actual exchange of sick between England and Germany was imminent. We prisoners always believed the good rumours.

I decided to try once more although, in baseball parlance, with three strikes against me, a home run was hardly likely. On the other hand, waiting to be interviewed by the Commission was always a great social occasion, some times lasting several days. There were candidates from all the other compounds of Stalag Luft III, from which we were segregated, as well as from other prison camps, and it was an opportunity to meet old friends one had not seen for a long time.

Hurriedly I prepared a new case, relying largely upon a medical encyclopedia and Digby Young who had once been a medical student.

This time the waiting room was overcrowded. All the regulars were there, including the genuinely sick. Among them was Bill Joyce.

I was delighted to see Bill and greeted him with a hearty cheerfulness. The heartiness was assumed and the cheerfulness forced. In reality I was shocked and appalled by his appearance. When I had last seen Bill at Dulag Luft, in the early days of 1942, he had hardly been a picture of health. Now he was skeletal. All the flesh seemed to have gone from his bones. His face was deeply lined and his blue eyes unnaturally prominent. He was still on crutches and moved with agonizing difficulty.

Bill smiled at me. It was not much of a smile, but there was still a trace of the vital personality I had known before.

'Come and sit here, skipper,' he said. 'It's good to see you again.'

'How's it go, Bill?'

I was so upset by the change in him that I was using conventional phrases to hide my emotion.

'I'm finished. They finally fixed me.' He was speaking calmly, with only a trace of desperation in his voice.

'Now I just hope they send me home . . .'

He left the sentence unfinished, but I knew the words he had left unsaid. I could have completed the sentence for him. There were only two words missing, '. . . to die.'

Gradually, because it took a while for me to recover from my initial reaction and to get Bill to talk, I got the story from him.

After Dulag Luft, he had passed through various prison camps and hospitals, gradually improving in health to the point where he could walk reasonably well without crutches. He had made a number of abortive attempts to escape and was getting more and more desperate after each failure. One dark night he had slipped out of his barrack block and started to crawl towards the fence, armed with a pair of wire-cutters. He was still a long way from the wire, well inside the camp, when the searchlights had picked him up and the sentries had opened fire. He was hit a number of times and one bullet had lodged in his spine.

Since then he had been in hospital. He was almost completely paralysed from below the hips and only with the greatest difficulty could he swing two useless legs between his crutches.

The bullet was still in his spinal column and the doctors had not dared to try and remove it.

As we talked, something of the old Bill Joyce I had known and admired came back. His sense of humour was still alive and his unquenchable courage was still there. The difference was that he now knew he was dying, but he desperately wanted to die at home.

I had the chilling thought that if the Commission should pass me for repatriation, and I was one of the biggest phoneys in the room, and at the same time turn down Joyce, I would never be able to live with myself.

I need not have worried. After the long and harrowing session with Bill Joyce, my appearance before the Commission was all comic relief.

As soon as I came into the room, the Swiss colonel, who was the chairman, rose to his feet to greet me.

'Ah, Major Calnan,' he said. 'It is a pleasure to see you again.'

He spoke excellent English and his welcome seemed to be genuine. This was the fourth time I had appeared before him and, in a certain sense, we were old friends.

'I hope that your tuberculosis has cleared up?' he continued solicitously.

This was one below the belt. On my last appearance before the Commission my story had been that I was an advanced case of tuberculosis. I had presented a remarkably well documented case history, all entirely false, which should have convinced any specialist that I was in the last stages of consumption. I had spent two weeks in hospital so that I could, three times a day, have a fake temperature recorded. After two weeks, my temperature chart was an exact copy of the typical chart of an advanced tuberculosis case presented in one of Digby Young's volumes on the subject.

The secret of achieving this result was to have a spare thermometer hidden under the pillow. The setting on the hidden thermometer could be arranged by dipping it into one's morning tea or by holding it under the hot tap. A little bit of sleight of hand, a momentary distraction of the nurse's attention and the thermometer one had in one's mouth could be switched for the other.

When they decided to X-ray my lungs, I had to choose where the cavities should be located. On the best available advice, I located a really big one at the apex of my right lung and a smaller one at the base of my left lung. To obtain the desired result on the X-ray plates, I painted the skin outside these critical points with white iodine. This was colourless and indetectable to the eye. It was the confident opinion of our most eminent medical students, Digby Young, Bob Cost and others, that the effect of the iodine would be to produce, on the negative, just that sort of dark haziness which the doctors would read as a cavity.

This complicated scheme was not successful, although I never did find out why.

The Swiss doctor was waiting for an answer to his kind enquiry. I mustered all my forces.

'As a matter of fact, colonel,' I said, 'it's taken a turn for the worse.'

I coughed disgustingly.

'But that was last time,' I started to say. This was a bad slip of the tongue.

'I mean,' I went on hastily, 'I've got a different problem now.'

'Oh, I'm sure you have. You must tell us about it. By the way,' he continued, 'how are your duodenal ulcers?'

The duodenals had been the time before. This man had too good a memory.

I clutched my stomach and bent forward. I was the hammiest of actors.

'Agony, doctor, agony,' I answered.

'You should drink a lot of milk,' he recommended. 'And are your eyes better?'

The Swiss doctor was now smiling broadly, almost laughing. He was referring to my first appearance in that room, nearly three years before, when I had blandly claimed to be blind in the right eye. I think that that had been the nearest I ever came to deceiving the Commission. The burns on my face were still livid and my right eyelid had a nasty, sinister droop. I really looked like a wounded man. But the specialist in Posen, with his bright lights, magnifying glasses and charts had destroyed that particular effort.

The Colonel had made it clear enough that, whatever my latest story might be, I was not going to be believed. I was not even disappointed. Rather, I was relieved. I would not have to go through with the embarrassing act I had planned to prove that I was mentally unbalanced. I felt that I might as well relax and enjoy myself.

My intention had been to present myself as a wire psychosis case. The problem which arose in selecting this popular mental ailment was that the rules of the game prevented the subject from diagnosing his own disease. All he could do was to describe the symptoms which should lead the board to the conclusion that he was mentally affected. For those who were natural actors and had vivid imaginations, this resulted in some quite remarkable presentations in front of the Commission which, I am sure, they found highly amusing.

The Swiss chairman was talking again.

'Now tell us about your latest troubles.'

On the desk in front of him was a thick file on my medical history which he had been studying.

'Well, doctor,' I started hesitantly, having abandoned my prepared script, 'I get delusions which are often very real and persistent.'

'Describe your delusions.'

'The strangest and most recent takes the form of an overwhelming conviction that all my illnesses in the past, the blindness, the ulcers, the tuberculosis, were all entirely imaginary.'

The colonel started to laugh. The German doctor joined him and soon the whole assembled board was laughing helplessly.

With a great effort of will, I kept a straight face.

'That's very funny, Major. It really is,' said the colonel as soon as he had recovered his breath. Then he corrected himself hurriedly.

'I mean, it's very interesting. What else do you wish to tell us?'

'I have many other delusions. Perhaps the most significant is that the Russians have broken through on the East Front and are on the outskirts of Berlin while the Allied armies have crossed the channel, occupied all of western Germany and have joined up with the Russians. That another million German soldiers have died.'

The German doctor, an old and respected enemy of mine, was staring fixedly at me. Nobody said a word.

'I even have the delusion that the fifty officers who were recently shot while attempting to escape were, in fact, cold bloodedly murdered by their captors and that these murderers have been tracked down, tried and hanged by the neck with a hempen rope.'

The Swiss Colonel interrupted me just as I was getting into the swing of my speech and developing a nice histrionic style.

'That will be quite enough, Major.'

'But I have many other interesting delusions,' I protested, 'one of which is that this Commission is just a farce. There are a number of very sick men outside that door who have been waiting for years to be repatriated.'

The Swiss held up his hand to stop me. He wiped his face with a spotless white handkerchief.

'In my opinion,' he said slowly, 'your delusions have no medical significance at all.'

The word medical was heavily underlined.

'As we have a very long list of cases still to consider, I will have to curtail this interview. Major Calnan, it is my judgement as chairman of this Commission, that your case does not warrant repatriation. That is all.'

He got to his feet and I rose as well. I wondered if I had offended him. But he held out his hand and gave me a warm handshake.

'Of course,' he said, 'there is nothing to prevent you from presenting yourself again, Major. But I would be happier if you did not contract any other serious diseases. You have more than enough to cope with already.'

When my guard ushered me back into the waiting room, forty-five pairs of eyes were staring at me, trying to read the verdict in my face. Quickly I made the gesture of pulling down the lavatory chain. Everybody's eyes immediately left me and conversation was resumed. There were the usual banal expressions of sympathy.

'Tough luck, Tommy.'

'Better luck next time.'

That moment of re-entry into the waiting room was always embarrassing. All the audience was searchingly alert to read the fate of the candidate in his expression. They seldom made a mistake. A successful candidate was a rarity and easily detected. Those of the failures who tried to hide their disappointment behind a too-cheerful smile, very seldom deceived that critical audience.

Bill Joyce's turn did not come until late in the afternoon. Refusing all offers of help he moved awkwardly and slowly through the door. Everybody wished him luck. He was the sickest man in the room and we were all confidently expecting that he would be passed without question. It did not seem that the Commission could do anything else.

Joyce was away a long time. Eventually we heard the sound of his crutches returning and he appeared in the doorway.

There was death in his face. A low moan of disappointment came from the audience, followed by a brittle, embarrassing silence. Nobody dared produce any of those meaningless platitudes which we had been using all day for the previous failures.

I got to my feet and walked across the room to meet Bill at the door.

His faint smile showed bitterness and resignation.

'That's my lot, Tommy,' he said very calmly. 'I'll never see auld Ireland again.'

Bill died before the war ended, still a prisoner.

Two

THE invasion had revived our spirits and suddenly every room in the camp had a new war map on which flags and arrows were moved forward eagerly to mark the Allied advances. But by Christmas the advances had slowed so much that the war maps were forgotten. In contrast, the Russian steamroller was crushing all German resistance in the East. Budapest fell on Christmas day, no more than 350 miles from us. Warsaw, a mere 250 miles away, was threatened. The prospect of the camp being overrun by the Russian armies began to look very real.

The Germans clearly thought the same because they moved us out of Sagan on 28 January 1945, one day after the Russians had taken Warsaw. For five days we marched through the snow. We had abandoned nearly all our belongings at Sagan and taken only food, clothing and blankets with us, which we dragged in sleds behind us. At night we slept in barns or empty buildings.

The snow thawed on the fifth day of the march and we left our sleds by the roadside, still piled with valuable belongings. A man can carry much less on his back than he can drag on a sled. When we finally arrived at Luckenwalde, we had little more than the clothes we stood up in.

Luckenwalde was a long established prison camp situated fifty kilometres due south of Berlin. It housed some 15,000 prisoners-of-war of all imaginable nationalities and each nationality was segregated by barbed wire. Of the long column of RAF prisoners which had started from Sagan, only a few hundred arrived at Luckenwalde. The remainder had been diverted northwards.

Conditions there were grim. We were crowded into filthy barracks and slept one above the other in three-tier bunks. The man on the top berth did not have enough head room to sit up in bed. There were no Red Cross parcels and the German ration was entirely inadequate. But there was a flourishing black market and for cigarettes one could buy food.

Our orders were not to attempt to escape but to await liberation by one or the other of the advancing allied armies.

By mid-April it was obvious that the Russians would reach Luckenwalde first. Although the Americans and the British were over the Rhine and advancing towards the Elbe, there was little hope that they would beat the Russians to Berlin.

I was not at all happy about the prospect of being liberated by the Russians. I preferred the idea of filtering through to the American lines as soon as they got reasonably close. I discussed plans with Digby Young, who was just completing his fifth year as a prisoner-of-war. For all his long imprisonment and many privations, Digby was one of the fittest and most cheerful men in the camp.

Digby was an Australian who had been studying medicine in England. Throughout his imprisonment he had continued his studies intermittently and had collected an impressive library of medical tomes. He was considered an authority and was very much in demand when the annual Repatriation Commission visited a camp. Digby was always glad to describe the symptoms of some suitably chronic disease which qualified for repatriation. He would also brief you how to answer the doctors' questions.

I do not know whether any of Digby's clients ever fooled the Repatriation Commission, but many tried. The popular diseases were tuberculosis, duodenal ulcers and wire psychosis. Every year scores of us went through the farce of pretending to be sick. It was accepted as a legitimate form of escape. I know a number of fit men who got home that way.

Digby was as nervous as I was about our situation and was anxious to take some action which would ensure his survival. We made our preparations together.

By 19 April the atmosphere at Luckenwalde was confused and excited. Rumours that the Russians were less than twenty miles away were insistent. Our German guards were unusually nervous and dangerous. The next day the sound of gunfire in the distance was distinctly audible. The war was arriving fast.

On 21 April, which was a Saturday, all the Germans suddenly disappeared in the middle of the morning. Within half an hour, the Russian prisoners had broken out of their compound and were looting the communal potato store. As this was one of the few major reserves of food for the whole camp, they had to be stopped. The RAF turned out at the double, armed with sticks and baseball bats. A hand to hand battle ensued and we saved the potatoes. There was little fight in the Russians, they were too weak. Out of pity, we distributed a generous ration of potatoes to them and sent them back to their barracks.

We then declared ourselves the rulers of the camp. Nobody protested.

But we had taken on an enormous responsibility. We had to feed more than 15,000 souls. Foraging parties were immediately organized, consisting only of air force officers, and we went looking for food. There was plenty to be found. We located a number of military warehouses stacked to the roof with flour, rice and canned foods. Soon we had commandeered some German trucks and were bringing tons of food back to the camp. Nobody was allowed out of the gates except the foraging parties, who had special passes, issued by the senior RAF officer. Naturally, I had one of these precious passes.

The rest of the camp, particularly our own RAF friends, who were not privileged to go foraging, were very resentful. Scores of prisoners of all nationalities went out over the wire to do their own foraging. There was little difference between foraging and looting.

We saw our first Russians two days after the Germans had left. An armoured column rolled down the road through the middle of the camp. Each gigantic tank was preceded by two running soldiers armed with tommy-guns. Most of these soldiers were squat, red-skinned Mongolians. I began to understand why the German population had such a fear of the Russians. We cheered ourselves hoarse to welcome the Red Army and, for a short time, fraternized with them. Then they were gone as suddenly as they had appeared.

For the next few days the countryside all around us was not safe. Isolated battles were in progress everywhere and the Russians were mopping up the many thousands of enemy troops who were in the area and still fighting desperately. It was a common sight to see exhausted German soldiers, some of them mere boys, running across country for the cover of the woods, pursued by Russians. They seldom escaped.

By 27 April the camp was strictly controlled by the Russians who had put armed sentries on all the gates and on the perimeter wire. We were prisoners again.

I decided that it was time to leave. Digby and I were both ready and during my foraging sorties I had liberated two excellent bicycles of Italian manufacture which were now safely hidden inside the camp.

The Russian officer responsible for the administration of the camp was Captain Medvedev, a very cultured Russian who spoke fluent French. He also liked his liquor. I went to call on him with Digby taking with me half a dozen bottles of French wine, which were also the fruit of one of my sorties. We had the wildest of parties which went on into the small hours. Medvedev had his own stock of liquor to keep us going when my poor contribution had run out. Before we were all stupified, I had obtained what I wanted, namely, two passes for the main gate signed by Medvedev. Without these there was no way out of the camp.

The price I paid was very high, the biggest hangover of all time and my Rolex watch.

I had made the crass mistake of wearing my watch on my wrist, although I knew well that any Russian soldier would be happy to cut my arm off to obtain possession of the watch. When I saw Medvedev eyeing it repeatedly I began to regret my thoughtlessness. But he gave me the passes I asked for. By then, the party had reached the sentimental stage of drunkenness.

'My dear major,' said Medvedev, 'we have a charming custom in Russia. When two people like us find we have such affinity, we swear eternal brotherhood. We shall now do that.'

Our glasses were refilled to the brim and standing, with our right arms entwined at the elbow, we emptied our glasses.

They were immediately refilled.

'To my brother,' Medvedev's voice was breaking with emotion.

'To my brother,' I responded trying to squeeze sufficient sentiment into my voice.

Again we emptied our glasses.

Medvedev looked me straight in the face and I suddenly realized that he was no more drunk than I was. There was a cold, calculating glitter in his eyes.

'To seal this eternal bond,' he announced solemnly, 'we now exchange gifts.'

He took his watch from his wrist. It was a sort of Russian Ingersoll, cheap and horrible, probably operated by a tired Russian beetle.

I looked into his eyes and knew I was defeated. I unstrapped my Rolex and gave it to him. It was the most cultured example of robbery that I have ever suffered. But it was still better than losing an arm.

Now that our business was done, we were all ready to call a halt to the drinking. Both sides had achieved their objectives. I had my passes and Medvedev had my Rolex. We parted in sentimental friendship. It was three o'clock in the morning

'We'll leave at dawn,' I told Digby. 'I don't trust that bastard not to revoke the passes.'

'What about food?' asked Digby.

'Let's forget it. In twenty-four hours we'll be with the Yanks. We'll have a huge breakfast and off we go.'

'Tommy, you're drunk. Where do we get breakfast?'

'Kanelakos,' I answered.

Jimmy Kanelakos was a Canadian air force officer of Greek origin. He was a master chef by nature. There was nothing he did not know about food and cuisine. For the last week he had been slaughtering and distributing the horses and cattle which the foraging parties had driven into the camp. Jimmy was well organized and would have no difficulty in rustling up a solid breakfast.

'He'll probably have eggs and bacon for us,' I went on, my mouth watering at the thought.

'Yes, but that's stuff for his mess. It will have cost him a lot of cigarettes on the black market,' objected Digby.

'Digby, we're leaving everything behind. We'll give it all to Jimmy and he can sell it on the black market. My sleeping bag alone is worth at least 200 cigarettes. That's five loaves of bread and ten eggs.'

THE END OF THE JOURNEY

Jimmy did not like being woken up at four in the morning, but when he heard what our problem was all his bad temper vanished. We ate the most magnificent breakfast I can ever remember. Then we went to find our bicycles.

Three

THE Russian sentry on the main gate was a Mongolian, the most dangerous and unpredictable of all the many races to be found in the Russian army. Not more than five feet tall in his boots, his skin was brick red in colour, his eyes tiny slits and his nose practically non-existent. The distance between his eyebrows and the hairline above his forehead could be measured in millimetres. His short tommy-gun was loaded and pointed at us. These little men were the toughest of all the soldiers in the Red Army. They were ruthless and efficient killers, apparently without any trace of fear in their make-up.

There was no British sentry on the gate. These were not posted until eight o'clock in the morning, which saved us the embarrassment of having to lie to one of our friends.

I had not yet met a Mongolian who could read and, when we presented our passes, I expected the worst. But my fears were unfounded. He did not hold the passes upside-down, which was the normal procedure for the many Russian sentries who could not read, but just glanced at them briefly and unlocked the gate. He patted each bicycle lovingly as it was wheeled past him. He longed for a bicycle of his own.

A moment later we were pedalling down the road to Juterbog. It was an exhilarating feeling which derived as much from the unfettered freedom of movement which the bicycle seemed to provide as from our intense conviction that we would never again see that dreadful prison camp.

Digby, like a small boy, was weaving from side to side of the road, thoroughly enjoying the physical sensation of bicycling. I was pedalling more sedately but only because I was trying to attach my briefcase to the cross bar. It was not yet seven o'clock in the morning, the sky was clear of cloud and it promised to be a perfect spring day.

Two miles down the road, when the camp was already out of sight, we turned to the right onto a narrow dirt road which would lead us in a westerly direction to Felgentreu. Our plan was to take a very circuitous route to Wittenberg using only the smallest and least important country roads. Had we stayed on the main road, we could have been in Wittenberg in less than three hours. But that particular main road promised a number of serious hazards. It was one of the major arteries between Berlin and Leipzig. It was unlikely that the Germans would still be holding it but it was certain that in their retreat they would have blown all the bridges and viaducts. If firmly in Russian hands it would certainly be closely patrolled. We preferred to avoid these dangers and were going to make a wide circle to the west and eventually approach Wittenberg from the north-west. Our route passed through no major towns and would, we hoped, avoid those areas where the advancing Red Army spearheads were in contact with the retreating Germans.

We had only just turned off the main road when the first minor disaster occurred. The front tyre of Digby's bicycle went flat. Pumping did not remedy the fault, the tyre was obviously punctured.

I waited patiently until Digby had exhausted his very considerable vocabulary of English and Australian oaths.

'You'd better get it mended quick, Digby. We can't hang around here.'

Digby kicked the offending bicycle viciously.

'Cheap, wop bog-wheel,' he said. 'Come on. Let's get off the road.'

'Where do you want to go?'

'Those woods over there. If any Russians come along this road they're going to hi-jack our bicycles. You know how they are. We'll never make it as far as Wittenberg on foot and I'm damned if I'm going back to that stinking camp.'

The woods lay about a quarter of a mile north of the road. We shouldered our bicycles and trotted across the intervening field, making for a thick clump of trees at the westward end of the wood.

I was about fifty yards behind Digby when he disappeared into the trees. Two seconds later he re-appeared signalling frantically.

From the gestures he was making I understood that I was to make no noise and to hurry. I did my best and joined him among the trees about twenty seconds later. He took my bicycle from me and laid it gently on the ground. Neither of us said a word. Tip-toeing, he led me into the wood.

Behind a clump of bushes there were three corpses, closely grouped. They had been mere boys, beardless and fair-skinned. They wore the uniform of the Hitler Jugend. The two who still had features looked angelic in death. The third had half his face missing.

Digby, the medical student, was fascinated by the corpses. He was examining them with a cold-blooded interest which was not in the least feigned. I was feeling rather sick.

'Look,' he said, 'all shot through the head and all with serious wounds in the stomach or the legs. These poor kids were wounded and couldn't move any further. They were finished off here, where they lay.'

'How long have they been dead?' I asked.

Digby started to lecture me. He assumed an exaggerated English accent and his best platform manner. It was a role he thoroughly enjoyed.

'The onset of rigor mortis,' he declaimed, 'depends considerably upon the ambient temperature. Bearing this in mind, it can first be detected in the jaw, between two and three hours after death. The arms and legs are affected from six to eight hours after death.'

He took the outflung hand of the nearest corpse and shook it. The whole arm flopped up and down loosely.

'Jesus Christ,' said Digby in pure Australian.

Rather gingerly he took hold of the jaw of the dead boy and pulled down. The mouth opened easily.

Digby looked at me. He was white in the face.

'On your bicycle, cobber,' he said. 'This is no place for us. These kids were shot less than two hours ago. Since dawn, in fact. I just don't want to meet the Russians who did the job. Let's go.'

We shouldered our bicycles and moved deep into the wood, our eyes searching for any sign of movement.

'This'll do,' said Digby. 'Let's get this puncture fixed and move on fast.'

Neither of us had mended a puncture since we were schoolboys, but we did a very fast job. Fortunately, the original owners of the bicycles had all the necessary kit in the little leather bags attached behind the saddles.

'Now where do we go?' asked Digby, when the puncture was mended and the tire pumped hard.

'Back the way we came,' I answered. 'There were no Russians on that side of the wood or we'd have seen them. They must be west of us. We'll meet them in due course, probably in the next village. Let's fix the flags on our bicycles and put on our armbands.'

We had brought with us small red banners which fitted on to a little mast on the front mudguards of the bicycles and two wide armbands of the same colour. We knew from experience that these were an effective insurance against being shot on sight. As the Russian armies moved into the country, the German communists came out of hiding and identified themselves initially by waving red flags. The Russians were looking for and expecting this reaction. Red was the colour of the day. Red kept the bullets away.

A few minutes later we were back on the dirt road, heading westwards towards Felgentreu. As we approached the village, Digby turned to me.

'I'll bet you anything you like we meet the Russians here.'

'I'm not betting. But don't forget the drill. As soon as we see them, we go into our act. We mustn't be stopped.'

Sure enough, as we entered the main street we saw a small group of Russian soldiers standing on the roadside. Automatically we went into our pre-planned routine.

We forced down on the pedals, working our speed up to the maximum, while still maintaining an upright and casual posture on our bicycles. We showed all our teeth in what we hoped would be taken for a happy smile. When we were thirty yards from the Russian group, we raised our right arms high in the air, fists clenched, armbands visible and shouted in unison.

'Zdrasti Tovarich.'

We had learned the phrase by heart. It meant 'Greetings Comrade.'

By the time the Russians had reacted we were past them, still with that inane grin on our faces and moving very fast.

The planned drill then called for us to swing round the next corner and disappear from sight. Unfortunately, there were no side roads in the village and we just had to keep going straight on. Every few seconds, one of us turned round, still grimacing, and waved a clenched fist in farewell.

It was primitive, but it worked. The last backward glance I had of the Russian group showed them standing stock still in open-mouthed astonishment. Then we were out of the village and out of their line of sight.

We were now making fast progress. The country was flat and we easily maintained the high velocity we had set up. We passed through Pechile without incident and soon reached Bardenitz, where we had to turn left for Klausdorf.

Bardenitz seemed to be completely deserted and there was considerable artillery damage. Rubble was lying in the streets and the church tower had collapsed. But there were no dead lying around and only a burned out Russian tank gave some indication of what had taken place.

'It was the Krauts who shelled this village,' observed Digby. 'There must have been a Russian armoured column moving through here and the Germans tried to stop it. The railway isn't far from here. They'd have been trying to hold the line open.'

In the village square was a newly painted signpost, incongruous among the dust and debris of destruction. We rode over to it, picking our way carefully between piles of rubble. We wanted to be certain of taking the right road.

The signpost was in Russian. Before pulling out of the village, the Russians had substituted the German signpost with one of their own. Fortunately, we had prepared ourselves for this possibility and were able to recognize the Russian characters which indicated Klausdorf. We turned left and cycled on.

After Bardenitz the road started climbing steadily and our pace slowed. Already we were getting saddle sore and my calf muscles were beginning to feel the strain. Bicycling was great fun in small doses, but we were beginning to have had our fill of it.

After a very long uphill struggle we emerged onto flat open heathland. It was delightful country, thickly spread with heather and gorse bushes and with occasional clumps of silver birch. The air was clean and invigorating. The sun, not yet high in a clear sky, promised warmth by noon.

We pulled off the road and found cover behind some gorse.

There we smoked our first cigarette since leaving the camp. It was a quarter to ten.

'I've got a feeling that there's trouble ahead,' said Digby. His English accent was back which meant that he was his usual calm self.

'You mean the railway,' I answered. 'You think the Germans may be trying to hold it to get their troops and supplies back to Berlin?'

Berlin had not yet fallen to the Russians. Hitler was in the city which was being defended tenaciously. Our theory was that all the retreating German armies would be pulled back to defend the capital.

'There is the possibility that the Huns have withdrawn to the autobahn, which can't be much more than twenty kilometres further west.'

This was Digby's opinion.

'Let's hope you're right, mate. Otherwise we aren't going to be able to cross the railway.'

Both of us were expert armchair strategists, as were nearly all the prisoners at Luckenwalde. We had our war maps pinned to the wall and every one of the rapidly penetrating Russian thrusts was plotted daily. Our information came from the BBC, the German radio and the German press. By extrapolating a little to allow for the staleness of the news and by collating local information which we had gathered at first hand, we had made a very detailed guess at the probable position of the line of contact between Russian and German forces. Our route to Wittenberg had been planned on this appreciation. If our guesses were right, our route would take us through an area which lay behind the front line, but ahead of the administrative and supply units of the Russians. Because of the rapidity of their advance, the Russian armour engaged with the enemy usually got far ahead of its logistical support formations.

'The way I see it is this,' continued Digby. 'Yesterday the Germans were still holding the railway and shelling Bardenitz. They were certainly holding Klausdorf. But it looks as if they've retreated to the autobahn. They must have done, or we would have run into the Russians by now. I think we can move on. The front line is some way west of us.'

We argued for a long time. Not because we were in disagreement, indeed our opinions coincided, but just to illuminate the situation for ourselves and to arrive at the most logical conclusion. We could not afford to make any mistakes.

'Let's go on to Klausdorf,' I proposed. 'If it's deserted, like Bardenitz, it must mean that the Russians have already crossed the railway. If the Russians are there with front line units, we've got to cut back eastwards.'

We cycled on at a leisurely pace. The road ran flatly across the high plain. There was an obstruction on the road, over a mile ahead of us. As we approached it became recognizable as an artillery piece, lying on its side. We pedalled cautiously up to it.

We were on the edge of a battlefield. In the ditch, near the big gun, were two corpses. Beyond the gun there was a large shell crater in the road.

Nervously, we looked around the heath. Everywhere there was the evidence of battle. Corpses, craters, burnt out tanks and trucks.

'Now, doctor,' I said. 'Tell me when this battle was fought.'

'Screw you for a Pommie bastard.'

Digby was suddenly very angry.

'Sorry, Digby. I didn't mean to be sarcastic. I really think we should know when this happened.'

Digby went to work on the corpses. After a while he delivered his verdict.

'It happened yesterday,' he said, 'probably early in the morning. It's a guess, Tommy. But it's not far wrong.'

He was no longer lecturing. There was no pomposity or bravura in his statement. Like me, he was just a lonely man, frightened by the proximity of death.

'Come on, Digby,' I replied, 'let's find a little bit of grass free of corpses and have a cigarette. We've got to plan some way of staying alive and of getting to the Yanks.'

We hid our bicycles and lay down behind some gorse bushes. Digby was silent. The medical student had had more than enough of corpses for one morning.

'I think we're doing all right,' I said. 'If we're about twenty-four hours behind the battle line, we're just where we wanted to be. It's nearly perfect. On our planned route, we should have a clear ride through to Wittenberg and the Yanks.'

Digby raised himself and flicked his cigarette in to the bushes.

'I'm going to find myself a pistol,' he said, 'and some binoculars. Frankly, Tommy, I'm dead scared. If anybody's going to shoot me—Russian or German—I'm going to be shooting too. I've got to have a gun.'

'We'll go together. I can't cover you because I couldn't give you warning if any Russians come along. We'll leave our bicycles hidden and keep out of sight.'

There were hundreds of dead men scattered all over the heath, amid the litter of war.

It did not take long to find two heavy automatic pistols. We took the belts and holsters from the corpses and strapped them on underneath our jackets, out of sight.

Digby was still determined to find a pair of binoculars. It was a long search but he would not give up. It meant identifying the corpses of the officers, and there were not many of them. But at last he found what he was looking for, a very fine pair of Zeiss. Their previous owner had been a major, but he would never use them again.

By this time we had strayed nearly a mile from the road.

'Let's go back and get moving,' I suggested. 'The scenery depresses me.'

'We'll try out the pistols first,' answered Digby. He had his automatic in his hand. 'It's no good carrying these unless we know how to use them.'

Digby found a German helmet and set it up ten yards away.

'See if you can hit it,' he said. 'Use a whole clip. We've got bullets to spare.'

I fired nine shots at the helmet and hit it three times. Digby did better. He hit it five times.

'I feel better now,' he said, putting away his pistol. 'If we run into trouble the argument won't be entirely one-sided.'

We recovered our bicycles and cycled cautiously across the heath avoiding the occasional hazards of shell craters. When the road started to go downhill again, after crossing the heath, we could see Klausdorf below us. We stopped to survey the scene through our newly acquired binoculars.

'I can't see any sign of life,' I said handing the glasses back to Digby.

Digby had another look.

'They've blown the bridges across the railway,' he reported. 'But there's a track leading off to the left, just short of the bridge. We'll follow that one and then find a way over. Shouldn't be any trouble.'

We freewheeled down the hill and into Klausdorf. Again the village was deserted, no inhabitants and no Russians. There was little damage to the houses. Meandering around the square, a solitary cow was bellowing in pain. The poor animal had not been milked. We did not stop.

We turned down the track Digby had selected, which ran alongside the railway. There were no Russian sentries patrolling the lines. After about a mile, we saw a road on the other side of the tracks which would lead us to Malterhausen, the next village on our route. We crossed the railway and got back onto our bicycles.

Until we rounded the corner, we did not see the Russians. There were four of them engaged in replacing a sign-post. At the side of the road was a horse and cart with all their equipment. There was another Russian seated on the cart.

We were moving slowly and there was not time to work up our famous burst of speed. We put our big grins on our faces, raised our clenched fists and shouted.

'Zdrasti Tovarich.'

The reaction from the Russians was a complete surprise to us. They all looked, smiled broadly and answered in chorus.

'Zdrasti Tovarich.'

They stopped their work and moved to intercept us, quite obviously friendly. Only one was armed with a rifle.

I suppose we could have pedalled on and ignored them, but we did not. We stopped and were immediately surrounded; our hands were shaken and the conversation became animated, if entirely one-sided. We just kept grinning.

Digby then uttered the only other Russian phrase he had learnt.

'Angliskii offitser,' he said proudly.

'Da, da,' they answered. They had already recognized us.

The man from the horsedrawn cart now joined us. He was carrying the inevitable bottle of colourless liquid. There was going to be a party. We all sat down on the grass verge of the road and the bottle was handed round. Digby got the first swig.

'Stalin,' he said and two inches of vodka disappeared. He handed the bottle back to a Russian.

'Churchill,' declaimed the Russian and tilted the bottle.

'The Red Army,' I said, when he handed the bottle to me.

The Russians drank in turn and, although we applauded their toasts, we had no idea what they meant.

When the bottle came back to Digby for the second round, we were out of vocabulary. I wondered what he would do.

'Tovarich,' he shouted, embracing everybody present with a sweep of his hand.

That one was a winner. The Russians were delighted and we emptied the bottle without further formality. Immediately, another bottle was produced from the cart.

'Digby,' I warned, 'if we get stoned now, we'll probably get shot later in the afternoon.'

'I'd rather die drunk than sober,' answered Digby, raising the bottle.

When the second bottle was empty, we got to our feet, determined to leave. We shook hands all round. But the Russians were not ready to let us go. They wanted a ride on our bicycles. Just one short ride each, they begged. By now there was a complete rapport between us and in mime or odd noises we could convey our meaning to each other.

I looked at Digby. He was as worried as I was. Our bicycles were the most precious property we owned.

'OK,' he said, 'one ride each. First you, then you, then you.'

He went round the circle making his meaning clear.

'Undo your tunic, Tommy. Let them see your gun.' He said this sotto voce.

I unbuttoned my tunic. I was feeling very hot anyway. It was probably the effect of the vodka.

Digby laid out a course. The starting line was where we stood and I was holding the two bicycles. Digby walked up the road and, on the way, took off his tunic and threw it carelessly into the grass verge. The big automatic was immediately evident. A hundred yards away Digby stopped.

'Two at once,' he shouted, 'and it's a race. The first one back gets a cigarette.'

I put his message over to the Russians. They jumped up and down in excitement.

The first two Russians stripped to the waist for the contest. They straddled the bicycles and I gave them a demonstration of how the brakes worked. Neither had ever been on a bicycle before. This was the case with most Russian soldiers. To them the bicycle was a boyhood dream which had never come true.

I decided that pushers would be allowed, indeed necessary. When I gave the word to go, two Russians propelled one of the contestants up the road towards Digby, while the fifth Russian and I did the same for his fellow. After about twenty-five yards they seemed to have got a sense of balance and we released them. They were pedalling furiously.

Digby wisely retreated, making frantic signs for them to turn. They both yanked at their handlebars and crashed into the hedge at the side of the road. Everybody collapsed in helpless laughter.

Anxiously, Digby and I recovered the bicycles. There was no damage except for a bent pedal which we battered straight.

'What do we do?' asked Digby. 'How the hell do we escape from this mess?'

'We'll run a few more races, straight ones, with no turns, and then we'll go.'

We set up a new course and posted two Russians to get the competitors started and one to help us stop them. Digby's jacket became the winning post, about 200 yards from the start and the two of us, with our Russian assistant, stood fifty yards beyond the winning post to catch the madmen before they crashed.

We played this silly game for more than two hours before the Russians were tired and had at last decided who was the champion bicyclist. The bicycles had been battered and bent, but they still worked.

We made our final farewells, with all the firmness we could command. They let us go reluctantly. As we pedalled away, all the Russians climbed into their cart and followed us at a smart trot.

Malterhausen was full of Russian troops, vehicles and tanks. We dared not turn back and we were afraid to go on. Somebody was bound to stop us and ask questions.

I looked back. The horsedrawn cart with the bicycling champions was less than a hundred yards behind us.

'Digby,' I said, 'let's get on the cart with our chums. They'll take us through and we can drink another bottle of vodka with them.'

'I could skip the vodka,' he answered, 'but I'm damned hungry. Do you think they'd have anything to eat?'

'Let's try.'

We let the cart catch up with us. Then we climbed aboard, pulling our bicycles after us. In sign language I made it clear that we wanted to be dropped the other side of Malterhausen. In sign language Digby made it clear that he wanted to eat.

Four

THE Russians had to erect a new sign-post just beyond the village and they dropped us there. Digby had obtained half a loaf of black bread and a slab of very fat, rancid bacon.

It was difficult to get away from the comrades. Another bottle of vodka was consumed in our honour and we distributed presents all round. Digby parted with his spare shirt and a pair of cuff links. I gave away a dollar bill, my collar-stud compass which had been with me on every escape I had made and my Gillette razor with two new blades. We also gave them a fresh pack of Player's cigarettes to divide between them. We had brought with us a good stock of cigarettes which, in those chaotic days, were the only valid currency in use.

What the Russians really wanted were our bicycles and the binoculars, but in the face of our generosity they did not dare insist. The fact that we were armed also discouraged them from being too greedy.

When eventually we were free of them we pedalled very fast for an hour to put distance between us. Digby threw away the Russian bacon. It was too rancid to eat.

'We're not going to make it,' he remarked. 'We'll have to find somewhere to sleep. We can't try crossing the line in darkness, both sides will shoot at us.'

I had already come to the same conclusion.

'Let's look at the map,' I answered, 'and see if we can get any ideas.'

We moved off the road and found a place to sit down, out of sight of any passing traffic.

'What we need is a village still occupied by its German inhabitants, but with no Russians. There we could get a bed and something to eat. We are usually very popular with the German civilian.'

'We'll go on as far as Kropstadt,' I suggested. 'It's less than fifteen kilometres ahead. If we haven't found what we need by then we'll just have to sleep in a barn and go hungry.'

We remounted and moved on slowly. We were both weary. The vodka and the strain of playing bicycle-rides with childish Russians had taken their toll of our reserves of energy.

We were about five kilometres from Kropstadt when we saw a cart on the road ahead of us. It was piled high with household goods and two women were sitting on top of the load. A man was leading the horse.

'Germans,' I said. 'Do you realize that these are the first German civilians we've seen all day. Where do you suppose they all went to?'

'They all pulled out westwards when they heard the Russians were coming. And I don't blame them.'

'Well, what are these doing here?'

'I don't know. Let's ask them.'

We overtook the cart and dismounted to walk beside the man leading the horse.

'Where are you going?'

'Kropstadt.'

'Where are you from?'

'Bardenitz. Our house was shelled.'

'Have you friends in Kropstadt?'

'My brother is there. He sent to tell us to come.'

'Are there many Germans in Kropstadt?'

'Yes, nearly all stayed. The burgomaster is a communist. He guaranteed their safety.'

'Will your brother give us a bed for the night?'

'I do not know, he has only a small house.'

The man we were talking to never looked at us. He just kept his eyes fixed on the road in front of him. He was perhaps sixty years of age, with short-cropped grey hair and the wiry physique of a farm labourer. He seemed to be in a state of shock.

'Did you lose much at Bardenitz?'

'My daughter was killed. And three cows. My two sons died on the Ostfront last year. All I own is on this cart.'

'Aren't you afraid of the Russians?'

'Yes, I am afraid of the Russians.'

He plodded on, his eyes still fixed on the road. We gave him a few cigarettes and cycled ahead.

In comparison with the other German villages we had passed through, Kropstadt was bustling with life. Red flags decorated most of the houses, there were scores of people in the street, nearly all wearing red armbands. Outside the baker's shop there was a long queue of women. This meant there was bread. Nobody looked particularly happy, but there was not that desperate fear in their eyes which had become so familiar to us since the Russians had arrived.

We found the mayor without difficulty in his office in the town hall. He received us at once. He was a tall thin man with a great mane of snow white hair which covered the back of his collar. In his late sixties and with a deeply lined face, he looked tired. But his eyes were youthful and the set of his jaw denoted determination.

He greeted us correctly but without deference. He was very sure of himself. We conversed in German.

'What can I do for you?'

'We would like a bed for the night.'

'Only one night?'

'Yes, we will leave early in the morning.'

'Do you wish the Russians to know you are here?'

'No.'

We felt that if the Russian authorities knew of our presence we would lose all freedom of action. Some long drawn out bureaucratic process would be initiated which would eventually take us back to the camp at Luckenwalde.

'Then you should not stay in the village.'

'Are the Russians here?'

'Not all the time. They have commandeered a house here. Often they sleep here. Today they are in Wittenberg.'

'Where should we go?'

'I will show you. If you do what I tell you you will not have trouble.'

I was inclined to trust the man. He seemed sincere and was, I thought, being justifiably cautious. I looked at Digby.

'Are you a communist?' Digby asked him.

'Today, I am a communist. If the Americans come, I will be a capitalist. I am only interested in survival and the best for the people of this village where I was born and where I will die. I wonder if you understand me?'

We understood him very well.

The mayor got to his feet.

'Come with me,' he said. 'We will walk through the village. It must be seen that you are my friends and you must be seen to leave. You know that there is a curfew from sunset until sunrise?'

We walked together the length of the village street. Everybody greeted the mayor respectfully and he duly introduced us. We stopped outside his house.

'Now I will bring some food. Then I will walk with you to the end of the village and wish you farewell. I will tell you where to sleep as we walk.'

The mayor brought us some boiled potatoes, apologizing that he could not offer anything better. I packed them into my briefcase. He also gave us a bottle of Schnapps. As we re-traced our steps up the main street he gave us our instructions.

Two kilometres outside Kropstadt we would find a large farmhouse, which was deserted. It was easily identifiable by the two tall elms which marked its entrance. Behind the farmhouse were three large barns. We were not to use the barns. They were not safe. There might be German soldiers or other fugitives hiding there.

At the back of the farmhouse we would find an iron door which led to the cellar. That was the safest place to sleep. We would find sacks there to cover us. There were also candles on a shelf just to the right of the door.

He also told us where to find the key of the iron door.

'Lock yourselves in,' he said. 'In the morning lock the door behind you and leave the key where you found it. You will be safe there. Tomorrow morning I will report to the Russians that you passed through here.'

We shook hands and mounted our bicycles. Looking back, we saw the mayor waving farewell. A crowd of villagers were behind him also waving. We knew what they were feeling. They were wishing that they had been liberated by the allies instead of the Russians.

Without any difficulty, we found the farmhouse as described and the iron door to the cellar. The key was in its hiding place.

'Shall we check the barns?' asked Digby.

'No point,' I said. 'If there's anybody hiding there, they won't come looking for us. Besides, it's too dark. Let's get inside the cellar.'

We found the candles and made our way down a steep flight of stone steps. The cellar was large and did not smell damp. The shelves which lined the walls were all empty. The floor was of brick. There was a pile of dirty sacks on one of the lower shelves.

We made ourselves as comfortable as possible and lit cigarettes.

'Do you think we can trust that burgomaster?' asked Digby. 'Or do you think he is going to send a platoon of Russians to pick us up?'

'Why should he? The Russian authorities won't be interested in us. If we don't make trouble and keep moving, they are not going to be bothered with us officially. They haven't the time.

'It's the Russian soldiery which present the biggest danger. There are too many of them about who wouldn't think twice about shooting us for our bicycles, the binoculars or your watch. Anyway, the worst that Russian authority could do would be to send us back to Luckenwalde.'

'That's bad enough,' said Digby. 'So we stay here?'

'Certainly. We'll leave at dawn and be in Wittenberg two hours later. If we find the Yanks there our troubles are over.'

In spite of the discomfort of the hard floor, we slept deeply. At dawn we were ready to leave.

I went first out of the cellar door, wheeling my bicycle. I looked around cautiously and was just about to give Digby the all clear when a Russian soldier appeared from behind the barn.

'Zdrasti Tovarich,' I said loudly so that Digby would hear me. Automatically I smiled broadly and raised a clenched fist.

The Russian walked slowly towards me without answering. There was no sign of welcome or recognition on his face. His eyes were mean and he had not shaved for some days. His rifle was slung over his shoulder and he had a pistol at his belt.

'Angliskii offitser,' I said loudly. Then looking directly at the Russian, as though talking to him, I continued in English.

'One hostile—stand by but stay hidden.'

It was good to know that Digby was in the background.

The Russian looked at me. I could read only greed and calculation in his eyes. He was considerably taller than me and had immense shoulders. A dangerous customer.

He put one hand on the handlebars of my bicycle and yanked it towards him. I had a firm grip on the saddle and immediately yanked it back.

'Niet,' I shouted, with all the authority I could command.

The Russian took no notice.

He now gripped the handlebars with both hands and jerked. I gave ground at first, still hanging on to the bicycle. Then I dug my heels and heaved back like the anchor man of a tug-of-war team. The Russian yielded ground but did not relax his hold. He had not yet said a word.

I watched him change his grip and settle himself for the final pull. He looked extremely confident. I held on grimly while he started to exert all his strength. Then, at the crucial moment, I let go completely.

The Russian went over backwards with the bicycle on top of him. Before he could disentangle himself and get to his feet I was standing over him with my automatic aimed at his head.

In a second Digby had joined me. The Russian was now looking into the barrels of two pistols.

He lay quite still, only his eyes moving from one to the other of us. He did not look afraid, only furious.

I yanked the bicycle clear.

'Roll over,' shouted Digby, making the appropriate signs. The soldier rolled over on to his face, with his hands outstretched above his head.

'What now?' asked Digby. 'We can't shoot him and we can't let him go.'

'Lock him in the cellar,' I answered.

'Right,' he agreed, 'I'll make him crawl there. You go and get my bicycle out and put the key in the lock. Stand by the door and be ready to slam it.'

I quickly recovered Digby's bicycle and covered the Russian again as he crawled towards the cellar door. The rifle sling fell off his shoulder and he was forced to leave the weapon behind. He still had a pistol in his holster which we had not attempted to take from him.

As he crossed the threshold of the cellar Digby kicked him violently in the rump. He fell forward, clear of the door which I slammed shut and locked.

'Come on,' said Digby. 'Let's get pedalling. The farther we get away from here the better I'll feel.'

'What about the key?'

'Throw it away.'

'I don't think that's fair on the burgomaster.'

'It's a bloody sight fairer than letting him go in there all innocently and find that mad Russian.'

'We'll leave him a note,' I said.

I tore a scrap of paper from a notebook and printed on it ACHTUNG RUSSE DRIN. I put the key back in its hiding place with the note wrapped around it.

We took the road moving as fast as we could.

'I wonder if we should have shot him?' asked Digby. 'It's quite possible that he'll shoot the lock off that door and raise the alarm.'

It was a worrying thought.

'We could not have shot him,' I answered. 'It would have been like starting a private war, we two against the whole Russian army. It's too stupid to think of. That iron door will probably hold. You know, we're less than two hours' ride from Wittenberg. Once there we'll be safe.'

'I hope you're right.'

We rode in silence, saving our breath. We were not more than twenty kilometres from Wittenberg and, if we evaded trouble on the road, might even arrive there in time for an American breakfast. Twice we encountered small groups of Russian soldiers, but in each case got by without being stopped, using our now well rehearsed technique of the Russian greeting, the broad smile, the clenched fist and a lot of velocity.

When we reached Wittenberg it was close to eight o'clock and the streets of the town were already thronged with people. There were Germans in plenty, all of non-combatant age, and scores of Russian soldiers. Red flags decorated all the buildings, but of the Stars and Stripes there was no sign.

'No Yanks here,' Digby commented bitterly, stating the obvious truth. 'What now?'

'We'll find the town major and get a pass from him. First let's get hold of an intelligent looking German and ask some questions.'

We made our way slowly to the centre of the town. There were some curious glances, but nobody tried to stop us. Everybody was particularly well dressed, even the Russians soldiers. I realized suddenly that it was Sunday, 29 April. Everybody was wearing his best suit.

In the town square we selected a German and accosted him.

'Where are the Americans?' I asked.

He shrugged.

'Perhaps across the Elbe.'

'Have they been here?'

'No.' There was considerable bitterness in his voice. 'Wittenberg was liberated by the Russians.'

A curious crowd had now formed all around us. The majority were Russian soldiers. Their envious admiration of our bicycles was beginning to be embarrassing. If something was not done quickly, it might become dangerous.

I made a short speech in Russian.

'English officers,' I said pointing to Digby and myself. 'Take us to the town major.'

The town major was the local Russian commandant, whatever his rank. It was a phrase I had learned from Medvedev and carefully memorized.

'The town major,' I repeated more loudly.

A Russian officer joined the group and the whole conversation had to be repeated for his benefit.

It was difficult to follow the officer's instructions, which were in Russian, although he used his hands freely to help make his meaning clear.

The German we had first interrogated intervened.

'I'll take you to the town major's office,' he volunteered.

We accepted at once and were able to withdraw with dignity from the ever-growing audience. The Russian officer saluted us and we returned his salute with due formality.

We were wheeling our bicycles and walking beside our German guide.

'Give him a pack of cigarettes,' I said to Digby.

Digby offered him a cigarette from a new pack and then insisted that he keep the rest.

'Never mind the town major,' I said, 'take us to the Elbe.'

Three minutes later we stood on the bank of the river. I stared at the great expanse of turgid water. It looked a mile wide. Possibly it was less, but I knew for certain that it was beyond my powers.

'What do you think, Digby? You're the swimmer.'

Digby found a branch of a tree and threw it far into the pale yellow waters. We watched it as it swept past us. It was moving at a rate of knots.

'Not for me, Tommy. If I were in training I might try it. But only with two rescue boats.'

Digby had swum for Australia in the Olympics.

We both turned back to the German.

'Where is the bridge?'

'The Germans destroyed it. I can take you there.'

'Don't bother.'

We sat down on the grass to consider the situation. The German sat with us.

'Now what?' I asked Digby.

'Back to the town major, I suppose.'

The German interrupted.

'The Americans are at Rosslau,' he said. 'I know for certain. If you take me with you, I can guide you. I have a daughter in Essen. I will go there.'

Both Digby and I knew where Rosslau was and we did not need a German guide, particularly as he did not have a bicycle. The town lay downstream and some forty kilometres west of us.

'No.' I said it brutally and with finality. 'You cannot come with us.'

He took the refusal stoically, with passive resignation.

'Will you give me a letter to say I helped you?'

'Yes,' I said.

Digby nodded agreement.

'Then I will show you the road to take and explain the route.'

I tore another page from one of my notebooks and carefully wrote out a detailed certificate. It recorded the man's full names and acknowledged the fact that he had given us valuable assistance. I read it to him in English and then translated it for him. He insisted on writing for himself a German translation.

By now it was nearly ten o'clock and we were anxious to go. Our guide led us via the back roads of the town until we came to the highway which led to Rosslau.

Our farewells were brief.

'Remember to avoid Coswig,' said the German. 'The Russian controls are very strict there. Keep well to the north of the town and then head for Klieken.'

We gave him two more packs of cigarettes and shook hands. A forlorn and rather desperate figure, he watched us pedal away.

About ten kilometres outside Wittenberg we found a promising road which led northwest. Our map showed that it would take us well to the north of Coswig and that we could re-join the main road without difficulty after a detour of some ten kilometres.

The new road climbed fairly steeply away from the Elbe valley. We fought the gradient for as long as we could but eventually had to dismount and push our bicycles. Walking, we felt exposed and vulnerable.

'If we meet any Russians now,' said Digby, 'we're going to be in trouble.'

'Come on,' I answered, 'it's not far to the top of the hill and then we can start moving again. Don't forget that when we turn back for the main road we'll have a long downhill run.'

We reached the top of the hill exhausted, but remounted immediately. The road was now level and running roughly parallel with the Elbe. At intervals we got a view of the river far below us on our left. When we came to the fork, we were in good spirits again.

The road to the right led to Düben, the one to the left to Klieken and Rosslau. Rosslau, our goal, was sixteen kilometres away.

We were freewheeling down a long gentle hill towards the valley when I saw the Germans. There were seven of them in single file, moving across the fields towards the road. They were about two miles away. We stopped abruptly and Digby raised the binoculars to his eyes.

'They're Luftwaffe,' he said, 'an officer and six men. And they have seen us. The officer has got his binoculars on us.'

'Armed?' I asked.

'Yes. Three with rifles and all with automatics.'

'Can we get by them before they reach the road?'

'I don't think so.'

I was of the same opinion.

'So what do we do now, cobber? Fight the Germans?'

'Don't be a clot,' I answered. 'They won't want to fight us. They'll want to surrender.'

'And what do we do with seven German prisoners?'

'We tell them to come back next week. Come on, we've nothing to be afraid of. They won't touch us.'

'Listen, Tommy, they outnumber us seven to two and they've all got guns. If we get into a fight, who do you think is going to end up in the ditch by the road side? Us or them?'

'Digby, we expected this. We foresaw it. The Germans are beaten. They don't want to fight us or the Americans. They just want to surrender to us and escape from the Russians. You know that better than I do. Give me the binoculars.'

I focused on the German officer. He was waving at me and pointing to the road.

'Come on, Digby. They're not hostile.'

'Don't let's take a chance, Tommy. They could hold us as hostages.'

'We can't turn back. Where would we go? There's nothing but trouble behind us, especially if that Russian has escaped from the cellar. We've got to keep moving. Why don't you stay here while I go and meet them? You can follow the proceedings through the binoculars. I'll signal you if it's safe.'

'No. We'll go together. But just watch it because if there's any trouble I'm going to start shooting.'

'There won't be trouble, Digby. You just keep calm.'

We checked our pistols and moved cautiously down the hill towards the enemy. Neither of us was feeling very happy.

Two minutes later we saw the Germans emerge onto the road ahead of us. The officer took up a position in front of his men who were drawn up behind him across the road.

'You drop back, Digby, and keep your eyes open. I'll handle this.'

'Negative. We'll handle it together.'

As we approached, the officer saluted. Then he drew his pistol from his holster and, reversing it, held it by the barrel, its butt pointing towards us. The six men stood rigidly at attention.

'Colonel Ritter,' he said in good English, clicking his heels and bowing stiffly. 'I have the honour of surrendering to you.'

Digby and I dismounted.

'Colonel,' I said, 'I can't accept your surrender. If you will give me your word as an officer that you will not use your firearms against us, then we can discuss the situation.'

'You have my word of honour.'

'Then get your men off the road and into the ditch. We're too conspicuous here.'

He barked an order and everybody moved into the ditch at the side of the road. Digby and I followed the German colonel. We had not drawn our automatics. The colonel's was back in its holster.

We looked closely at the man. There were rivulets of sweat running down his face. He was in full uniform, including a long leather greatcoat. It was obvious that he was near exhaustion. But he was fully in control of himself and very calm.

I offered him a cigarette and Digby threw a pack to the soldiers.

'I want to surrender to you, with my men,' he insisted.

'Why, colonel?' I asked. 'Do you think we save you from the Russians? Be realistic, if you want to survive. We ourselves are trying to evade the Russians. We have no power to protect you. We'll be lucky to reach the American lines without being shot by the Russians. If we take you with us, we'll certainly all be shot. You know that, don't you?'

'But the Russians are your allies, major.'

'Yes, but not yours. How they treat prisoners-of-war is their own affair and they certainly know nothing of the Geneva Convention. I repeat, colonel, we can do nothing to save you.'

'So what do you suggest, major?'

'Surrender to the Americans. You are not far from their lines now. But don't move openly across the countryside. We could see you from miles away.'

'I'll take your advice. Where are the Americans, exactly?'

'The other side of the Elbe.'

'But how do we cross the river?'

'I'm afraid that's your problem, colonel.'

'You don't think there are American units this side of the Elbe?'

'I'm quite sure there are. But I don't know where their bridgehead is.'

'May I ask you where you are going?'

'No, my dear colonel, you may not. Now, we have to be moving. You and your men will leave first. Which direction will you take?'

He pointed towards Rosslau.

'Right. Move off into that wood, at the double. Remember, I have your word of honour.'

'I'm nearly beaten, major, we've been marching all night. I have little strength left. It would have been a great relief to surrender.'

He paused. Then he looked at me obliquely and smiled.

'But suppose I took you prisoners? We outnumber you.'

Digby's pistol was suddenly in his hand. It was pointing straight at the German's stomach. There was a tenseness in his expression, a whiteness round his mouth, which frightened me. It frightened the German far more.

'Drop your pistol on the ground, kraut. And don't make any mistake. If you open your mouth I'll fill it with lead.'

The viciousness in his voice was like a whiplash. It was not in the least assumed but was the climax of five long years in prison camps. Digby was ready to kill on the slightest provocation.

The German threw down his pistol.

'Now on your feet, hands high above your head. Tell your men to throw their guns on to the road. Don't look at them. Look at me.'

The colonel did exactly as he was told and shouted his orders. The soldiers obeyed without hesitation. Three rifles and six automatics dropped on to the dirt road. Throughout the whole scene not one of them had moved. I had been covering them anxiously with my automatic. But they were tired and beaten men. They did not want to fight.

'Now march,' said Digby, 'that way.'

He pointed up the road in the direction from which we had come.

'March until I say halt.'

I picked up a rifle and slid a bullet into the breech. The click of bolt was audible to everybody.

The colonel marched his men down the road. Digby collected a rifle and loaded it.

When the Germans were 200 yards away, he threw the rifle into the ditch.

'Come on,' he said, 'let's get out of here.'

We picked up our bicycles and moved away fast. When we looked back, we saw the Germans standing stationary in the middle of the road watching us.

I waved.

'Bloody krauts,' said Digby. 'God, how I hate them. You know I damn nearly shot that man. I wanted to kill him. All that my dear colonel, my dear major stuff was too much for me. They're just a lot of murdering bastards.'

'I feel exactly the same, Digby. I just thought it was the moment for diplomacy. But your ploy with a gun solved our problems much quicker. Christ, it was damned dangerous, though. I don't think it would have worked if it had not been so plain from your face that you wanted to kill. Mate, when you point a pistol, you really are frightening.'

'I'm sorry, Tommy. I know it was dangerous. You would have talked us out of trouble anyway. I'll have to watch it in future.'

'Let's keep our heads cool and try to stay alive for another few hours. We haven't got far to go and I really would hate to stop a bullet at this late stage in the game. The idea is to get us back alive.'

Five

Twenty minutes later we were approaching Klieken. Out of caution, we entered the village on foot, pushing our bicycles. We were both badly shaken by our encounter with the Germans. We could see nobody on the main street and there was absolute silence which indicated that the place was deserted. The sound of our footsteps re-echoed from the walls.

As we rode through the village we saw that there was no artillery damage and the houses were all intact. But nearly every front door had been broken open and most of the windows were smashed. Everywhere there were signs of looting. Furniture and household goods were scattered and smashed in the street. Empty bottles and broken glass lay everywhere. Klieken had suffered its night of pillage. Probably it had suffered murder and rape too. As we left the village I wondered whether it would ever come to life again.

'Let's stop,' said Digby after we had been cycling for five minutes. 'I'm getting nervous. I'd like to look at the map.'

When we had spread out the map and examined it, we lit cigarettes.

'We're nearly there,' I said.

'We're damned close,' agreed Digby. 'Just how are we supposed to cross the line?'

'I've no experience, chum. What do you think?'

'Like the porcupine, very, very carefully. If necessary, I'll crawl on my belly for a mile.'

'Let's climb that hill and have a look. If we can actually see American trucks or tanks or something, then we can make a definite plan.'

We hid our bicycles and took to the fields. Half an hour later we were high above the valley and had a commanding view of the countryside for miles around.

'You look, Digby,' I said. 'I'm going to take a nap.'

I lay on the grass, comfortably relaxed. I was too tired to light a cigarette. I must have dozed off.

'Tommy, Tommy.' Digby was shaking my shoulder. 'I've seen them. They're there. Come and look.'

I rubbed the sleep from my eyes and took the binoculars. Digby gave me directions.

Less than three kilometres away, between us and Rosslau, was a park of American vehicles. The white stars were clearly visible on their sides. I counted twenty trucks, six half-tracked personnel carriers and three heavy tanks. They were grouped together near a small hamlet consisting of five or six farmhouses. Beyond the hamlet was a group of camouflaged tents.

'What a wonderful sight,' I said, handing back the binoculars. 'It's a long way from Pearl Harbor to Rosslau-on-the-Elbe. I can hardly believe it. Pick us a route Digby and we'll call on them for lunch.'

Digby settled himself comfortably with the binoculars and reported what he saw.

'The main road's no good, there is a big road block and lots of Russians. It's damned lucky we stopped. There's a small track about a kilometre north of the main road which leads directly towards the Yanks. I can't see any sentries on it. Shall we try that?'

'Let's go. I'm very hungry.'

'Do you think the US Army is dry like their Navy? I'm just dreaming of a large gin and tonic, with masses of ice.'

'Stop it, Digby, you make my mouth water. Anyway, I'll settle for a beer. They're bound to have that.'

'Do we take the bicycles?' asked Digby.

'Too right we do, cobber. Those bicycles have saved our lives more than once and I'm not giving mine up until I'm physically surrounded by a lot of GIs.'

We moved fast down the hill, taking advantage of all the cover there was. Our bicycles were where we had left them, by the main road. It was a laborious business to heft them across the fields to the dirt track we had selected for our crossing, but now we had renewed energy. We knew we were nearly at the tape.

When we got to the road we stopped to recover our breath. 'How far from here?' I asked.

'About three kilometres. But they'll have patrols out nearer than that.'

'Do we go fast or slow?'

'We go balls out,' said Digby, 'full boost, max revs.'

'Red flags or not?'

'Dunno. Would the Yanks shoot at a red flag?'

'Let's leave them on,' I suggested. 'They've been good luck so far.'

'Guns?' asked Digby.

'We keep them. We're not home yet.'

Soon we were tearing down the road like racing cyclists, heads down and bottoms up. Ahead of us was a narrow bridge with a long rising approach to it. We were 200 yards from the hump of the bridge when a Russian sentry stepped into the road, right in the middle of the bridge.

Long before we could go into our act he had his rifle pointed and was calling on us to halt. Cautiously we cycled up to him. He made us dismount.

'English officers,' I announced in Russian.

I pointed down the road indicating where we wanted to go.

'Amerikanski,' I said.

'Papieren,' he demanded in German.

We showed him all the passes we had. It was no good, we needed a special pass from the town major in Wittenberg.

'Cigarettes,' I said to Digby.

As we smoked, trying desperately to keep the conversation alive, Digby persuaded the Russian to accept a couple of packs. He let him view a couple more packs, to excite his greed. The Russian became friendlier but still remained firm. We could not cross the bridge without a pass from the town major.

'Where are the Americans?' I asked.

I gathered from his answer that they were only a few hundred metres down the road.

He was the last Russian.

The frustration of being so close to freedom was almost too much to bear. I saw a wild glint in Digby's eyes and feared that he might try something rash.

'Come on, Digby, let's go back. We'll cross by the fields. This bastard isn't going to soften.'

Reluctantly we turned around and walked back wheeling our bicycles. We were dejected and must have looked it.

'As soon as we're out of sight we'll dump our bicycles and go on foot. The line here must be wide open.'

I had hardly finished speaking when there was a shout from the Russian. We looked over our shoulders. He was waving to us to come back. He beckoned insistently.

Hardly daring to believe what we hoped, we hurried up the incline. The sentry's rifle was safely over his shoulder. When we got to him he waved us past with a sweeping gesture.

'Churchill khorosho,' he said.

'Stalin khorosho,' we answered.

Digby gave him two more packs of cigarettes. He gestured that we should go quickly.

Digby was already astride his bicycle. I paused.

'I'm going to give him my bicycle,' I announced. 'Can I ride on the crossbar of yours?'

'You're a clot, Tommy. But go ahead.'

The Russian did not believe it at first. When he realized I meant it, he embraced first the bicycle and then me. When I left him he was polishing it lovingly with his sleeve, his rifle forgotten against the bridge parapet.

I settled myself uncomfortably on the crossbar of Digby's bicycle and he pushed off. We had gravity to help us and were soon moving fast. Just as we reached the flat a shot rang out and a bullet whined over our heads. Digby put us straight into the ditch. We crashed with a violence which winded me. The handlebars hit me in the chest and Digby's full weight hit me in the back. When I had recovered my breath and untangled myself from the bicycle I saw Digby prone with his head raised cautiously above the edge of the ditch.

'You trigger-happy son of a bitch,' he yelled and added a number of other unprintable insults. 'Watch what you're doing. We're British.'

Another bullet whistled over our heads.

'Watch you' mouth, white trash. Ah got you covered.'

Digby looked back at me, grinning from ear to ear.

'The voice of America,' he said.

There was a long pause.

'On your feet and start walking. Keep your hands real high.'

'Can I bring my bicycle?' Digby shouted back.

'Negative. Now git movin'.'

We walked slowly down the middle of the road, our hands in the air. A giant of a negro stepped into the road. He had a rifle pointed at us.

'Against the wall,' he ordered. 'Lean on your hands.'

We did as we were told. We heard movement behind us. Turning our heads slightly we saw a sergeant approach with a short tommy gun at the ready. He was a white man.

'These two tried to break through on a bicycle. They claim to be Limeys,' the negro reported.

'Whar youall from?' The sergeant's accent was deep Georgia, more southern than the negro's.

'Major,' said Digby to me, giving an excellent imitation of the traditional southern colonel, 'these ain't no Goddamned Yankees. This heah's the Confederate Army.'

He started to whistle Dixie.

'Cut it out, Digby,' I said.

'We're British air force officers, escaped from a prison camp.'

'Drop those pistol belts on the ground.'

We obeyed.

The negro collected them.

'Turn around. Now sit down.'

We sat.

'Youall bin a long time in the cage?'

'Too long, sergeant. More than three years for me. Digby here much longer.'

We both looked at Digby. He was so full of repressed excitement, so wildly happy that it showed all over him. He could not talk seriously.

Still playing the role of the Confederate colonel, Digby addressed the sergeant.

'When they took me prisoner, Sergeant, General Lee commanded your outfit. How is the old bastard?'

The sergeant ignored him.

'So you're fliers. What'd you fly?'

'Spitfires,' I answered.

'A real little killer, they tell me. Where'd they git you?'

I told him and the interrogation went on. The sergeant was an extremely intelligent man and was not asking questions at random or out of curiosity. He was checking on us, patiently and methodically.

'Sergeant,' I said, 'I want to see your commanding officer as soon as possible. It's important.'

'Why?'

I told him.

'He's at divisional headquarters right now. Might be back in an hour. You can talk to him then.'

'Who is he?'

'He'll tell you.'

Digby had come back to the world of reality.

'Sergeant,' he asked, 'could we get something to drink. It's five years since I tasted good liquor. Just one shot, well, maybe two?'

The sergeant smiled and, for the first time, the smile was friendly. He called over the negro.

'Jason,' he ordered, 'turn in those guns and get a receipt in my name.'

'Let's go,' he added, 'you'll get your guns back later.'

We got to our feet. Digby looked at the private.

'Jason,' he said, 'how would you like a bicycle? There's mine up there in the ditch. If you want it it's yours.'

'Yessir, you bet. Sarge, can I take it?'

'Sure. Go ahead and break your neck.'

Digby never did get his drink; the unit commander arrived back too soon and we were summoned to see him. When we were shown into his office, which was set up in one of the farmhouses, he was talking on a field telephone. He waved us to two chairs.

I studied the man, although I hardly noticed his features. I was examining his dress. The uniform was immaculate, so expertly and recently pressed that any tailor's dummy in Savile Row would have looked well in it. The trousers had knife-edge creases. The shoes were polished to brilliance. The crewcut was severe but stylish. The hands carefully manicured. He was a full colonel.

What impressed me most and completely destroyed my morale, was his shirt. It was so spotless, so freshly ironed, that it was a work of art.

Suddenly, I felt ashamed. I was unshaven and my hair had not been cut for nearly three months. My hands were grimy and the

nails black. My uniform was stained and shapeless, my boots
muddy and dusty.

All these things, I could forgive myself, but a dirty shirt, and
mine was filthy, was inexcusable.

I began to realize how far we prisoners had let ourselves go,
how calamitously our standards had deteriorated. We had never
bothered about our personal appearance, we were always scruffy
and untidy and made no attempt to dress correctly. We had, of
course, a variety of excuses for our behaviour but they would have
seemed trivial to a man who had fought every inch of the way
from the Normandy beaches to the Elbe and could still look as
if he had just stepped off the parade ground at West Point. I admired the man and began to suspect that re-adjustment to normal
military life might not be quite so easy.

The colonel put down the telephone and turned to us.

'Yes, squadron leader? You asked to see me.'

The voice was precise and coldly impersonal. As he looked us
over his face remained blandly impassive, but I thought I detected
a fleeting expression of fastidious distaste. Immediately I decided
to make the interview very short. I was in no mood for sufference
or condescension.

I caught Digby's glance. He was near boiling point.

'Colonel,' I said, 'I just want to tell you this. At Stalag IIIA at
Luckenwalde, which we left yesterday, there's a large number of
very sick American air corps officers, nearly all pneumonia cases.
There are no medicines or drugs, no nursing and food is very scarce.
Their condition gets more serious every day. If you could send trucks
in to evacuate them, you might save a number of lives.

'That's all I have to report, colonel. Now we'd like to be on our
way, we're in a hurry to re-join our units. If you have any transport
going west, perhaps we could get a ride.'

I got to my feet as I said this and Digby followed my example.

'Can't let me cobbers down,' he said, in an atrociously exaggerated Australian accent. 'Got to give them a hand to finish this
war.'

He started whistling 'Waltzing Matilda' through his teeth.

We both saluted.

'Now just one minute.' The colonel was very upset. 'We need
more information on this. We need more detail.'

'I've told you all I know, colonel,' I answered. 'Luckenwalde is the place. If you don't know it I'll point it out on the map. But now we must go.'

'Now, please,' and the word was music to us, 'let's just consider this calmly. OK, you're in a hurry, but you've got vital information which I need. I'll send you back to division in a jeep after we've talked this over. From there you can get a ride to practically anywhere. I'll ring the general myself.'

He looked at his watch.

'It's just ten minutes of noon. We can talk for half an hour and then you'll have lunch with me. By two o'clock you can be on your way. You can't make it any faster. How about that?'

'Good on you, sport,' said Digby.

The trouble with Digby was that once he started an act he could not be stopped. He was now playing the wild Australian from the outback and his diction was a horrible caricature of the original.

It was all too much for the colonel, so I intervened.

'That's a very generous offer. Of course, we'll give you as much assistance as we possibly can. And we'll be very glad to accept your invitation to lunch. We're pretty hungry.'

'And damned dry, too,' added Digby.

Having satisfactorily reduced the colonel to normal dimensions, we were able to apply our full attention to the more serious task of telling the Americans how to get to Luckenwalde. The colonel called in his operations and intelligence staff and we all stood around a large scale map.

It took me ten minutes to describe the conditions at Luckenwalde, the route we had taken and the hazards to be avoided. Everything I said was carefully noted. We answered the questions asked by the colonel and his staff officers as exactly as we could. After twenty minutes the Americans had formed a very clear picture of what was involved.

'This is for division,' said the colonel after a pause. 'I don't have enough transportation or drivers. And if we are going to evacuate the British too, it's way beyond my resources. I'll talk to division now.'

Within a few minutes he had the divisional commander on the line. He reported the situation most precisely and in very few words. He was on first name terms with the general.

'Fifteen-thirty, Joe? OK. They'll be there. See you in Berlin.'

He replaced the field telephone and turned to us.

'You'll report personally to the general. Tell him exactly what you've told me and he'll look after it. Now we'll go and get something to eat. You'll leave here at 14.15. Is that OK?'

We assured him that it suited us perfectly.

The officers' mess was located in the kitchen of another farmhouse some 200 yards distant. They had no gin, nor tonic, but Scotch, Bourbon and beer were offered.

Digby and I settled for Scotch.

Rather to our surprise, the colonel drank Bourbon with us and his staff joined him. I was left, however, with the impression that this was an unusual occasion and that the colonel normally did not encourage the consumption of hard liquor before lunch.

Digby had relaxed entirely, which meant that he was again talking in good English. He was giving a highly coloured account of our bicycle ride to an attentive group of officers and the colonel was listening with half an ear as he talked to me.

'I thought your friend was an Australian?'

He was a little bewildered.

'He is Australian,' I answered, 'and a very good chap. But English is his favourite language.'

I tried to explain Digby to the colonel. He appeared to understand at least to the extent that he had the coloured mess-man re-fill Digby's empty glass. He also had his own glass re-filled and, long before lunch started, we had all become close friends. The tension had gone, the suspicions had evaporated, everybody was being natural. I discovered that I knew the colonel's brother who had been shot down over Berlin.

When the jeep arrived to take us to division we were sorry to leave. It had been a very enjoyable interlude.

Precisely at 15.30 we were wheeled into the general's office. During the long jeep ride we had had time to recover from the effects of drinking too much whisky before lunch.

We spent more than an hour with the divisional commander, who was a close-cropped, grey haired, two star general, fighting his age as well as the war.

We told the whole story once again.

'I'll send in a convoy of fifty trucks,' the general announced.

'That should be enough to get out all the Americans and the British.'

We agreed.

'Don't you worry any more. They'll be on their way tomorrow or the day after at the latest.'

We were not worrying. We just wanted to get home. We had done all we could for the boys back at Luckenwalde, now all we wanted was Piccadilly Circus.

We were given a billet for the night in the divisional BOQ and by seven o'clock that evening were down in the bar, freshly bathed and looking nearly immaculate in our new outfits. The general had arranged for us to draw anything we needed from the quarter-master's stores. My shoes, shirt, tie and socks were all new and a negro batman had performed miracles in cleaning and pressing my uniform. I had also had a hair-cut. At a casual glance I could have been mistaken for an RAF officer.

It was a very happy evening. We drank a lot but remained comparatively sober. We made friends with everybody and re-told our stories with false modesty. We boasted, laughed and enjoyed ourselves. But we still concentrated singlemindedly on finding the quickest solution to our problem, which was how to get home.

We were drinking with a most sociable and well-informed US intelligence officer, who had probably been detailed to keep an eye on us, when Digby asked him the direct question.

'What happens to us now?'

'It's just routine,' replied the American. 'We've liberated so many prisoner-of-war camps and handled so many evaders, that we've had to set up an organization to take care of it.'

'So what happens?' we insisted.

'Tomorrow you'll be taken to the cage, which is about seventy miles west of here—just a reception centre, you understand?'

We understood.

'There you'll be processed and, when you're cleared, you'll be shipped back to the UK.'

Both Digby and I bravely kept happy smiles on our faces on hearing this but, behind our smiles, was a cold dread. We could guess exactly what lay ahead of us unless we acted quickly—an American-run prison camp, de-contamination, de-lousing, vaccinations and endless stupid questions. It was not for us. We bought our friend a drink and moved off in search of different company.

Eventually we found USAAF pilot, a major, who was flying to Eindhoven early next morning. Our planned destination was, in fact, Brussels, but Eindhoven was near enough and we now knew what threatened us if we did not get away from the area very quickly.

We drank with the air force major until it was long past midnight and we were all blood brothers. He promised to give us a flight to Eindhoven and to ignore the fact that we had no written authority for the journey. We arranged to meet him in the car park at six o'clock next morning. Just to be on the safe side, Digby and I escorted him to his room and noted where he lived. He was our lifeline and we did not intend to let him slip through our fingers.

We went back to the bar and remained there until the coloured barman said that he could not keep awake any longer. He asked our permission to close down. We let him go. Both of us were extremely tired, but we had no desire to sleep.

By half past five next morning we were showered and ready to go. We went round to the major's room to wake him. He had a nasty hangover. Ours had not yet started. We carried his luggage out to his jeep and rode with him to the airfield. By seven thirty we were on our way to Eindhoven in an old clapped-out C-47. We slept soundly all the way.

In the mess at Eindhoven we met a lot of Dutch officers who were serving with the RAF. There had been so many Dutch officers in Stalag Luft III that we were soon able to establish that we had many friends in common, after which all was plain sailing. Our new friends cured our hangovers and gave us an excellent lunch. More important still, they arranged for us to fly to Brussels.

We landed at Evére, just outside the city of Brussels, at about four o'clock that same afternoon. Nobody checked on us and we thumbed a lift into the city in the back of an RAF truck. From the driver, I learned that the name of the local town commandant was Peter Stansfield, a very old friend of mine. This was just the little bit of luck we needed. Peter and I had served together in No 2 squadron before the war and I knew I could rely on him to help us in every possible way. We got the driver to drop us outside Peter's office in Brussels.

Peter welcomed me like a brother. Nothing was too difficult for him to arrange and the next morning we were in an aeroplane bound for Croydon.

I have never had a more frightening trip. The aircraft was a very tired Anson and the weather was nasty, with a cloud base of about 600 feet and drizzle below. The pilot was a happy-go-lucky character who flew across the whole stretch of water between Dunkirk and Ramsgate at about fifty feet. There were twelve passengers in the aircraft, which was about four more than I would have dared carry. If one of those ancient engines had seized, we would all have been swimming for our lives.

But, of course, he made it and landed at Croydon with a professional smoothness which I was forced to admire.

Digby and I climbed down from the aircraft thoroughly shaken men. We had forgotten how ridiculously dangerous flying could be. We followed the other passengers over to the buildings.

The turf was wet and springy beneath our feet. The grass was a luxuriant English green, a colour I had not seen for years. If I had not been masquerading as a 2nd RAF squadron leader on leave, I would have rolled on the grass and kissed it. I felt a strong urge to make a close physical contact with it.

Inside the reception hall we were faced with an array of customs benches which looked more formidable than any Abwehr search in a prison camp. The customs officers who stood behind the benches looked as bloody-minded as ever. This was really England.

Our lack of luggage aroused no comment and we presented ourselves to a tired immigration official. He glanced briefly at the leave passes with which Peter had so thoughtfully provided us and handed them back. We turned to go.

'Your identity card, please.'

That did it. We had no identity cards.

There was a long pause. We could not think of anything intelligent to say.

The official looked up and examined us carefully.

'You're evaders,' he said. It was more a statement than a question. 'Come this way, please.'

We went that way and were handed over to a flight lieutenant of the MPs, a typical ex-policeman. He interrogated us at length and wrote down our answers at even greater length. When he had finished, he started to lecture us on the correct way for evaders, as he insisted on calling us, to return to England. We should have done this and this and this. Everything we had done had been most irregular. We evaders were causing a great deal of unnecessary work and trouble. He was just starting to develop this theme when Digby interrupted him.

'That's enough from you, copper,' he said curtly. 'Now suppose you get on with your job and get us cleared. I've been five years a prisoner and I'm in a hurry. I want to be in town by the time the pubs open.'

The policeman was hurt.

'It's going to take longer than that,' he said, boot-faced.

'What's your name, chum?'

There was an icy hostility in Digby's tone.

'Rogerson. John Rogerson.'

'Well, listen, Rogerson, me old cobber, if you don't have us out of here by five o'clock, I'm going to come looking for you one day very soon and I'm going to beat the guts out of you. That's a promise.'

Digby was in a towering rage. The policeman was obviously scared and I could not blame him. Digby was a powerfully built man and the look of fury on his face was not something you could put down to indigestion.

The policeman appealed to me.

'This is most improper, sir. I refuse to be talked to like this.'

'You heard what he said, Rogerson. You might as well believe him. He always keeps his promises. Now, let's calm down.

'I'm in just as big a hurry myself, so you get to work. Here's a list of very senior officers who will vouch for us. We're both easily identifiable and well known. You won't have any difficulty in clearing us. Just you get on with it because, whichever way it goes, we're going to be in town tonight. You might as well play ball and get some credit for it.'

'Yes, sir. I'll certainly do my best. Now, I'm sorry, but I'll have to lock you up.'

This was something I had not expected. After all, we were in England, the land of liberty. But there was no point in complaining. This was the English way of doing things, this was our bureaucracy at its best, this was what we had been fighting to preserve.

We were spared the indignity of being put into the cells and were shepherded into an unoccupied office. The door was locked behind us; there were bars on the window. We settled down to wait.

Our first visitor was the medical officer. He and Digby knew one another well, they had been medical students together. They greeted one another warmly and exchanged a lot of banter.

'Are you ever going to qualify, Digby? Or are you going back to the flying game?'

'I don't know, Ross. I've lost a lot of time. I'm not sure if I'd have the stamina to complete my studies. I'm going to take some leave and think about it.

'Tell me, are you going to hold us in quarantine, or are you going to clear us?'

'I'll give you a routine check and, if you haven't been in close contact with any epidemics, I'll clear you. Strip off and we'll get it over.'

The doctor examined us with admirable professional rapidity.

'No contagious diseases where you've been?'

We assured him there had not been any.

'Well, you're both fit and I'll give you medical clearance. You're thin and underweight, but that will pass.'

He turned to me.

'You'll have to go into hospital. Not now, but I wouldn't delay it very long. I'll give you a chit to report in three weeks time.'

'What for, doc?' I asked.

'Your face. You've got to have some skin grafts, particularly around the eyes. Your eyelids don't close properly. And there's a lot of skin tension which will have to be slackened off. You could have serious troubles with your eyes if you don't get the eyelids properly adjusted.'

I must have looked alarmed.

'Don't worry,' he said. 'McIndoo and his staff will handle you and they're the best in the world. A couple of small skin grafts won't give you any trouble at all and afterwards you'll look much better and feel much more comfortable. You won't be in hospital more than ten days.'

'Where will they do the job, doc?'

'I don't know. Maybe East Grinstead, but it could be Cosford or Halton. It doesn't make any difference, they're all first-class hospitals.'

'Ross,' asked Digby, 'when will they let us go, now that you've cleared us?'

'It depends on the security boys. Who's handling your case?'

'Rogerson.'

'He's a good lad. A bit of a plodder, but he's thorough.'

'Yes, but we're in a hurry. Could you make a couple of telephone calls for us?'

'Certainly, I will. And I'll tell Rogerson to get some action.'

'Thanks a lot. The truth is that if we're not released by teatime, I'm taking off anyway. After five years in the bag, I'm not about to spend my first evening of liberty locked up.'

'I understand, Digby. I'll do what I can, but you know people do spend a day or two here waiting for a clearance. By the way, I'll give you some comfortable beds in the sick quarters tonight, if you're still here.'

'Don't worry, Ross, we won't be here.'

By four o'clock in the afternoon, Digby was beginning to be un-controllable. I had promised him, and I was sure that it would work out, that we would be in the bar of the RAF Club by seven o'clock. But now he was losing faith in my promises.

He was pacing backwards and forwards.

'Come on,' he said, 'we're going to get out of here. You get working on the door. You can open it, can't you?'

I nodded. The lock was simple.

'We can be in town in an hour. London, here we come. There are at least twenty pubs I've got to drink in tonight and I also want the best dinner in the West End.

'Come on, let's go.'

'Take it easy, Digby,' I answered. 'We're no longer prisoners-of-war, so we haven't got any more escaping to do. If we break out now, they'll hit us with everything in the book—absence without leave, disobeying lawful orders, conduct unbecoming to an officer and a gentleman, the lot. There'll be a quick summary of evidence, followed by a court-martial.'

'Don't be bloody silly,' Digby started to protest, but I cut him short.

'And do you know how your defending officer is going to plead?

He's going to plead insanity. He's going to say that you've been so long in the bag that you're way round the bend. So they'll acquit you and put you in the nuthouse for a couple of years. How would you like that?

'No, Digby,' I continued, 'it's all over.'

I kicked the door so violently that the bottom panel split.

'Don't you realize that we're free at last?'

Beschriftung der Erkennugsmarke	Charaktereigenschafte
Nr. ═══	

Lager: ....

	Datum	Grund der Bestrafung
Strafen im Kr.-Gef.-Lager	18.5.42	Fluchtversuch ¹⁸/₅ Spangenbg.
	2.7.42	„ „ 2/7. 42
	15.3.43	„ „
	22.11.43	Flucht aus d:Lager 20.11.43

Schutzimpfungen während der Gefangenschaft gegen _S. auch_

Pocken	Sonstige Impfungen (Ty. Paraty., Ruhr, Cholera usw.)		K
am	am	am	
Erfolg	gegen	gegen	
am	am	am	Zahnsa
Erfolg	gegen	gegen	2. Beot
am	am	am	
Erfolg	gegen	gegen	
	am	am	
	gegen	gegen	

	Datum	Grund der Versetzung	Neues Kr.-Gef.-Lager
Versetzungen	17.2.42		Oflag IX A/H
	28.4.42		Stalag Luft
	7.9.42		Oflag XXI B
	31.3.43		Stalag Luft